K·I·S·S

DK

The Only Guides You'll Ever Need!

THIS SERIES IS YOUR TRUSTED GUIDE through all of life's stages and situations. Want to learn how to surf the Internet or care for your new dog? Or maybe you'd like to become a wine connoisseur or an expert gardener? The solution is simple: Just pick up a K.I.S.S. Guide and turn to the first page.

Expert authors will walk you through the subject from start to finish, using simple blocks of knowledge to build your skills one step at a time. Build upon these learning blocks and by the end of the book, you'll be an expert yourself! Or, if you are familiar with the topic but want to learn more, it's easy to dive in and pick up where you left off.

The K.I.S.S. Guides deliver what they promise: simple access to all the information you'll need on one subject. Other titles you might want to check out include: Living with a Dog, the Internet, Microsoft Windows, Managing Your Career, and Astrology.

GUIDE TO

Managing Your

Career

KEN LAWSON

Foreword by Martin Yate

Author of the internationally acclaimed *Knock 'em Dead* books

A Dorling Kindersley Book

Dorling Kindersley

LONDON, NEW YORK, SYDNEY, DELHI, PARIS,
MUNICH, AND JOHANNESBURG

Dorling Kindersley Publishing, Inc.
Editorial Director LaVonne Carlson
Series Editor Beth Adelman
Editor Matthew Kiernan
Copyeditor Kristi Hart

Dorling Kindersley Limited
Managing Editor Maxine Lewis
Editorial Director Valerie Buckingham

Jacket Designer Neal Cobourne

Created and produced for Dorling Kindersley by
THE FOUNDRY, part of The Foundry Creative Media Company Ltd,
Crabtree Hall, Crabtree Lane, Fulham, London SW6 6TY

The Foundry project team
Frances Banfield, Lucy Bradbury, Josephine Cutts, Sue Evans, Douglas Hall, Sasha Heseltine,
Dave Jones, Ian Powling, Graham Stride, Bridget Tily, and Nick Wells.
Special thanks to Polly Willis, Jennifer Kenna, Karen Fitzpatrick, and Anna Amari.

Copyright © 2000
Dorling Kindersley Publishing, Inc.
Text copyright © 2000 Ken Lawson
2 4 6 8 10 9 7 5 3 1

Published in the United States by
Dorling Kindersley Publishing, Inc.
95 Madison Avenue
New York, New York 10016

Library of Congress Cataloging-in-Publication Data

Lawson, Ken.
    KISS guide to managing your career / Kenneth A. Lawson. -- 1st American ed.
        p. cm. -- (Keep it simple series)
            Includes index.
            ISBN 0-7894-6138-2 (alk. paper)
    1. Vocational guidance. 2. Career development. 3. Job hunting. 4. Success in business.
    I. Title: Keep it simple series guide to managing your career. II. Title. III. Series.
        HF5381 .L3435 2000
        650.14--dc21
                                                                00-009446
Dorling Kindersley Publishing, Inc. offers special discounts for bulk purchases for sales promotions or premiums.
Specific, large-quantity needs can be met with special editions, including personalized covers,
excerpts of existing guides, and corporate imprints. For more information, contact Special Markets Department,
Dorling Kindersley Publishing, Inc., 95 Madison Avenue, New York, NY 10016 Fax: 800-600-9098.

Color reproduction by David Bruce
Printed and bound by Printer Industria Grafica, S.A., Barcelona, Spain

For our complete catalog visit

www.dk.com

Contents at a Glance

CONTENTS

PART ONE Thinking Seriously About Your Work 24

CHAPTER 1 Managing Your Career Today 26

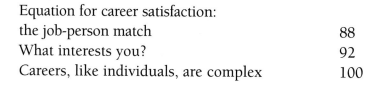

APPENDICES   404

Foreword

AS A CAREER MANAGEMENT EXPERT, *I've seen a lot of job applicants who are just looking for work. Some aren't really sure what they want to do, and some know exactly what they want but don't know how to get it. Too many of us think of a career as a series of random chances and lucky breaks. We work hard and wait for great things to happen. But sometimes they don't. Then what?*

This book is the answer. The K.I.S.S. Guide to Managing Your Career will show you how to take control of the process. You start by understanding that you do have choices. You next job doesn't have to be something that just happens you. It can be your first step (or your next step) in shaping the kind of career you really want. Examine your skills, look at your interests, and choose where you want to go. It's in your hands.

There are many reasons people look for jobs. Some people get bored, some people get laid off, some people want more responsibility or more money or a different boss. Some are looking for their next job; others for their first.

Whatever your situation, when you realize that you can drive the car, the whole picture changes. You can make your own choices, and then work to make them happen. How do you identify the industries that are right for you and the companies you want to work with? What skills do you have and how can you put them to work right now? Where can you look for jobs, and where can you place yourself so that employers are looking for you? What's the best way to communicate to others exactly what you're capable of doing? How do you network so that it really produces results?

The K.I.S.S. Guide to Managing Your Career will guide you through the process. You'll learn how to make the best of the skills and talents you have, how to minimize your weaknesses and showcase your strengths. But best of all, you'll learn how to take control of your career.

This book is upbeat and positive without being sentimental or phony. Ken will not fill you full of motivational aphorisms, but instead will equip you with real tools that you can use to decide what you want from your career and how to go after it. The rest is up to you.

MARTIN YATE

Introduction

BECAUSE YOU'VE PICKED up this book, it's a pretty safe bet that you have some questions or concerns about your career. It's another safe bet that those questions or concerns are pretty serious and complex because right now, in the early part of the 21st century, managing your work life is more difficult and more demanding than ever before. In fact, it's anything but simple – which is why there's a K.I.S.S. guide on managing your career: The more complicated work lives become, the greater the need for clear thinking, straightforward strategies, and uncomplicated guidelines to help you manage your career thoughtfully and effectively.

Maybe you're bored with your job. Maybe you've been at it too long, and everything about it has started to feel wrong: the work itself, the physical environment, the people, the pay. Or maybe you don't have a job right now. If you've been in the workforce for even just a few years, chances are you've seen or felt the impact of corporate mergers and downsizings. Maybe you've been personally affected by one of those events, and it has left you without work.

Maybe you've been out of the workforce for a while raising a family or pursuing your own business. Or maybe you're transitioning out of school and trying to figure out how to break into the work world for the first time.

Whatever your career situation, you may have a sense that you need to do some things differently in your work life. If so, you're ready to stop reacting to whatever may come at you along the career highway and to start managing your work life more intentionally. That's a vital frame of mind to maintain because, when it comes to the world of work, one thing is as sure as sundown: If you don't take the time and trouble to manage your career, your career will manage you.

The K.I.S.S. Guide to Managing Your Career will train you to think of your career not just in terms of your current work situation but the sum of your work experiences across your lifetime. And it will train you to anticipate and plan your career moves and to navigate through that big-picture context. It will help you bring careful thinking, planning, and order to your work life – and help you avoid or halt a career free-fall. This book will be valuable if you're thinking seriously about your career for the first time or if you're wondering about where to take your career next.

By the end of the book, you should feel empowered to take command of your career and gain control over its progress. And if you stick with the principles and guidelines in these pages, you'll soon be skillfully navigating your mapped-out career path by choice, not by chance.

KEN LAWSON
New York

Dedication

This book is dedicated to my family, with love and thanks for their encouragement and support, and especially to Katie, because life and careers can bring what you'd like to have – if you ask.

K.A.L

What's Inside?

THE K.I.S.S. GUIDE TO MANAGING YOUR CAREER is organized to provide you with career management guidelines to use right away – and in the future. Wherever you are in your career, you'll find information, ideas, and strategies to help you manage your work life purposefully and effectively.

PART ONE

Part One explains the shape of today's work world, how it got that way, and what to do about it. You'll learn how to take responsibility for your own career and how to design the important changes or moves that you may be considering.

PART TWO

In Part Two you'll learn how to take inventory of your career interests, skills, and values and to relate them to your personal style qualities to find the work life and environment that suits you best. The many exercises provided will help you examine your traits and personal attributes thoughtfully now and as they evolve in the future.

PART THREE

There are actually several types of career moves you can opt to make, and Part Three helps you consider courses of action that you can take whether you're in transition or currently employed. You'll learn how to build a solid foundation for a major career change and how to investigate and pursue working as an entrepreneur. You'll also design an action plan that will serve as your blueprint for short- and long-term career progress.

PART FOUR

Part Four sets you up with simple guidelines and tactics for managing an effective job search campaign. You'll learn strategies for maximizing your job-search efforts, including presenting yourself forcefully in print (with your résumé) and in person (in interviews).

PART FIVE

Finally, in Part Five, you'll learn how to manage your career while you're working – how to move ahead while you're hunkering down. There are plenty of practical pointers on how to develop and enhance your career reputation, how to think and act advantageously at work, and how to maximize your career vitality.

The Extras

IN THE MARGINS YOU WILL see some icons scattered throughout the book. There are four of these icons:

Very Important Point
This symbol points out a topic I believe deserves careful attention. You really need to know this information before continuing.

Complete No-No
This is a warning, something I want to advise you not to do or to be aware of.

Getting Technical
When the information is about to get a bit technical, I'll let you know so that you can read carefully.

Inside Scoop
These are special suggestions and pieces of information that come from my experience.

You'll also find some little boxes that include information I think is important, useful, or just plain fun.

Trivia...
These are simply fascinating facts that will give you an insight into all aspects of careers and career management.

DEFINITION
Here I'll define words and terms for you in an easy-to-understand style. You'll also find a glossary at the back of the book with career-related lingo.

INTERNET
www.internet.com

I think that the Internet is a great resource for career-minded individuals, so I've scouted out some of the best web sites for you to check out.

PART ONE

BE QUICK OFF THE MARK IN MANAGING YOUR CAREER

THINKING SERIOUSLY ABOUT YOUR WORK

IF YOU WANT SUCCESS and satisfaction from your career, put yourself in command of it. If you've never given much thought to managing your career, now is the time to begin. When it comes to your *relationship* with work, you have a choice. You can work in any job that comes  along, and just let your career happen. Or, you can take *control* of your relationship with work, and make your career happen.

The first part of this book explains the shape and nature of the work world today, how it got that way and how to respond to it. We'll also look at it from a very systematic perspective so that you can gain a clear *understanding* of what it takes to plan and accomplish change and manage your career successfully.

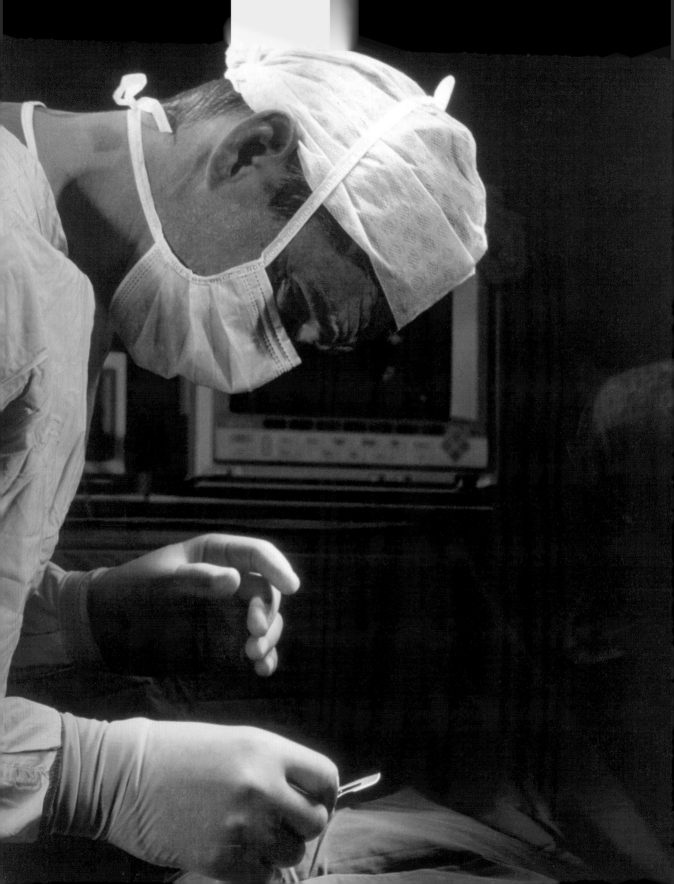

Chapter 1

Managing Your Career Today

MANAGING YOUR CAREER effectively means taking control of the forces and factors of influence that you are capable of acting upon. And it's tougher and more demanding now than ever before. However, because of the shape of the work world in the early 21st century, taking command of your own career is crucial if you are going to meet your goals and achieve the success you desire.

In this chapter...

✓ Influences from inside and outside

✓ It's your responsibility – and yours alone

✓ How we got this way

✓ The old mindset about moving up

✓ The transformation of the work world

✓ If you stand still, you don't stand a chance

YOUR CAREER IS A PRECIOUS THING – AND THE RESPONSIBILITY FOR IT IS IN YOUR HANDS

Influences from inside and outside

LOTS OF FACTORS INFLUENCE *your work life and how successful or unsuccessful your career is. Basically, there are both internal and external influences. The internal influences are those that are native to you: your interests, skills, work values, and personal qualities. The external influences on career success are the characteristics of the world around you: where you live, the vitality of the economy, the shape of the job market, the career choices and histories of your family members, and other forces that are mostly beyond your reach (including just plain luck and coincidence – or the lack of them).*

■ **Your interests** *play a major role in the type of career you choose.*

While all of these factors play some role in career success, it is safe to say that careers are shaped by a combination of forces within your control and forces beyond your control. We're not going to be concerned with the second category. Instead, we're going to take a good, hard look at the first category – the career influences that are within your control. There are many more of these than you might think. We'll look at all of them in some detail throughout this book, but for now let's consider one idea that's the foundation of effective career management: You need to apply time, effort, and energy to all of the success factors that you can touch and influence.

Okay, that's easy enough to say. But what does it really mean? Think about whether or not you achieve career success just by saying yes to a job offer. Accepting an offer of employment usually is a success by itself, but in terms of the career big picture it's only the first of many hurdles to jump. By the same token, do you achieve total career success when you're given a promotion and a raise? Once again, those events can represent a nice milestone in your career, but they hardly add up to total career success.

INTERNET

www.careervoyager.com

www.planetclick.com

These two easy-to-use portals offer hundreds of links to career management sites.

■ **When it comes** *to your career, you are the only one who knows what is best for you, so have some enthusiasm for it!*

It's your responsibility — and yours alone

TO MANAGE YOUR CAREER STRATEGICALLY and effectively over *the long haul, you need to take charge of all work-related influences that you can control. That means thinking seriously about the following:*

1. The kind of work you want to do

2. Where you want to do it

3. What kinds of people (if any) you want to work with

4. How you find meaning and satisfaction in your work

5. How easily you're able to separate your "work self" from your "personal self" (if you can do that at all)

Once you do the thinking, you'll need to make decisions and choices, develop short- and long-range action plans, and begin to follow them. No one can accomplish these things for you. No organization will build your road to career success.

No matter how talented or skilled you are, no corporation, plant, institution, foundation, association, or professional society is going to set you up to succeed. You have to do these things yourself.

Designing your career path (and pursuing success on it) is no one's responsibility but your own.

■ **Are you** *happier working alone, or as part of a team?*

How we got this way

MANAGING A CAREER *hasn't always been so much of a personal mission. Anyone aged 35 or over can easily remember a time when the world of work seemed far more secure, gentle, and protective than it seems now. Back then, you could take a job with a company, manufacturing plant, or retail store and reasonably expect that if you showed up on time every day, worked diligently, and generally kept out of trouble, you'd be able to keep that job for life.*

In fact, companies encouraged that kind of thinking. Throughout most of the 20th century, employers wanted their workers to believe that in return for loyal service and good performance, they'd provide a lifelong cushion of support. For a long time, that's how the world of work really did function. Companies encouraged employees to invest their entire careers in one place and rewarded their loyalty and dedication with security, annual raises, and a shining gold watch at their retirement parties.

■ **Things have progressed** *significantly since the days of turning up day after day to do the same mundane job.*

Playing by new rules

It's a different work world now. Individuals entering the workforce for the first time can typically expect to work in at least two or three different fields before they reach retirement age. And, within those fields, individuals can typically expect to work in ten or 15 different jobs, or more, before they retire. In fact, retirement itself is becoming an obsolete idea. Many people will continue working in some capacity throughout the course of their entire lives.

Companies and organizations are no longer taking care of their employees as they once did. It's up to you to navigate the new world of work and manage your own career. How did things ever get this way? Like just about everything else in life, the world of work evolved. There's no need to go all the way back to the invention of fire to track the changes. Let's just skip to the last chapter or two of the story.

How the stage was set

The Industrial Revolution exerted a profound and lasting influence on the world of work. As machines made it easier to produce goods and products in mass quantities, a new emphasis on high-output manufacturing took hold. More and more workers were attracted to production plants and factories, and the face of the labor force changed

■ **The question of money** *has always been a major part of the world of work.*

forever. Throughout the 19th century, relations between employers and employees alternated between fast-changing periods of benevolence and antagonism as the work world took on an expansive new shape to accommodate the demands and priorities of high-output manufacturing.

The Industrial Revolution resulted in many benefits to the labor force and to the world of work in general, despite the fact that periods of remarkable economic prosperity alternated with periods of economic downturn. In the 20th century, an economic slump that began in 1907 eventually gave way to a period of inflation that followed the World War I, and then the giddy economic boom of the Roaring Twenties.

The stock market crash of 1929 produced the long and terrible Great Depression that stretched through the decade of the 1930s and touched everyone. It produced chaos and uncertainty in the workplace, and created levels of unemployment that were far-reaching and disastrous. Then, as the Depression was running out of steam, World War II gave the American economy the boost it needed.

Prosperity produced stability

When World War II ended in 1945, the United States was on the brink of a long period of prosperity and stability that extended all the way to the last quarter of the 20th century. That period gave shape to the work world that was dominated by the fathers of *Baby Boomers*, and eventually by the Boomers themselves.

During that prosperous period, workers could feel comfortable and safe by joining a reputable organization and remaining with it until retirement, 20 or 30 years later. Organizations took on many benevolent characteristics and came to be viewed as providers by their workers. Employees and their families could feel protected and secure by virtue of their relationship with their employer. Many organizations encouraged their employees to think of their coworkers as extended families and their workplaces as homes away from home.

The mutual understanding at the heart of that work contract was something like, "Be good for us, and we'll be good for you." In other words, if you contributed to a company in some measurable way, it would take care of you – and manage your career to your advantage and benefit. Generations of workers played out their careers just that way. Was that poor career management? No. It was effective career management, given how the world of work was shaped for so long.

DEFINITION

Individuals born between the years 1946 and 1964 were part of the largest boom in infant births in American history. They are commonly referred to as Baby Boomers. *The year 1957 marked the zenith of the baby boom.*

The philosophy that dominated the work world during those years was *upward mobility*. Workers were encouraged to think about their careers in terms of climbing a staircase or ladder – and earning more and more money with each step toward the top. For many years this benevolent, wealth-increasing work world did not include many women. Eventually, it stretched and changed to include more and more females in the workforce.

The old mindset about moving up

YOU'VE HEARD CLICHÉS AND PHRASES *about "moving up the ladder," "climbing the stairs," "making it to the top," and even "hitting the ceiling." Notice how all of them refer to a gradual upward movement, as if careers can only be like rising escalators. It's not an accident that phrases like those found their way into everyday language. Instead, it's one result of how people were conditioned to think about careers for so long – and a reflection of how companies were structured and designed.*

During the mid-20th century, companies and institutions steadily expanded in order to advance their business and the marketing of their products and services. To meet business goals and objectives efficiently, companies typically organized themselves in very orderly, structured ways. More often than not, the structure that employers put into place at their organizations resembled the chain of command in the military: a select few leaders making key decisions at the very top, with many layers of increasingly less powerful links beneath them. This kind of highly militaristic, bureaucratic organizational structure is typically called a hierarchy.

■ **There is now much** *more to career success than climbing the corporate ladder.*

Beginning at the bottom

Back during the stable, prosperous mid-20th century, hierarchy was just what the world of work needed. It provided workers with lots of opportunities to "start at the bottom" and "work your way up." It produced lots of middle-level positions and stations that ambitious workers could set their sights on as they advanced in the organization and in their lives. And, it meant having a real shot at a few powerful positions at the very top of the pecking order. In a work world characterized by hierarchy, it's a natural condition for employees to want to move up. Because, typically, moving up means earning more money. In fact, to earn a larger salary you have to move up. And for a long time, organizations that wanted to reward loyal employees would do so by giving them just what they wanted – promotions and pay raises.

Choosing the right employer

For generations, modern organizations promoted one view of the work world for employees to look at: the view north. The unspoken (but well understood) work contract implied that you could be as successful as you had a mind to be – if you kept working, kept out of trouble, and kept climbing the ladder.

■ **Once, choosing** *your employer was the only career decision you would have made.*

With that kind of career playing field in place for so much of the last century, hundreds of thousands of employees over several generations had one key decision to make. In fact, managing a career came down to the first (and often the only) question to answer about the world of work: Which employer will I sign up with?

The pace accelerates

Compare that 20th-century picture of the work world with the one you see today. What has happened? How did it change from a protective, nurturing environment into a landscape that produces anxiety and insecurity? The answer lies in one word: Technology. And in particular, computer technology.

So what? We all know that computers have changed our way of living once and for all, but what does it have to do with the shape of the work world? Everything. The pace of work picked up speed when the electric typewriter made its debut in the 1960s. When photocopying was introduced into the workplace, it revolutionized the way information was spread around. Telecommunications grew more sophisticated, enabling us to connect instantly by phone with just about any location in the world. Later, fax machines enabled us to transmit written messages. But none of these technological innovations changed the world of work so drastically and quickly as the personal computer. It changed the way we live and work. In fact, it changed almost everything.

Speed breeds new workplace needs

During the remaining years of the century, the personal computer and its technological cousins appeared everywhere: in offices, factories, stores, restaurants, churches, synagogues, and, of course, homes. It transformed the way we work as no other innovation before it. It influenced all professions, turned entire industries inside out, and redefined how to do just about every job that involves getting a paycheck. Why? Because of what the computer brought into the workplace: speed.

Never has the world of work been such a frantic, fast-moving place. Transactions are completed with a quickness that would have caused heads to spin during the slower-moving, deliberate post-war period of economic prosperity. Now, there seems to be no limit to what can be accomplished during the course of a day, both in the workplace and outside of it.

Working at a number of activities simultaneously is called multitasking. For better or worse, multitasking is no longer the joke most people used to laugh at. It's our way of life.

Computerization has shortened our attention spans along with the amount of time it takes to get most things done. We have responded by taking on more and more tasks each day, each hour, each minute. Are things getting done as thoroughly and as intricately as they used to? Probably not. But many people would argue that there's no real need to be thorough and intricate, just as long as a goal is accomplished or an end is reached in some reasonable fashion.

This tendency is at the heart of new challenges confronting the world of work in the 21st century. It has triggered a decline in the value of and regard for accuracy. It has also exerted a profound impact on (and discussion about) the definition of quality. As we march into the new millennium, there is no consensus on the possible long-term effects of favoring quantity over quality.

■ **No matter how** *quickly something has to be done, you should always try to produce quality work.*

Trivia...

Here's a story about one way that the world noticed the impact of computer technology. In the early 1980s, Time magazine broke with a publishing tradition it had established and preserved since the 1920s. Time had selected a person or persons that had influenced the world most sharply during the previous 12 months as Man or Woman of the Year (now called Person of the Year). As 1982 drew to a close, the magazine chose not to spotlight a person, but an object. The year-end cover story featured not a man or a woman, but a Machine of the Year. And what machine, in particular, was the newsmagazine bringing to the world's attention? The personal computer.

The transformation of the work world

WHETHER YOU AGREE OR NOT, *there's no denying that the work world has been completely reshaped by technology and the many benefits – and drawbacks – it has triggered. The resulting changes have been more widespread, far-reaching, and profound than any since the Industrial Revolution. Many of its characteristics have had and will continue to have a direct impact on you, your career, and your opportunities for career growth.*

We've already lived through several waves of corporate downsizing brought on by surging trends toward mergers, acquisitions, and increased profitability. In the 1980s and early 1990s, companies and agencies eliminated jobs by the hundreds of thousands. Nearly every worker was touched in one way or another by this movement to reshape the work world. Those who didn't lose their jobs or have them redefined were the exception, not the rule. Yet during the last five years of the 20th century, unemployment in America reached its lowest point in over 50 years.

■ **Computer technology** *has revolutionized the way we work.*

Many other trends have gathered momentum as a result of advancing technology. Together, these trends are what give the work world its new shape and definition. You're probably more familiar with the trends than you might realize, but let's take a quick look at just a few of them.

The shift to service

Throughout the robust economy of the later 1990s, people were working, but in what kinds of jobs? What happened to the hundreds of thousands of workers who were "right sized," or enticed to change their career situations by generous early-retirement packages? Increasingly, they became involved in service-oriented roles.

One of the most important, bottom-line facts about the changes in the work world over the past few decades is that America has shifted from a manufacturing-oriented to a service-oriented economy. That means that the vitality of our economy is no longer measured by the goods that we produce but rather by the services we provide. It also means that the vast majority of jobs in the country involve providing services that others are willing to pay for.

A surge in small business

■ **The move away** *from more traditional types of employment has given rise to countless new opportunities, such as desktop publishing.*

The trend toward service orientation has enabled countless individuals to try their hand at starting and running their own businesses. The ventures range from desktop publishing to running small hotels or bed-and-breakfasts, from dog-walking services to party-planning teams. Countless kinds of startup ventures have been tried, many that have worked, and many others that have failed miserably. The point is that small business is the fastest-growing sector of the American economy, and the trend is spreading internationally. Even as early as 1995, small business accounted for 1.5 million new jobs. Today it continues to provide opportunities for workers who want the kind of career that is not linked to a large organization.

Flatter structures, shorter ladders

Many organizations are moving toward flatter, less hierarchical structures, which means there are fewer rungs on the corporate ladders that employees used to hunger to climb. Organizations now are moving steadily away from the kind of structuring that produces lots of top-heavy bureaucracy and toward more efficient structures where fewer levels separate management from line employees.

One positive result of this trend is that recognition for contribution is not reserved for just a few upper-echelon management stars. The flip side is that there are far fewer middle-management jobs for organizational workers to strive for. As a result, advancement, promotions, and increased compensation have to be determined in ways that have nothing to do with bumping up to another title.

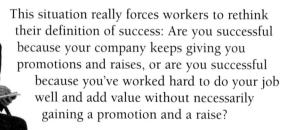

This situation really forces workers to rethink their definition of success: Are you successful because your company keeps giving you promotions and raises, or are you successful because you've worked hard to do your job well and add value without necessarily gaining a promotion and a raise?

■ **The workplace** *is seeing a move away from the old top-heavy management structure, meaning there are fewer middle-management positions.*

Outsourcing

Another trend that has resulted from advancing technology is outsourcing. Many jobs that organizations formerly did internally are now being "farmed out" for completion by independent contractors, entrepreneurial companies, or service agencies. One example is the payroll function. Many organizations now rely on an external accounting firm to make sure that their employees receive their paychecks on time. Another example is training. Many large companies have shifted the responsibility for training and developing employees to external consultants and firms, which are typically hired on a contract or per-project basis.

When companies choose to outsource projects or functions, it's usually because the work can be completed over the long haul less expensively than by retaining full-time employees to do it. Outsourcing is almost always a cost-saving decision, although in terms of productivity it sometimes costs companies more to rely on business relationships with external service providers. The most significant result of the trend toward outsourcing, though, is the creation of the "contingency" workforce – professionals who are hired on a time-defined or per-project basis.

■ **It is increasingly** *common for businesses to hire a consultant for his or her particular area of expertise on a short-term basis.*

The growing use of contingency workers has reduced the number of permanent jobs that organizations have to offer, it has increased the number and caliber of job opportunities that exist in the workplace. Some of them may be right for you.

Win-win arrangements

Other workplace trends triggered by the impact of technology on the work world include job sharing and flex time.

Job sharing means that the actual duties and responsibilities of a particular job are shared by two employees, with each working roughly halftime. One might work from 8 a.m. to noon, and the other from 1 p.m. to 5 p.m. Or perhaps one employee works Monday, Tuesday, and Wednesday, and the other works Thursday and Friday. Companies may choose this option if it means that they get to tap into the talents and contributions of two workers while paying out the equivalent of just one salary. And from the employees' point of view, job sharing usually works because it enables the sharers to earn a paycheck (and perhaps even qualify for health benefits) without devoting 100 percent of their available work week hours to a single employer. It's an employment arrangement that leaves plenty of room for other priorities.

It's often much easier these days to work from home, and many employers are structuring arrangements with workers that take into account different lifestyle requirements. For example, workers who are raising young children or pursuing advanced studies are sometimes able to perform their duties on flex time, meaning that their work does not necessarily have to be done in the office between 8 a.m. and 5 p.m., Monday through Friday. The worker may instead work mornings at home and afternoons in the office.

■ **Many organizations** *now recognize that employees have other commitments and are much happier working certain hours in the office – mornings only, for instance.*

Cyberspace in the workplace

It's possible that the single most profound change in the world of work has been generated by the Internet.

Cyberspace has become increasingly relevant to and meaningful in our everyday existence. Think about e-mail and e-commerce.

Think about all the information people get from the World Wide Web. Think about the countless number of web sites that have been established over the past five years, and how many have become part of our daily experience.

Think about how often web sites are mentioned in television and print advertising. The 1990s ended with a surge of "dot-com mania" that shows no signs of subsiding. Today, even the smallest organizations and enterprises consider a web site essential to doing business. A Web presence is seen as a sign of credibility.

And, of course, the Internet is transforming the way people look for and find work. Employment agencies, search firms, and headhunters are being forced to change the ways they provide services to people who are looking for work. Job postings are now readily available at any number of career-related web sites on the Internet (see Chapter 16 for a few recommended sites). Employment information is now readily available on the Web to anyone who wishes to access it.

If you stand still, you don't stand a chance

ALL OF THESE TRENDS, *all of the contours in the new shape of the workplace, mean that managing your career is more challenging and more demanding than ever before. In many ways, you're in uncharted territory. Because, as quickly and as drastically as the work world has changed over the past 15 years, it will change again in the next ten. And then again, in the following five.*

■ **Workplaces constantly change** *as technology demands that our working methods change.*

At the beginning of the 21st century, what we know best about tomorrow's shape of the work world is that it won't look the same as it does today. In fact, the two things we can be sure about are that change is the only constant and it will keep happening – fast and furiously. The workplace of 20 years ago is practically as far away from us now as the days before automobiles. And 20 years from now, we'll be twice again as far away.

INTERNET

www.altavista.com/careers

www.excite.com/careers

www.hotbot.com/careers

www.msn.com/careers

www.snap.com/careers

www.yahoo.com/careers

If you're serious about managing your career in the age of cyberspace, you'll need regular access to one or more of the career portals on the Web. These sites are among the most useful career links of the major search engines and will serve you as Internet pathfinders for career management information and resources. Visit all of them, choose your favorite, and add it to your bookmarks or favorite sites list.

So how can you possibly manage your career if the work world isn't standing still? The answer is simple: You have to keep pace. As the work world continues to change, you need to change with it.

■ **Perhaps the** *notion of spending a day in the office will become obsolete in the future.*

You're on your own

Managing your career effectively means creating visions. Setting short- and long-term goals. Thinking and re-thinking what you want and need out of your relationship with work. Developing action plans and strategies. Overcoming setbacks. Savoring small successes as well as large ones. Riding with a little good luck, and shaking off the doses of bad luck – however large or small.

■ **You know the** *style of work that suits you best, and it's up to you to make sure you achieve it.*

If you want to succeed, you're on your own.

Managing your career today is not about climbing ladders or staircases; it is about taking charge and taking initiative.

Managing your career means relying on yourself. It means growing, developing, and adapting, both personally and professionally. It means continually acquiring new skills, improving the ones you already have, and letting go of the ones you no longer need.

Managing your career today means changing along with the work world and continually evolving. If you choose not to, sooner or later it will control you, as well as what happens and doesn't happen to your career. If that sounds appealing, you need to do nothing. Just sit back and let your career happen to you.

If it doesn't, you need to get to work.

INTERNET

www.dol.gov/dol/asp/ public/futurework

For a wealth of information and insight about current and future workplace trends, visit Futurework, maintained by the U.S. Department of Labor.

■ **It may mean** *not always going for the easy option, but taking charge of your career is the most important step you will take in your working life.*

■ **By taking quite** *simple steps, you can often begin to take charge of your career in a positive way.*

A simple summary

✓ Managing your career effectively is more important, and more demanding, than ever before. It requires ongoing investment of thought and effort on many fronts.

✓ Career management is your own responsibility. No one, and no organization, is going to do it for you. However, people and organizations can help and support you with your career management initiatives.

✓ The world of work is defined today by time-limited relationships between employers and employees – a new work contract. Managing your career effectively requires you to navigate those temporary relationships and leverage them to your benefit.

✓ The new landscape of the work world has cleared a career management playing field that is broader than ever before. Important trends that have reshaped the world of work have also produced a wealth of new opportunities for career success.

✓ In the workplace of the 21st century, the only constant is change. How well you tolerate and adapt to it will help determine how successful you are in your career.

Chapter 2

Your Career Canvas

NOW THAT YOU KNOW you're accountable for your own career successes and satisfaction, it's time to view career management through a wide-angle lens. In this chapter, you'll see how your career and your life are intertwined and mutually influential. You'll understand the benefits of the "long view" of careers and why it's best to avoid situational perspectives. Because it's important to begin managing your career from where you are right now, you'll learn to ask some very basic, tough questions about the ground you're currently standing on, and how to answer them. Got your paintbrushes ready?

In this chapter...

✓ You're in it for the long haul

✓ Working well takes work

✓ Designing your own track

✓ Asking yourself the tough questions

✓ The age factor

YOUR CAREER CANVAS IS FILLED WITH DIFFERENT COLORS AND TEXTURES

You're in it for the long haul

HOW DO YOU THINK ABOUT YOUR CAREER? *If you're like most people, you think about it as the bundle of activities and routines you do in order to earn a living. The hours of your workday, the days of your workweek, the weeks of each work month, the months of each business quarter or sales season, the seasons or cycles of each fiscal or calendar year. Chances are you can visualize yourself working away in each of these settings.*

Or, you can think about your current or most recent employment situation and remember it in its different phases. The early phase when you first started working in that setting and everything felt new and different, may have been slightly intimidating and maybe even exciting. Later, after the newness had worn off, perhaps you began to feel entrenched in the job. Then a promotion introduced a new or revised set of responsibilities, followed by some successes and setbacks. Maybe there was another promotion, or maybe a demotion, or maybe just nothing at all. Maybe it all turned into just an ongoing string of days that felt pretty much the same, and still do now as you think back on them.

■ **You will not** *always feel the same about your job as you did when you first started.*

But what's wrong with these pictures? If either one comes close to how you think about your career – everything! The scenarios described above focus on the present or the recent past. People tend to view their career in terms of what's going on right now in their work life. That's what's called a *situational view* of careers. It's thinking with mental blinders on: You can only see what's right in front of you. I prefer a longer view of careers, and I hope that after some thought and consideration, you will too.

Managing your career effectively means managing for the long haul – not just for a particular situation. It means getting the most out of your current situation (whether you're employed or not) and planning for getting the most out of your next situation – and the next, and the next.

A long view of career management makes it easier to accomplish those goals, because it will afford you a context that goes beyond today.

Your career story: a work in progress

What goes into a long view of career management? To find out, let's get to a definition of career. Think about your career not in terms of just your current or most recent situation – or any one situation at all. Think of your career as the sum of all your work experiences, throughout life. Each one of them adds something to the pool of knowledge you have about what work you enjoy, what you do well, what you don't do well, where you will thrive, and where you will barely survive.

Your career is your progression through the variety of work situations you involve yourself in throughout the course of your life. A career is a long journey across a sprawling landscape of hills, valleys, mountains, and plains. You may even have to cross a desert or two. Your career is not limited to just your current livelihood. It's the sum of all your working experiences.

If you take that view, every job you've ever held factors into your career – beginning with your newspaper delivery route or your babysitting nights. Of course, your career really kicks into gear when you make the transition from being a student to earning a living, but all work experiences play some influential role, however large or small, in your career story, because all of them tell you something about the kind of work that works for you. And that's what you need to know in order to manage your career thoughtfully and purposefully.

Perhaps the best thing you can do to begin managing your career effectively is to think of it as a series of connections and relationships. What you learn and experience in one situation shapes your next situation, how you approach it and what you get out of it.

Your various past work experiences inform the options you will have and the decisions you will make about your work experiences in the future.

What's more, you're going to find (if you haven't already) that the progression of your career takes on a certain measure of the domino effect: One situation will lead to another that is somehow related, and that one will lead to another related situation, and so on. Typically, this pattern picks up momentum as a career progresses. Breaking out of it usually requires a drastic and momentous overhaul – what most people call "a career change."

Once you take the long view of your career, you'll need to be clear in your perception and description of change.

You won't be able to say, "I'm thinking about changing careers," any more than you'd be able to say, "I'm thinking about changing lives." But you can plan and achieve a major change (or changes) within your career. The accurate way of planning for that goal and describing it would be to say, "I'm thinking about making a career change." Which is about the same as saying, "I'm thinking about making some real changes in my life."

The age-stage theory

Some career theorists (academics, psychologists, sociologists, historians, and others who research, study, and write about people's relationships with work) argue that careers progress in very neat, orderly chunks of time and experience. For example, there's the early career, then the midcareer. At some point just before or just after that, there's the peak career. Later on there's the early late career, and finally the late career itself. This view of career advancement that ties into phases of adult growth and development is called an age-stage career theory.

■ *The notion of "early" and "late" career is tied to stages of adult development.*

Career theorists who advocate an age-stage view of careers always tie it into phases of adult growth and development. "Early career," for instance, always refers to the first set of working experiences, usually collected in adolescence and the early 20s. "Late career" typically refers to those working experiences that individuals have while they're approaching or anchored in the later part of adulthood, a stage that originally meant the 55-to-65 age bracket. When you think about adults who are living late in life these days, however, it usually means adults who are 75 and older.

The fundamental flaw of classic career theory is that it relies on a view of adulthood that is obsolete. Individuals don't become certified adults at age 21, middle-aged at 40, older at 60, and elderly at 75. Life expectancy is much longer than it was when classic career theory came into being. People also are marrying later, raising families later, and working later in life. For many adults, retirement is not an option – either because they want or need the income or because they don't want to stop working. For retirement-age adults who keep working, work can be a source of satisfaction as well as income. Not everyone is able to enjoy that kind of relationship with work, but many do.

Boundaries that don't bind

Lifestyles have evolved so much over the last few decades that the start and end points of so-called predictable life stages have become very elastic. Some individuals move into their version of middle age around their 30th birthday (you may know a 30-year-old who seems miles away from being young). Others don't start behaving like middle-aged adults until they're pushing 50.

There's also the other end of the spectrum, those adults in their 60s who seem "old." They may have very low energy, be impatient with some of the physical symptoms of aging, be chronically pessimistic, or have all of these characteristics. On the other hand, you probably know of adults who always exude youth and vitality, whether they're in the 40s, 50s, 60s, or beyond.

Different approaches at different times

There's truth to the idea that career development is tied to adult development. What you're capable of doing in the workplace, what you need from your relationship to work, and what you're able to attain are different at different stages of life.

INTERNET

www.aarp.org

People over 50, individuals seeking a late-career change, and anyone approaching or enjoying retirement can find a wide range of useful information and services at the web site of the American Association of Retired Persons (AARP).

What works for you in your 20s is not likely to be what works for you in your 40s, and what seems right in your 40s isn't likely to be right in your 60s. Why is this true? Because even if you don't go looking for it, change will come to you; and adult individuals have an amazing ability to learn, grow, and evolve. As life happens, change happens and your life experience broadens.

The long view of career management takes into account your evolution as a person and a professional, starting with a fundamental assessment of who you are and what makes you tick: your career values, your interests, your skills, and your personal qualities. The details of your self-assessment will serve as building blocks for your career management strategies. It will give you a solid foundation of knowledge about yourself that is essential for exploring career options, making choices and decisions, and designing workable action plans to reach your goals.

■ **Think about who** *you are and what you want as a positive start to managing your career.*

Working well takes work

*AS **SHOULD BE VERY** clear to you by now, where you are in life has a lot to do with what you need from your career – and how you go about getting it. You may be in a phase of your career where you experience an urgent need for change. That calls for intensive work and a great deal of focus and dedication.*

■ **You may wish to** *think about a change of direction in your career.*

Or, you may be just beginning to sense that you'll need to make a change somewhere down the line. That gives you the luxury of more breathing room and a more deliberate approach. If you're looking to enter the workforce for the first time or re-enter after a long period of absence, your quest for change will probably be paced somewhat moderately.

Wherever you are in your career, you'll want to set a priority for your career management activities. It could be that nothing is more urgent right now, especially if you've just lost your job or you're experiencing intense frustration or dissatisfaction in your current job. More likely, though, it's one of several aspects of your life that demand a significant investment of time, energy, and focus – your family, your lifestyle, your fitness, your finances.

■ **Take time out** *to consider what's really important to you.*

Assign a priority to your career management activities. Where you rank that priority has a lot to do with what else is going on in your life at any given moment. How you proceed with managing your career is up to you.

No matter where you are in your career, no matter how satisfied or successful you are or aren't, you must put some time, attention, and energy toward managing your career on an ongoing basis. That's a fundamental guideline for managing your career effectively, and it's nonnegotiable.

Designing your own track

IT'S EASY TO THINK ABOUT QUITTING *your current job and finding another one. It takes absolutely no work to decide that your career doesn't amount to a hill of beans and that you're ready to overhaul it like a car you've driven 75,000 miles.*

Or, if you're not currently employed, it's easy to think that you can latch onto one of those opportunities you see in the classified ads or on the Internet. After all, those are real jobs just waiting to be filled by qualified people, aren't they? (Not necessarily; see Chapter 14 for a discussion of the "public" job market.) Surely there must be a job hidden in that haystack of ads that calls for just the set of qualifications you have. All you have to do is comb the haystack carefully enough, right? Wrong.

■ **Don't become** *another cog in the corporate machine.*

While help-wanted ads do contain some jobs that are eventually filled by people just like you, your chances of actually landing one of those jobs are pretty small. And even if you do, your chances of finding real career satisfaction in it are even smaller.

Responding to help-wanted ads is the equivalent of pursuing potential work situations just because they are there (or may be there). In many ways, that's the career course of least resistance – like hitchhiking along the career highway and grabbing a ride with the first vehicle that comes your way.

What's wrong with landing a job through the classifieds? For many people, absolutely nothing. Navigating the classifieds has successfully employed millions of people. Very few of them, however, wind up in a job they really want.

Here's the point: Managing your career effectively, and for maximum success and satisfaction, means avoiding the course of least resistance. Opt instead for a track that's designed by you and around your needs. Obviously to accomplish that you're going to have to do some difficult work, perhaps over a fairly long period of time.

■ **Your ideal job** *is out there, but it may take time and effort to find it.*

The good news is that even though it may be difficult, it's not work that hurts; it just requires time and concentration. The bad news is that there are no guarantees that it will pay off the way you want it to. But if you do the work and dedicate yourself to it over time, you will increase your chances of attaining the career success and satisfaction you want. In other words, doing the work may not make your career success a sure thing, but not doing the work will make your lack of success a sure thing.

■ **Time spent managing** *your career is certainly time well invested.*

Asking yourself the tough questions

BEGIN BY CONFRONTING THE REALLY TOUGH QUESTIONS *about your career, and let your answers inspire you to action. Work to come up with thoughtful, detailed answers to the following tough questions.*

What's good about what I have?

No matter how desperate your current situation is, no matter how bleak, bland, or boring it may be, there's a good chance that there's something about it that works for you. Maybe it gives you the opportunity to get things done your own way, without following a format or a routine. Or maybe you enjoy many of the people you work with, enough so that you'd miss them if you were to change your job.

■ **Your coworkers** *may be the best thing about your current job.*

Identify the positive qualities of your current situation. Count those as things you'd like to have in your next situation. And if it feels like that's a long way off, concentrate on the positive qualities of your current job to make it more bearable – and perhaps, in small but significant ways, enjoyable.

What aspects are missing?

I'm not talking solely about money. Sure, your time, efforts, and services have value to an employer, and it may seem to you that you're not being paid what you're worth. Welcome to the club! Most people feel that they deserve to earn more money – and many really do. (Teachers and social workers head the list of underpaid professionals.)

But the issue of compensation is very tricky, and it's influenced by a host of factors. Each industry has its own standards of pay (which are by no means commensurate with the importance of each industry to society or the good of the world), and even within each industry pay scales fluctuate by organization. Large, established companies are generally likelier to pay on the higher end of the scale than smaller startup firms, which usually need to count every penny for their first few years in business, and often beyond. Several other factors influence compensation levels, too, most of them well beyond your control.

Apart from pay, however, there are many other factors that form your relationship with work. Each of them contributes to the level of contentment you experience with your career. Creating a list of the things you need and do not have in your current situation can help you clarify the vision of what your next situation should be.

For example, do you want to perform a large part of your work as a member of a team, or are you more comfortable working by yourself? What about your coworkers – do you feel as if you fit in with them, or do you feel uncomfortable when you mix with them? Do you have enough workspace? Resources to get your job done? Time to manage your work well? Thoroughly evaluate and identify exactly what is missing from your current situation, and write them down. (For assistance in creating this list, refer to the "Career Values" section in Chapter 7.)

What alternatives are available?

Determining what the alternatives are to your current work situation may require some serious research and legwork. You need to begin by asking yourself what limitations you have. For example, if you cannot work outside of a 20-mile radius from your home, you don't have as many options as you might if you could expand your radius to 40 miles. Likewise, if you are unable or unwilling to relocate, your options are going to be limited. If you absolutely must earn a certain level of income no matter what, obviously the situations that don't offer that kind of compensation are not viable options.

It gets harder when the question "What's available?" means "What other kind of work is out there?" There is no way you're ever going to understand or even know about every single way of earning a living. But rather than trying to understand jobs, try understanding yourself and the work activities you enjoy doing.

INTERNET

www.bls.gov

To look at current and projected demographic trends in the workforce, check out the extensive web site maintained by the U.S. Bureau of Labor Statistics. This site also provides online access to an indispensable career guide, the Occupational Outlook Handbook (see Chapter 11).

First, ask yourself whether you most enjoy working with objects, information, concepts, or people. Then rank those categories, assigning 1 to your highest interest and 4 to your lowest. Second, concentrate on expanding your top two categories. For example, if your top category is people, what activities in particular that relate to people do you most enjoy: teaching, helping, managing, persuading, collaborating? If your second category is information, what kinds of information do you typically enjoy working with: financial accounts, research findings, statistical trends, scientific data? (For assistance in creating this list, refer to the "Interests" and "Skills" sections in Chapters 5 and 6, respectively.)

■ **If teaching others** *is what you enjoy, make the most of your skill.*

Rather than trying to shape your career from the top down by trying to find out information about jobs or situations, grow your career from the ground up by starting with yourself and what your own characteristics and preferences are.

Once you have a handle your unique set of qualities, you'll be able to make connections to jobs, professions, and career paths that are likely to involve them. There are plenty of resources to help guide you through that process, including *The Complete Guide for Occupational Exploration* and *The Occupational Outlook Handbook*, both easy-to-access reference works that bridge interests and skills to job profiles.

What expectations are realistic?

This could be the toughest question of all, because a truly honest answer might mean some unpleasant revelations. Many motivational speakers and writers will urge you to adopt the view that you can do anything you want to – anything that you're really passionate about – and the money will automatically (and easily) follow. But the truth is that you can't and the money won't. There are many earthly influences that stand in the way of dreams.

You need to look at your career in the context of your life (more about this in Chapter 7). Ask yourself where you are in your life and what changes you can make, permanently or temporarily, in order to achieve new career goals. Ask yourself what responsibilities and commitments you already have in place and how negotiable they are. Do you have a family to support? A mortgage to finance? Tuition to pay off (or save for)?

In other words, ask yourself what is your level of required income and how much wiggle room does it leave you. Can you afford to change jobs if there's a pay cut involved? Can you really take on the expense of earning an academic degree? What are the long-term consequences of a major career change that will require you to start over at the lower end of the pay scale?

■ **It is now much** *more common to have one or more changes of direction during your working life.*

The age factor

APART FROM FINANCIAL CONCERNS, *there are other factors that have a major influence on career decisions, regardless of whether those decisions involve changing the kind of work you do or just where you do it. A big factor is your age. Don't make the mistake of thinking that age places no limits on what you can do to earn a living and what you can't. It does.*

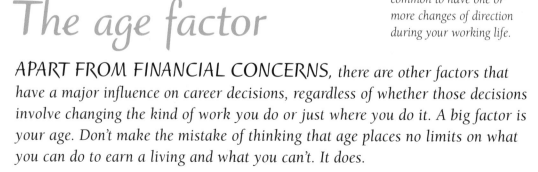

Even apart from the unfairness and injustice of *ageism*, the limitations an employer places on an employee based on its perception of the employee's age, advancing in life brings into the work-world picture issues that affect you personally regardless of your career status. As you mature, you're likely to experience changes in your health, energy level, skill levels, and, very importantly, how you look at the world and perceive your place in it, and you should consider all the facts as you develop your self-assessment and career plan. This is not to say that your age will necessarily impose restrictions on your career development. It is likely that you will match well with different work situations and opportunities as you get older. In fact, your age may open more career possibilities for you than it closes.

> **DEFINITION**
>
> *Discrimination in the workplace based on an individual's chronological age is called* ageism. *Although ageism is technically illegal, it is fairly pervasive throughout the world of work.*

A useful exercise is to take stock of the age-related considerations that are imposed on you by external influences (factors that you have no control over, such as the youth-orientation of American culture, the tendency in the corporate world to "hire young," and the inevitable changes to your body and health). You should also distinguish them from age-related considerations that are internal influences on your career. These are the influences that come from within and are prompted by you alone. They include evolving attitudes about what's important in life and your own decisions about what you can and can't do. Here are a couple of examples.

Passion can produce new possibilities

Stan was 30 when he began thinking about pursuing a major change in his career. Up to that point he'd been making a living as an advertising writer. Stan's self-assessment work brought to light, among other things, a passion for baseball. He thought about what it would take to pursue the sport as a player, even to experience it for just a couple of years before he reached middle age. Yet he hadn't played a lick of baseball since his elementary school days.

It didn't take long for Stan to conclude that, even if he devoted one hundred percent of his time to developing his baseball skills and talents for several years, playing baseball professionally did not represent a viable career choice for him at that point in his life. (Basketball superstar Michael Jordan, one of the most talented athletes ever to play professional sports, attempted to convert his skills to the baseball diamond at a relatively advanced age. Even he was not able to reach the level of athletic success as a baseball player that he envisioned.)

So, Stan found himself face-to-face with one of the external age-related influences: limitations on his pursuit imposed by the age-related falloff of athletic skills. In a creative maneuver, he eventually bridged his interest in baseball with his skills as a writer and went to work for a sports magazine. He hopes to eventually write exclusively about baseball and to research and complete a book on the sport.

Is not working an option?

Susan was in her early 50s when the book publishing company that had employed her most of her professional life initiated drastic cutbacks and a severe downsizing, eliminating her position and dozens of others. A generous severance package supported Susan's transition for many months and gave her the luxury of time to do serious career evaluation and explore her options carefully. She was, at that point, situated at a major crossroads in her life. Her children were grown and on their own, her husband was successful in his own career, and Susan might have entertained the idea of retiring to pursue her many leisure interests. But she wanted no part of that.

Instead of turning away from her career, Susan looked forward in her life and calculated how many more years she would be working. She startled herself with her answer. Susan could not envision the day when she would not be working at something very intensely and with the fullest energy she could summon. Her conclusion? That it was not too late in life to embark on a radical career change, one that required a long period of professional training and an even lengthier period of apprenticeship that could be brutally stressful and competitive. At 52, Susan researched law schools, prepared for and successfully completed the LSAT, and received three offers of admission to prestigious law programs. She accepted one and is now at work pursuing a new profession – and midlife career dreams.

Among Susan's challenges in the process of redirecting her career were the internal influences on age-related career limitations. She needed to confront a series of key questions about herself before finalizing and committing to her decision. Would she have the resolve to complete a rigorous three-year professional program before she could begin working in her new field? Did she want to be among the oldest students in the program? Would she be able to

■ *If you see your working life only as a series of days – make the change!*

enjoy working in her field as a junior professional at her relatively advanced age? And, perhaps most significantly, would she be able to find meaningful employment over the next 15 to 20 years? For Susan, the answer to all these questions was yes. Other people might reach different conclusions – and their decisions would be right for them.

A celebration for the ages

As 1999 drew to a close, one middle-aged professional reached the culmination of an extraordinary plan to observe the arrival of the new millennium. More than ten years earlier, after working halfheartedly in his family's business for years, Michael decided to pursue a new profession. He set career goals and focused on them single-mindedly. In 1990 he marked his first milepost: he gained admission to medical school. His dedication to his newly chosen profession was unwavering throughout the long years of academic training and then a formal internship. By the end of the decade, as the year 2000 approached, Michael was able to realize a goal that he'd set years before: to perform his first surgical procedure before the 21st century. In 1999 he was 56.

When asked if his age would work for or against him in his new profession, he said, "Definitely it will work for me. I think I have a lot more empathy at my age than most people who are younger than me."

So the question of what's realistic in your career has a special meaning for you, which can be a different answer from everyone else's. The answers are shaped both by external influences that are beyond an individual's control and internal influences that are different in everyone. Confronting both sets of influences will give you a lot of information about yourself and the extent of your appetite for managing your career in a forceful, satisfying way. Whether you're considering a radical career change or simply ways to grow and develop in your current career, you'll need to ask yourself how much time, energy, resources, and resolve are at your disposal to get your career the way you want it to be.

A simple summary

✓ Your career, like your life, has phases. In order to manage it effectively, you need to take the long view and avoid situational perspectives.

✓ You'll be more purposeful in managing your career if you develop an appreciation for process. Significant, major career goals just can't be achieved overnight. Typically, they take careful planning and deliberate pursuit over a period of time.

✓ Career development is linked to adult development. The work situation that's completely right during one period of your life may be completely wrong for the next one.

✓ Your career is likely to yield greater successes and satisfaction if you avoid the course of least resistance in making key decisions and commitments.

✓ Grow your career from the ground up. You have no choice but to begin with what you have right now. Ask yourself what's good about your current situation, what's missing, what's available, and what's realistic. Let your answers inspire your actions.

Chapter 3

Identifying With Your Work

YOU CAN USUALLY TELL HOW people feel about their career by the way they describe it. How you think about and talk about your work tells others a lot about you. In this chapter, you'll learn about the different ways to align with your work and why your choice of alignment will influence how you manage your career.

By examining carefully the world of work as a system of different contexts for your career, you'll understand why it's important to invest time and energy in each. You'll also see how and why one of them holds a special key to your career continuity and vitality.

Got your thinking cap on?

In this chapter...

✓ The inevitable question

✓ Planet Work

✓ Your profession: choosing for the long haul

✓ What about change?

THINK CAREFULLY ABOUT HOW YOU RELATE TO YOUR WORK

The inevitable question

YOU'RE AT A PARTY, *or on line at the grocery store, or riding a bus, or posting mail in town. You fall into conversation with someone you don't know. It's a pleasant conversation, and before a lot of time passes, your new acquaintance asks you a question that seems as inevitable as rain on a cloudy day:*

"So what do you do?"

How do you respond? Do you mention the name of your employer? Do you describe the business field you're in? Do you talk about a role you play in the private or public sector? Do you refer to a profession? Do you say that you're in transition? Or do you recite what's on your business card?

How you describe your work says a lot about who you are. People basically know this and usually go to great lengths to portray themselves in the most impressive way imaginable (sometimes at the expense of accuracy). Let's look at just a few of the many ways to answer this question:

1. I'm in sales.

2. I work for American Express.

3. I'm a teacher.

4. I do financial stuff.

5. I'm a secretary.

6. I have my own business.

7. I write for Jay Leno.

8. I have a job at the post office.

9. I'm a dentist.

10. I sell insurance.

11. I'm with Lucent.

12. I'm an account manager.

13. I work at Macy's.

■ **Do you run** *your own company, or do you work for yourself?*

■ **Do you work** *in finance, or are you an accountant?*

Which of the answers provide the most information, and the clearest picture, of a person's work life? Which provide the least information – and the fuzziest picture? Now, while you're in a thoughtful mood, ask yourself this: Which answers tell you the most about a person's needs for recognition? Apart from how appealing these work situations may be, which of the options comes closest to the way you describe your work?

Talking about work

There are lots of ways to talk about your livelihood. Most of them say a lot about how you identify with your work and your career. What, exactly, do you know about a person who says that he's "in sales"? You might presume that he deals with people, is fairly persuasive, has a solid measure of self-confidence, and does a lot of traveling. Accurate or not, that summary approximates a typical, reasonable perception of an individual who is in sales. And maybe that's just what this guy wants you to think.

What about the individual who replies, without missing a beat, "I work for American Express"? What would you know about the work this person does? Basically nothing. The Director of Global Marketing could say that she works for American Express, and so could the woman who answers the customer complaint hotline. And so could the guys in the mailroom.

The person who replies "I work for Macy's" is hoping to strike a familiar chord with you, because everyone has heard of Macy's. And the person who says "I'm with Lucent" is presuming that you know it's a hugely successful telecommunications firm.

Identifying with work

People *align* with their work in different ways. Often the ways people describe their work contain hints of information about their career satisfaction. Many people take real pleasure in aligning themselves with an organization that enjoys renown – in the hope that some of the renown will rub off on them. Others feel genuinely proud of the goods or services their organization provides and hope that you'll find a way to feel as favorably about them. And some people identify with an organizational name or image to evoke prestige.

DEFINITION

You align with your work when you think about your career in relation to yourself and your needs.

What's wrong with tying your career image to an organization? Not a thing. In fact, identifying your work in the same breath as a company or institution that has high name recognition can be one of the small, steady pleasures of a career. However, it's important to remember that identifying strongly with a single organization doesn't say much about you and your own unique qualities. And when people ask you about your work, they usually ask because they're really interested in finding out more about you and what makes you tick. (How you reply provides a lot of information about you!)

If it seems like I'm picking on fine points here, try to keep an open mind. The idea that's key in this chapter, and throughout the rest of this book, is that managing your career effectively means paying attention to several different contexts for your work. Whether you realize it or not, you participate in several contexts at once. For example, think for a moment about the many ways in which you are "a citizen," an active participant in an organized body of persons. You are a citizen of your community, your city or town, your state, and your country – all at the same time. What I'm describing are different roles within several contexts that range from very focused (community) to very broad (country).

Planet Work

WHEN LEARNING A NEW CONCEPT, *an analogy can help convey the necessary information. Let's think of the work world as a planet and call it Planet Work. The terrain of Planet Work poses several geographic locations (contexts) in which you must navigate your career. To thrive on the planet and to gain the kind of satisfaction from your career that you want and deserve, you must understand its geography.*

A systematic view of the work world

Caela Farren, an internationally known consultant and educator, has done pioneering work in career development and management for more than 25 years. She has developed and refined a systematic view of the work world that makes clear distinctions between professions, industries, organizations, and jobs – and how working individuals relate to each. In her book *Who's Running Your Career?* (Bard Press, 1997), Farren summarizes her broad experience in career management by demonstrating how this system of work relationships impacts new workers, individuals in career transition, and experienced workers.

Farren's system of the work world and its interdependent relationships is summarized by the idea of Planet Work, which has a system of geography that is similar.

In simplest terms, your career involves four different contexts for the work you do. In ascending order, or smallest to largest, they are:

 Your job   Your organization

 Your industry   Your profession

When you think about going to work, you probably think about going to your job. You think about the day-to-day activities and routines that you get involved in to earn a paycheck. Your job can be very consuming, because it presents you with a neverending stream of tasks to accomplish. Along with the tasks come unanticipated crises to manage, "fires" to put out, actions to initiate, and processes to manage. All of these add up to a bundle of activities that comprise what you know and think about as your job.

■ **What tasks constitute** *your job?*

In the geography of Planet Work, your job is the equivalent of your home.

Your home is the place where you live: it is the most immediate context for the experience of living – the one you know best, and the one that commands the bulk of your time, attention, and energy. It's only natural to lose sight of the larger geographic scheme by focusing on the tasks and responsibilities of your home. It's equally natural to lose sight of the larger scheme of your career by focusing on the tasks and responsibilities that are most immediate to your work experience – your job.

But there's a catch: Just as your home is likely to change during the course of your life, your job is going to change, too.

Jobs come and go in the workplace at a fairly rapid clip. Those that do not disappear altogether are constantly evolving. Change in the workplace demands that they do. And, as you saw in Chapter 1, change is happening at such an accelerated pace that jobs are appearing, evolving, and disappearing more quickly than ever before. If you've been laid off, or downsized, you know this all too well. If you've been in a single job for a long time, think about what your job entailed five years ago – or even three. Chances are that your tasks, duties, and responsibilities took a different form than they do now.

■ **Today your job** *may be totally different from the one you were first employed to do.*

61

Looking at Planet Work from above

Let's look at Planet Work from a bird's-eye view, starting with the largest context and working our way toward the smallest and most focused.

1 *Profession* = country. By far the largest context for your work is your profession. It's the equivalent, in the geography of Planet Work, of identifying with your country.

2 *Industry* = state or province. Your industry is the next largest context for your work. On Planet Work, your industry is the equivalent of the state or province in which you live. It's a more narrowly defined context for your career – a smaller area of land.

3 *Organization* = hometown. Your organization is an assembly of people who are clustered together within an industry to work toward well-defined goals. It could be a manufacturing company, retail store, nonprofit foundation, hospital, telemarketing firm, or any other aggregate of individuals who are working toward a common purpose. On Planet Work, your organization is the equivalent of your hometown. You may hail from a major city or a small rural town. Similarly, you may work in a large corporation or a five-person business.

4 *Job* = address. Finally, your job is the smallest, most immediate, most changeable, and most consuming context for your career. On Planet Work, your job is the equivalent of your home address at any given point in time. It's likely that you'll have several addresses (and at least as many jobs) during the course of your lifetime.

Now that I've defined the different locales on Planet Work, let's visit them and look at how effective career management relates to each of them.

Your profession: choosing for the long haul

JUST WHAT IS MEANT BY PROFESSION, ANYWAY? Caela Farren describes a profession as a discipline of work activities that exists in response to enduring human needs. She identifies 12 basic needs that have remained and will remain constant over time:

BASIC HUMAN NEEDS

Home and shelter

Family and kinship

Work and career

Social relationships

Physical and mental health

Financial security

Learning

Transportation and mobility

Environment and safety

Community

Leisure

Spirituality

■ **Think of your health** *when considering a career change.*

■ **It is important** *to consider the environment you will be working in before accepting a job.*

Think of a profession as a discipline of work activities that exists to serve one or more of the basic human needs. Professions last over time and evolve along with the times. Becoming a member of a profession usually requires a long period of specialized education or tutelage, or a lengthy apprenticeship that involves formal supervision. Some professions are easier to learn and enter than others, but achieving true excellence in any given profession usually takes about 15 years or longer.

Many people use the term profession to refer exclusively to those disciplines that require an extensive amount of formal, specialized academic training, such as doctors, dentists, lawyers, psychologists, and teachers. But in the world of Planet Work, professions also include trades and crafts, which require a different kind of preparation and, often, long apprenticeships. In other words, professions include many different kinds of work that are sometimes called "blue collar."

■ **"Profession"** *is a loose term that can refer to lawyers and sculptors alike.*

An easy way to think about professions is to think about people in roles, rather than in fields or areas of expertise. For instance, "interior designer" is a profession, but "design" is an industry. Professions usually refer to the individuals that specialize and earn a living in particular career roles – professionals. Here are some examples:

PROFESSIONS

1. Accountant
2. Animal trainer
3. Architect
4. Athletic coach
5. Auto mechanic
6. Beautician
7. Biologist
8. Cosmetician
9. Electrician
10. Engineer
11. Home nurse
12. Interior designer
13. Landscaper
14. Lawyer
15. Marketer
16. Musician
17. Occupational therapist
18. Painter
19. Photographer
20. Physician
21. Pilot
22. Plumber
23. Politician
24. Salesperson
25. Sanitation worker
26. Sculptor
27. Social worker
28. Software designer
29. Teacher
30. Tree surgeon
31. Television producer
32. Veterinarian
33. Writer

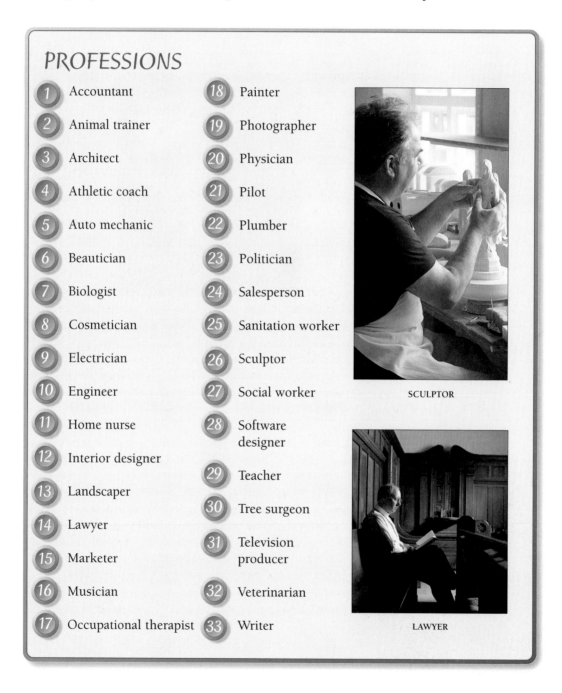

SCULPTOR

LAWYER

How professions shape careers

Although some of the professions listed above sound like jobs, notice that they are not confined to a particular context or situation. A writer can write for the entertainment industry or the healthcare field. A social worker can practice in a big city or a rural town.

Professions are portable – they can travel across industries and organizations.

Professions endure over time, whereas jobs spring up and then change or disappear like dandelions. Also, professions do not typically pose age barriers, unlike many jobs. In any given profession, there is room for junior participants and senior practitioners.

Caela Farren's ideas and overarching philosophy about managing careers can be summarized by a slogan she quotes in her writing: "Take a job and you'll work for a day; craft a profession and you'll work for life." Choosing and identifying with a profession is perhaps the most important career decision you'll ever make.

Over the long haul, what counts for the most in managing your career well is what you work as, not where you work. If your job is to read and route customer complaint letters for the FineWrite Pen Company, your profession is customer service. When it's time to look for another job, you'd want to investigate all opportunities that enabled you to have direct contact with customers, not just jobs at pen companies that required you read and route complaint letters.

Industries and organizations require a blend of professions to achieve their goals and missions. It's important to remember that professions can apply directly to many different industries and organizations. Organizations often bring together a number of different professions.

Professions are always evolving as technology advances. Think of the medical profession, which includes physicians, nurses, surgeons, and other specialized care providers. Although medicine has existed from time immemorial, it has continually changed and been refined as advances in technology have allowed. By their nature, professions provide individuals with room to grow, develop, improve, and become more proficient – which is what mastering a profession entails.

■ **You may have** *the role of accountant in a marketing company.*

You've already seen that a career is like a life – you get only one and, if you're lucky, you'll have it for a long time. By far the smartest choice you can make in your career is your choice of profession. Your profession will allow you to be portable, and it will offer you as much stability as is reasonable to expect on Planet Work in the 21st century. In addition, your chosen profession will provide you with two career factors that are important beyond measurement:

① The opportunity to continue to grow and develop in your career

② A sense of identity that carries the potential for deep and lasting satisfaction

INTERNET

www.iccweb.com

This is a noteworthy site for career-minded individuals. It features a wealth of career-related categories, which link to clusters of related sites such as business for sale, career articles, job sharing, networking, older workers, self-employment, and others. It's a comprehensive and useful site.

What about change?

SOME PEOPLE NEVER HAVE TO *make a single career decision. They know from childhood what they want to be when they grow up. They go through law school or medical school, or enter military service, and then establish themselves and stay in their chosen profession until they retire. Such individuals are the exception, not the rule. Most of us will change our profession at least once during the course of our careers, and many of us will change several times.*

■ **Most of us will** *end up making numerous decisions about our careers during our working lives.*

Can you change professions as readily as you can change jobs? No, you can't.

Remember that a profession is a discipline of career activities that requires extensive preparation through education or training, or both, along with a period of apprenticeship. You can work in more than one profession during the course of your career, but think of a profession as requiring at least ten years of dedication. So, you do the math. Think of how many years you'll be working, and then think of how many changes of profession you can reasonably succeed in during that time frame.

In the next chapter, you'll learn more about Planet Work and encounter other contexts for your career, which relate much more closely to where you work: industries, organizations, and jobs.

■ **Choosing your profession** *may be the most important career decision you'll ever make.*

A simple summary

✔ There are many ways to talk about your livelihood and identify with your work. How you think about and describe your work says a lot about who you are and how satisfying your career is.

✔ The world of work is a system of different contexts for your career. To thrive, you must make choices about each context – and take ongoing initiatives in each.

✔ Choosing and dedicating yourself to a profession is probably the most important decision you will make during your career. It exerts a powerful influence on your career continuity and vitality.

✔ You should remember that it's the work you do, and not the places where you do it, that holds the key to enduring career success and satisfaction.

Chapter 4

Choosing Where You Work

BECAUSE SOME WORK contexts represent the best bets for smart career management, while others are more risky, where you work is just as important as what you do. In this chapter, you'll learn how industries and organizations bring together various professions. It will become clear to you how and why jobs are really packages of tasks and activities that come and go quickly. Ready for a closer look at the geography of Planet Work?

In this chapter...

✓ Industries

✓ Gauging career stability

✓ Organizations

✓ Jobs

IDENTIFYING YOUR PLACE OF WORK INVOLVES SEVERAL KEY DECISIONS

Industries

WHAT DO YOU THINK OF WHEN *you hear the word* industry? *Smokestacks? Manufacturing plants? Railroads? If we were living at the dawn of the 20th century, rather than the 21st, those images would be accurate. They portray some of the most typical working conditions and situations of earlier times.*

You should recall from the previous chapter that in the geography of Planet Work, industries are the equivalent of the state or province where you live. A state or province is a smaller area of land than a nation. It has a more confined locale. States and provinces can vary greatly in their character, appearance, population, economy, and history.

> **DEFINITION**
>
> *An industry is a field of work. It has definite boundaries, just like states or provinces. Industries exist to provide essential products or services. They endure over time. Industries do change and evolve, but not as rapidly as organizations or jobs.*

Fields of work that reach far and wide

In the previous chapter, you looked closely at professions. These are best described by referring to people (lawyers, electricians, musicians, etc.). Industries are most accurately described as fields of work.

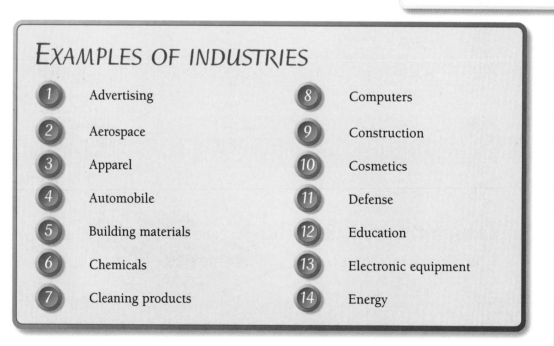

EXAMPLES OF INDUSTRIES

1. Advertising
2. Aerospace
3. Apparel
4. Automobile
5. Building materials
6. Chemicals
7. Cleaning products
8. Computers
9. Construction
10. Cosmetics
11. Defense
12. Education
13. Electronic equipment
14. Energy

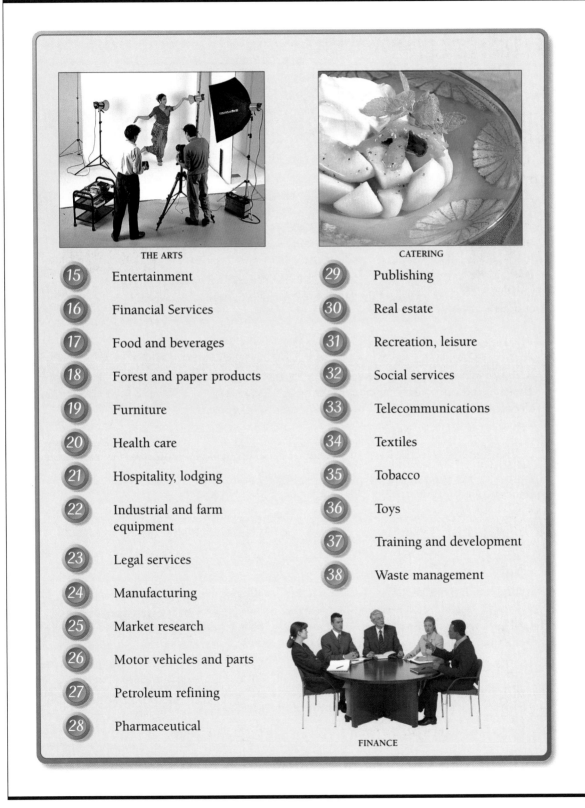

THE ARTS

CATERING

15 Entertainment

16 Financial Services

17 Food and beverages

18 Forest and paper products

19 Furniture

20 Health care

21 Hospitality, lodging

22 Industrial and farm equipment

23 Legal services

24 Manufacturing

25 Market research

26 Motor vehicles and parts

27 Petroleum refining

28 Pharmaceutical

29 Publishing

30 Real estate

31 Recreation, leisure

32 Social services

33 Telecommunications

34 Textiles

35 Tobacco

36 Toys

37 Training and development

38 Waste management

FINANCE

Industries typically provide a wide range of opportunities. For example, think of all the ways to work in the entertainment industry and all the roles in the health care industry. Many people launch or reshape their careers by choosing an industry to work in without necessarily having a full understanding of the many specialized roles and occupations within it. Is there anything wrong with that? It depends.

If an individual is truly passionate about the product or service provided by an industry, it might not matter what role he or she may have within that industry. Just being "around" a particular product or service and participating in the process of presenting it to the world may provide a deep sense of career satisfaction and meaning.

■ **Think about** *the kind of job you really want to do.*

Because industries typically house a broad spectrum of roles, many people who allow their careers to be guided by their choice of industry find themselves working in the right field but the wrong job.

If that describes you, one of the most urgent career steps you should take is to look at the other roles in your industry and ask yourself if any of them holds a greater potential for satisfaction.

Professions within industries: primary or secondary

While navigating the geography of Planet Work, it's important to understand that industries attract clusters of different professions. Accountants, for example, work in virtually every industry. (And when payday comes, you're thankful that they do!)

Every industry attracts both *primary professions* and *secondary professions*. The primary professions are those that truly represent the essence of the industry. In newspaper publishing, for example, reporters and editors do the work that the world associates with newspapers. They represent the primary professions of the newspaper industry. But to thrive, the industry needs people to perform secondary professions: marketers, salespersons, human resources managers, accountants, auditors, and administrators.

■ **Being an editor** *is only the tip of the newspaper industry's iceberg.*

DEFINITION

Primary professions *are those that are core to the industry and indispensable.* Secondary professions *are those that are farther away from the core of the industry and not necessarily indispensable.*

Gauging career stability

IS THIS SPLITTING HAIRS, DO YOU THINK? *No, we're looking carefully at the geography of Planet Work because it has very important implications for you and your career. To gauge the stability of your career, you need to understand that every industry has what can be called primary professions. They're closest to the essence of the industry, and the ones that will not change.*

It's important to know where your profession fits into the scheme of your industry and whether it is essential to the industry.

If you work in one of the professions that is primary to your industry, your role is probably more stable within that industry. If you work in a profession that is secondary to your industry, your role is potentially less stable within that industry.

As you move through the process of career planning, you should take a serious look at the industry you're currently working in or the one you're thinking of entering. Think about what's going on in the industry: Is it growing or declining? Is it a newer industry, like e-commerce, or an aging one, like heavy manufacturing? What are its prospects for expansion and change? What are the important recent trends in the industry? Carefully research your industry in relation to your profession, as well as to the larger context of your career.

Organizations

ORGANIZATIONS ARE COLLECTIONS OF PEOPLE *from various professions who are united – organized – to pursue a well-defined set of goals and objectives. Usually the goals are shaped by commercial or philanthropic concerns. Organizations can take the form of small businesses, medium-sized companies, or huge corporations with divisions that cut across several industries. Organizations can also take the form of foundations, associations, institutes, and even small neighborhood enterprises.*

On Planet Work, your organization is the equivalent of your hometown. Whether you hail from a major metropolis or a small rural town, you have intimate knowledge of what makes it tick: the culture, customs, and people. Chances are you feel very comfortable there – right at home. And whether you do or don't feel like you belong there, you know exactly why you feel that way.

Organizations have distinctive cultures

The organization you work for will provide you with similar senses. It's an immediate context for the work that you do. Every organization has a distinctive culture, a personality all its own, which has significant implications for your career.

To attain and preserve the career success you want and deserve, you'll need to find the organization that makes you feel right at home. That could be the leading company in a particular industry, or it could be that company's fiercest competitor. It could be an exciting startup business or a more mature firm. It could be a franchise that excites you. Or, it could be your own enterprise.

Like many people, you might feel inclined to shape your career around a particular organization. Many, many people are enchanted and seduced by the public image of an organization and assume that being on the inside will fill them with a personal measure of what they see on the outside. Unfortunately, this rarely happens because there's a vast difference between perception and reality. One of the places where this difference is most obvious is in the organizational sector of Planet Work.

In general, it's usually not a good strategy to target a particular organization as the focal point of your career.

Why not? Two main reasons stand out. First, organizations undergo change relatively often, sometimes very quickly. Second, as you saw in chapter 1, organizations no longer provide a context of support for the span of their employees' careers.

The rules of the "contract" between organizations and individuals are far different from what they were a generation or two ago. The bottom line of that contract is that you cannot rely on an organization to advance your career and ensure your success and stability.

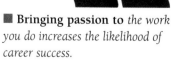
■ **Bringing passion to** *the work you do increases the likelihood of career success.*

Evaluating organizations

The final decades of the 20th century repeatedly dramatized the new work contract as many corporations that had remained constant for generations transformed, reshaped, reorganized, reinvigorated, or expired. For instance, until the century was about three-quarters over, AT&T had a monopoly on telephone service. Today, the company is still successful but on a much smaller scale.

The Woolworth Corporation, which built an empire of retail household goods stores in the early part of the century, shifted its core business to athletic apparel and footwear as consumer needs changed over the years. Finally, in the mid-1990s, as the dwindling number of Woolworth stores became increasingly irrelevant to contemporary lifestyles and purchasing patterns, the company reorganized to concentrate fully on its other lines of business. The Woolworth name, so prevalent in American consumers' lives during the early part of the century, disappeared from the retail landscape.

Think about businesses you know that have come and gone over a period of time, both neighborhood enterprises as well as nationally known businesses. Newspaper and news web site headlines are full of dramatic signals of change in the organizational landscape. Some organizations evolve slowly over generations, while others transform virtually overnight. Even organizations with a history of stability can be thrown into sudden turmoil if they are bought by or merged with other organizations. Inevitably, major organizational deals result in staff shakeups. Drastic reductions in staff are common as the merged companies identify areas of overlap and redundancy. Placing a single organization at the center of your career planning is placing too much of your career destiny beyond your reach – and out of your control.

INTERNET

www.career-index.com

www.CareerPerfect.com

Several web sites bring together a variety of career- and job-related resources that are useful to individuals considering a major change or planning a search campaign. At these sites you'll find advice and direction on many issues relating to work.

■ **It is unwise** *to place your destiny in the hands of one company.*

You will, however, have to carefully evaluate specific organizations so that you made important decisions about your career. Depending on your current circumstances, you may be asking yourself questions like these:

1. Do I stay here and see what the next few months or years bring?

2. Do I look into the competition and see if I can land a job there?

3. Can I find a position with a smaller or larger organization?

4. Can I work at a place where I'm more than just a cog in a wheel?

5. Would I be able to succeed if I took on a franchise?

6. Could I make a go of it on my own?

7. Should I quit now and see what comes along?

8. Should I approach a particular organization to see if they're hiring?

Notice how each of these questions involves two key ingredients: your career success and the context – the organization – that best facilitates that success. The answers to these questions are essential for you to make intelligent decisions about where you fit best. And because organizations are constantly changing, you must continually evaluate your present work situation and what the alternatives might be.

■ **Don't lose sight** *of your role in your place of work.*

Measuring your organizational vitality

Throughout your career, three key questions will trigger valuable insights and intelligence about the relationship between you and the organization that presently provides your paycheck:

1. What is my place within this organization?

2. What is the place of this organization within its principal industry?

3. How will an association with this organization enrich and enhance my career?

You also will need to ask yourself some other tough questions. What's good about your current organization, and what's missing? Or, if you're gathering information about another organization, you should create a detailed picture of what it would be like to work there. Here are ten pros and cons to help you with your assessment.

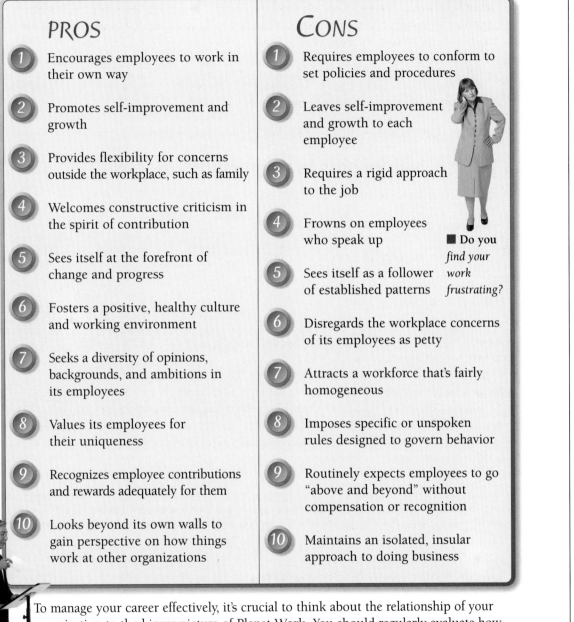

PROS

1. Encourages employees to work in their own way

2. Promotes self-improvement and growth

3. Provides flexibility for concerns outside the workplace, such as family

4. Welcomes constructive criticism in the spirit of contribution

5. Sees itself at the forefront of change and progress

6. Fosters a positive, healthy culture and working environment

7. Seeks a diversity of opinions, backgrounds, and ambitions in its employees

8. Values its employees for their uniqueness

9. Recognizes employee contributions and rewards adequately for them

10. Looks beyond its own walls to gain perspective on how things work at other organizations

CONS

1. Requires employees to conform to set policies and procedures

2. Leaves self-improvement and growth to each employee

3. Requires a rigid approach to the job

4. Frowns on employees who speak up

■ **Do you** *find your* *work* *frustrating?*

5. Sees itself as a follower of established patterns

6. Disregards the workplace concerns of its employees as petty

7. Attracts a workforce that's fairly homogeneous

8. Imposes specific or unspoken rules designed to govern behavior

9. Routinely expects employees to go "above and beyond" without compensation or recognition

10. Maintains an isolated, insular approach to doing business

To manage your career effectively, it's crucial to think about the relationship of your organization to the bigger picture of Planet Work. You should regularly evaluate how well you fit, or align, with your current organization, as well as how your organization fits in the larger context of Planet Work, particularly its health and vitality means looking at the organization in relation to its industry, to your profession, and to your career plans as you currently envision them.

■ **You do not have** *to make a speech to voice your concerns.*

Jobs

WHICH TITLE IN THE FOLLOWING LIST *comes closest to describing the job you have or the job you want? If none of them comes close to describing it, write the title in one of the blank spaces following the list.*

50 JOBS

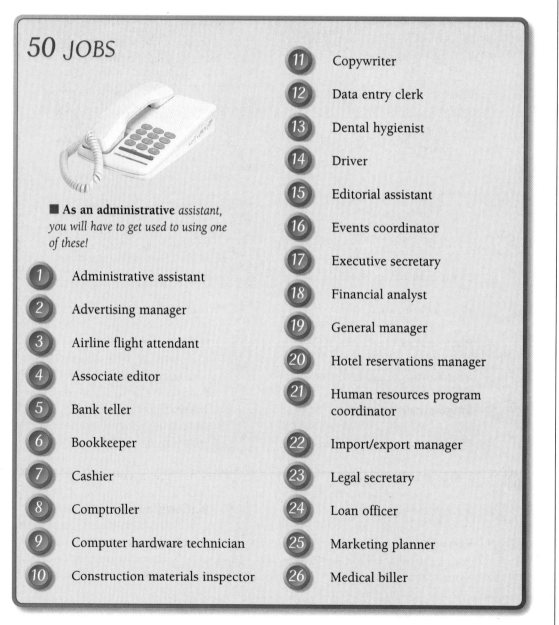

■ **As an administrative** *assistant, you will have to get used to using one of these!*

1. Administrative assistant
2. Advertising manager
3. Airline flight attendant
4. Associate editor
5. Bank teller
6. Bookkeeper
7. Cashier
8. Comptroller
9. Computer hardware technician
10. Construction materials inspector
11. Copywriter
12. Data entry clerk
13. Dental hygienist
14. Driver
15. Editorial assistant
16. Events coordinator
17. Executive secretary
18. Financial analyst
19. General manager
20. Hotel reservations manager
21. Human resources program coordinator
22. Import/export manager
23. Legal secretary
24. Loan officer
25. Marketing planner
26. Medical biller

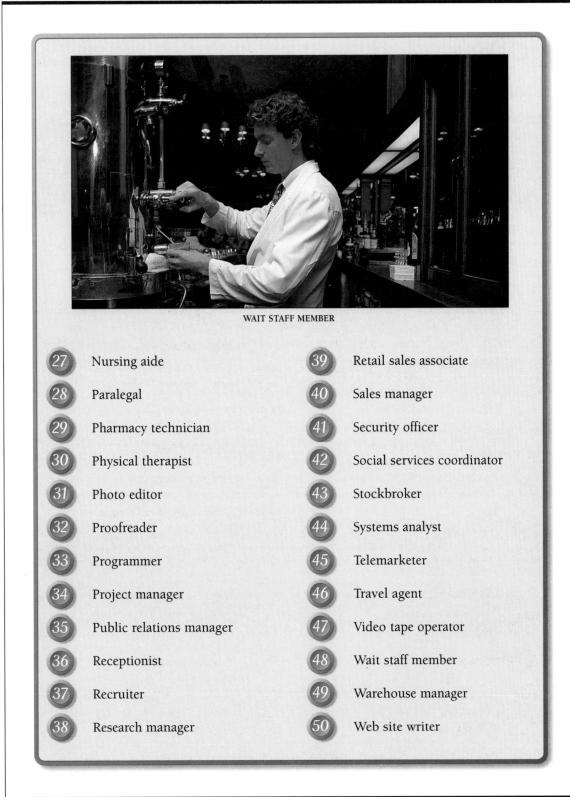

WAIT STAFF MEMBER

Don't worry if you didn't find your job or the job you want on this list. I could have produced a completely different list that might have included your current job or your fantasy job. And a different list after that, and another one after that.

Tasks and activities

It's important to understand that your *job* is not likely to stay constant over time. As the goals of your organization are met or as they evolve, your job too will evolve into another collection of tasks and activities – perhaps slightly different, perhaps radically different. Eventually, a particular job may become unnecessary in the changing context of an organization's goals. When that happens, an individual is likely to hear the words that will ring in his or her ears for a long time: "Your position is being eliminated."

DEFINITION

A job is *a set of tasks and activities that help an organization reach its goals.*

Jobs evolve over time. They are volatile due to outside forces (the needs of the organization). And because they are, it's not a good idea to place them in the forefront of your career planning. Managing your career effectively means much more than attaining or excelling in a single job. It means paying attention to a bigger picture – the larger contexts of work.

But hey, we all need to work, right? Most of us need to earn a living, and so most of us need to hold a job. Many people need to hold two. Throughout your working life you'll need to manage the delicate balance between your job and your career. Here's a fundamental question you should regularly ask yourself because the answer will have a great impact on the measure of success and satisfaction you'll get from your work: Do I focus my energy on my job (tasks to be done now) or on my career (life to live over many years of time)? You'll be glad to know that it's possible to apply energy toward both simultaneously, but only if you don't confuse your career with your job.

Chances are that you will hold a lot of different jobs throughout the course of your working life, but you have only one career.

If and when you decide to pursue a different job, be mindful of how the new job will influence (and possibly reshape) your career.

■ **Your career is** *more than just the routine tasks you undertake in your job – think about it!*

Getting a job: getting into gear

An interesting thing about jobs is that they're plentiful in your field when you're at the beginning of your career and scarce when you're deeper into your career. Or so it seems. Most people can tell you stories about how they fell into their first job or how they answered a classified ad and got hired.

Sometimes student internships convert into real-world job situations. When you're first starting out, it's usually not difficult to land some job in your field. This could be true because you may not be sharply focused on what work you'd really like to do, because your salary requirements are relatively low, because you're impressionable and "trainable," or all of the above. Most people latch onto at least one job simply by coincidence or good (or bad) luck, like hitchhiking and grabbing the first ride that comes along.

However, the farther along you are in your career, the more challenging it probably will be for you to find and keep the job that's truly right for you. Why? There are many reasons.

■ **Keep in mind** *your long-term goals, no matter what your first job is.*

■ **The kind of job** *that you want and the kind of job you can get later in your career may not be one and the same.*

■ **It is perfectly** *normal to assume that what interests us at age 20 may not capture our attention at age 40.*

Experiences count – at work and in life

As adults, we grow and change based on our life experiences. In our careers, we grow and change on our work experiences. What we can do in our 40s may be far different from what we could do in our 20s. And, what matters to us most in our 40s is likely to be far different from what mattered most in our 20s. The same pattern holds true also for adults in their 60s when compared to those same adults in their 40s.

As we advance through our personal life and career, our financial needs also change, and typically we look to our work for greater and greater compensation. Our interests also change, and along with them so might our desire to focus on a specific field or organization.

What you need to know is that the deeper into your career you go, the harder it is to land the job you really need and desire. Not impossible, just harder.

You may also find that your chosen career path presents many opportunities at the entry level, but few opportunities for growth and advancement to the middle and upper levels. If you find yourself running in place after a substantial investment in one career path, you may need to rethink your career direction.

You've probably heard the expression, "Get a job!" Roughly speaking, it means, "Get with the rest of the world and get to work." It's fairly easy to get a job. It's far more difficult to get the right job – the one that's strategically great for you and your career.

■ **Getting a job** *is relatively easy; developing a career is much more difficult.*

Most people on Planet Work don't see the differences between jobs and careers and generally don't care – as long as they're earning a paycheck somewhere. For these people, career management means checking the classified ads or job web sites every few months (or weeks) to see "what else is out there." They hop from job to job, performing the tasks and activities attached to each until they either grow tired of them or the organization grows tired of their contributions.

If you're reading this book, you've already decided that's not good enough for you. Read on and capitalize on the investment you're making in yourself.

A simple summary

✓ Industries bring together different professions, providing a variety of career opportunities for individuals from a variety of backgrounds.

✓ Every industry attracts both primary and secondary professions. The closer a profession is to the core of the industry's activities, the more indispensable it is within that industry. Your choice of industry will have a great influence on your career stability.

✓ Organizations are situated within industries. They bring together groups of individuals from various professions to pursue a well-defined set of goals and objectives. Every organization, large or small, has a distinctive culture or "personality".

✓ Jobs are sets of tasks and activities that help organizations reach their goals. Jobs are formulated, reconfigured, and eliminated over time. Jobs alone typically do not represent viable opportunities for long-range career planning.

✓ Managing your career effectively means investing not only in the job you have (or want), but also in your organization and your industry.

PART TWO

LOOK AT YOURSELF AND REMEMBER WHAT YOU SEE

THINKING SERIOUSLY ABOUT YOURSELF

PART TWO OF THIS BOOK IS DEVOTED to *self-assessment*, the process of looking at and learning about yourself and your career-related qualities in a careful, deliberate way. Most of us get so caught up in our daily routines that we never think about what makes us tick. But that process  *informs* all good career management decisions, so it's vital to devote time and energy to it.

Self-assessment is not a one-time event. Although some of your qualities will remain constant, others will change and *evolve* during the course of your life. The process of self-assessment is the opportunity for you to take note of those changes and enable you to understand their implications for smart career management. What you know about yourself is central to identifying the work situations that will be satisfying and meaningful to you.

Chapter 5

Who Are You – and What Moves You?

SMART CAREER MANAGEMENT begins with smart self-assessment. In this chapter, you'll learn about the Job-Person Match, a simple career management equation that provides a framework for smart self-assessment, and why it's vital to your success and satisfaction at work. You'll then begin to work the equation by looking carefully at your interests – the things that capture your curiosity and attention. You'll classify your interests into four general categories and draw conclusions about which of them attract you the most. It will be easy to see why integrating your interests into your work can bring lasting satisfaction to your career. Finally, you'll use the interest categories to bring into focus work situations and career pathways that may be worth pursuing.

In this chapter...

✓ **Equation for career satisfaction: the job-person match**

✓ **What interests you?**

✓ **Careers, like individuals, are complex**

$$a = b^2 \sqrt{x + y - 3^2}$$
$$(3)^3 - (2)^2$$
$$27 - 8$$

Equation for career satisfaction: the job-person match

HAVE YOU EVER THOUGHT ABOUT *the differences between people who love their work and people who hate it? Somehow, people who hate their work always seem sad, forlorn, angry, or bitter. They express negativity toward everything that relates to their work, to their job, and to the ongoing process of participating in a livelihood. People who hate their work always seem to be struggling – as if they're pushing a huge boulder up a steep hill. If you've talked with anyone who's in this category or if you include yourself in it, you may have the sense that people who hate their work are captives in an earthly hell.*

■ **Don't hate your** *work: life is too short!*

In many ways, you'd be right. People who are unhappy in their work are often unhappy with themselves. They may be unable to change their work situation for any number of reasons, or they may not know how to change it. Either case would inevitably deepen their dissatisfaction with work and make them feel even worse about their ability to take charge of their lives.

The flip side of that distressing picture is the typical portrait of people who are happy in their work. Somehow, they always seem positive and upbeat, confident of their ability to achieve meaningful goals, and content with themselves and the world around them. People who love their work have ease about them. They're the people who simply have to give a boulder a little push from the top of a hill and watch it gather momentum and speed on the way down.

■ **Plan a career** *that makes good use of your interests and skills.*

People who love their work often seem born to be doing the job they're in. They seem to be using every inch of their talent, personality, intelligence, and skills to support and advance the work they do. Even during stressful or frustrating times, people who love their work show different behaviors than people who don't. They seem to be equipped with better tools for solving problems and responding to challenges. And, they typically keep a genuinely positive attitude that goes a long way toward achieving success.

In short, people who love their work seem to "fit" perfectly with their job, like a hand in a tailor-made glove.

VIP Looking at all the angles

*When the traits and characteristics of an individual's personality match up well with those of a particular work situation, career counselors call it career **congruence**.*

■ **If everyone had** *their ideal job, just think what a happier place the world would be.*

In other words, matching a job's requirements with a person's qualities is like aligning the wheels of your car. If your wheels are properly aligned, your car rides smoothly. If your personal qualities and your job requirements are aligned, your career rides smoothly.

> **DEFINITION**
>
> *Simply put, congruence is the state of being in agreement or in a state of harmony.*

That concept is fairly easy to propose, but fairly difficult to realize. Reaching congruence with work involves achieving a delicate balance of many factors and traits – those of the individual and those of the work he or she does. The Job-Person Match that career counselors frequently use to describe the ideal work situation is called the Job-Person Match. The model looks like this:

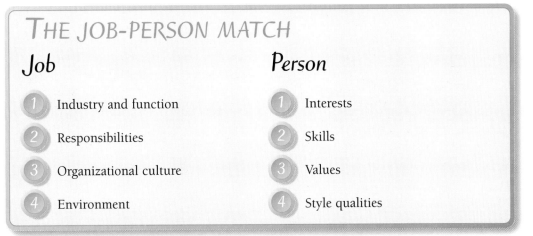

THE JOB-PERSON MATCH

Job

1. Industry and function
2. Responsibilities
3. Organizational culture
4. Environment

Person

1. Interests
2. Skills
3. Values
4. Style qualities

The table shows a correlation between the facets of a work situation and the facets of a human personality.

A good match produces a win-win situation: It works well for the individual because it tends to generate a high degree of career satisfaction, and it works well for the organization because a satisfied employee tends to be a more productive contributor.

To gain the satisfaction and sense of meaning that you want and deserve from your work, use the Job-Person Match to inform your career decisions. It's a model and a standard that's worth revisiting at many points along the way as you manage your career. You'll need to ask yourself, at strategic career checkpoints, "How well is my Job-Person Match working?"

Planning career pathways

So how does this apply to the real world – Planet Work – and your place on it? Let's take a look at some typical occupational roles by interest category. Remember: professions, trades, crafts, and specific jobs usually combine two areas of basic interest, sometimes more. But here are some examples listed by their primary interest category:

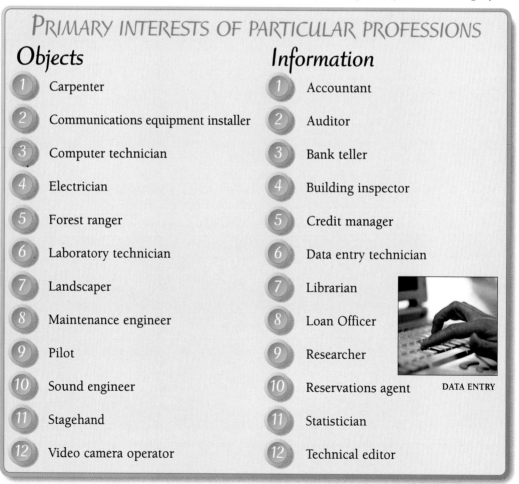

PRIMARY INTERESTS OF PARTICULAR PROFESSIONS

Objects

1. Carpenter
2. Communications equipment installer
3. Computer technician
4. Electrician
5. Forest ranger
6. Laboratory technician
7. Landscaper
8. Maintenance engineer
9. Pilot
10. Sound engineer
11. Stagehand
12. Video camera operator

Information

1. Accountant
2. Auditor
3. Bank teller
4. Building inspector
5. Credit manager
6. Data entry technician
7. Librarian
8. Loan Officer
9. Researcher
10. Reservations agent
11. Statistician
12. Technical editor

DATA ENTRY

Concepts

1. Advertising copywriter
2. Architect
3. Brand manager
4. College professor
5. Consultant
6. Corporate communications manager
7. Economic analyst
8. Graphic artist
9. Industrial psychologist
10. Interior designer
11. Policy analyst
12. Strategist

People

1. Account executive
2. Business broker
3. Career counselor
4. Corporate trainer
5. Customer service representative
6. Events planner
7. Executive recruiter
8. Human resources manager
9. Real estate agent
10. Receptionist
11. Sales representative
12. Social worker

■ **There are many** *career paths open to you if you enjoy working with others.*

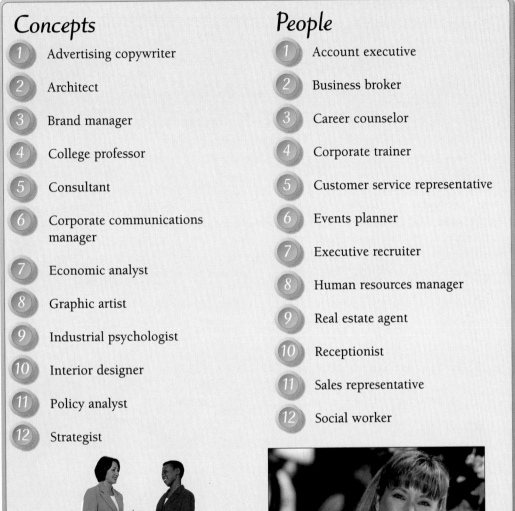

■ **If you like** *to meet and greet, then perhaps reception work is for you.*

Striving for a career ideal

Achieving perfect congruence is like reaching nirvana. It's not likely that you'll find perfection in a job, because every work situation involves some measure of compromise.

Think of the job-person match as a career ideal to strive for.

If career perfection is out of your reach, a career ideal is the best possible situation that's within your reach – the one that involves the least amount of compromise with your interests, skills, values, and style qualities.

To form a picture of viable career goals in the real world, think for a moment of career congruence as four tall glasses. They represent your interests, skills, values, and style qualities. In a perfect world, a job would fill all four of those glasses to the brim – and fulfill all of your needs and requirements in each of the four key areas. But since you don't live in a perfect world, that's not likely to happen. Instead, it's likely that you'll have to compromise in one or two of the key areas – and perhaps, to some degree, in all of them.

That doesn't mean you shouldn't use the Job-Person Match to design and pursue your career goals. Filling each glass as full as possible will enable you to achieve the greatest congruence that may be attainable. Remember, there's a difference between a work situation that's perfect and one that's ideal. Appreciating the difference is one of the most subtle, and most powerful, keys to managing your career effectively.

■ **It could be that** *your ideal career pathway leads you to scuba diving!*

What interests you?

WHAT DO YOU DO TO RELAX AND DECOMPRESS? *Here's a scenario to consider and a question to ponder. Imagine your busiest, most frantic day, filled with tasks, activities, objectives, schedules, and accomplishments – one of those days where you just barely make everything happen. Now, imagine that you have one hour to spend any way you'd like – just a single hour to yourself, to fill in any way your heart desires. How would you spend it?*

Would you work out at the gym, shoot some baskets, or go for a run? Would you chop wood, knit a sweater, or rake leaves? Would you read a book, practice speaking another language, or surf the Internet? Would you listen to music, flip through a fine art book, or watch a sitcom on TV? Would you call a friend, engage in conversation with your spouse, or get together with neighbors?

This is not a quiz, and there are no right or wrong answers. The purpose is to look at where your

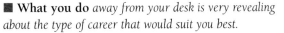

■ **What you do** *away from your desk is very revealing about the type of career that would suit you best.*

interests lie and where they generally direct you. Obviously, there are many things to do with a single, precious hour in the midst of a very demanding day. But the activities listed above are meant to reflect in a general way some very basic, but very different, categories of interests.

Your attention, please

Just what are interests, anyway? Many people believe that all activities they do well qualify as interests or that interests describe only activities they're good at. But that's not the perspective I want you to take. Think of an interest as a topic you're naturally curious about, something you're drawn toward. I'm not talking here about your ability to do something or to complete a task. An interest is simply something that captures your fancy.

Confused? Look at it this way. It's possible that you have a high degree of interest in music. You may be very knowledgeable about the history of jazz, for instance, and have numerous jazz CDs in your collection. If that's so, it's likely that listening to jazz makes you feel a connection with the music and provides you with some measure of pleasure and relaxation. It could be the way you choose to spend that precious, coveted hour of free time in the middle of the day from hell.

■ **Are you interests** *based indoors, or do you like to get into the big wide world?*

Does it necessarily follow that you're a skillful jazz musician – or even an aspiring one? No.

Don't make the mistake of confusing interests with skills.

It's possible to have a deep and passionate interest in music of any sort without having a lick of innate musical talent. On the other hand, you might possess a natural gift for playing the piano – and not an ounce of inclination to do so.

Interests are different from skills. Skills always involve proficiency in some activity, however large or small. (You'll get a closer look at skills in the next chapter.) Your interests play a huge role in your relationship with work – and in managing your career successfully. In fact, interests are where the self-assessment process begins, because they define the areas that present you with a connection, a sense of purpose and meaning.

Points of direction

In terms of managing your career, interests are general thematic categories of activity that represent the object of your curiosity. Think of them as categories that pull you in a particular direction. Just as there are four basic points of direction on the compass – north, south, east and west – there are four basic categories of interest:

1. Objects

2. Information

3. Concepts

4. People

Think again about how you'd spend your hour of free time. Which of the four categories would command your attention and your curiosity? Which "world" would you be likeliest to visit in order to relax and decompress? Let's take a quick survey of each of them.

The world of objects is the world of tangible things. It typically involves action and physical exertion, rather than mental or intellectual effort. Sports, woodworking, sailing, and knitting are all examples of hands-on activities in the realm of objects.

The world of information is the world of facts and figures. Usually, it refers to analyzing numbers or trends, or to finding patterns and making connections between facts or data. Doing a budget, researching a thesis, forecasting the economy, and editing text are all examples of activities that involve hard-and-fast information.

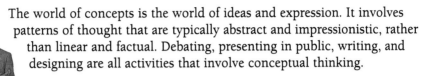

The world of concepts is the world of ideas and expression. It involves patterns of thought that are typically abstract and impressionistic, rather than linear and factual. Debating, presenting in public, writing, and designing are all activities that involve conceptual thinking.

The world of people involves a high degree of interaction and exchange. Usually, it involves leadership or service in relation to others, often anchored by humanistic concerns. Teaching, demonstrating a skill, persuading, and counseling are all activities that involve interaction with people.

■ **Perhaps your chosen** *career could involve presentations, if you thrive on that kind of challenge.*

Going with the grain

Okay, so what does all this mean when it comes to managing your career? Look at it this way:

It's generally acknowledged that the level of career success you attain has a lot to do with how you approach your work. What's not so obvious is that how you approach your work has a lot to do with what your natural interests are.

In other words, what engages your curiosity is likely to command your attention – and define your interests. Becoming involved in activities that relate to your interests, however directly or indirectly, is likely to feel fairly enjoyable and natural. If it does, there's a high degree of probability that you'll excel in that activity.

■ **Teaching skills** *can be put to use in almost all work situations.*

Wait a minute, you're asking – what about the person interested in music who can't even carry a tune? He or she can indulge that interest in another kind of work that relates directly to music and can excel without having to carry a tune. For example, he or she could write or edit music criticism, book musical talent, represent a regional orchestra, or work at a record company. Any of those activities would put that person close to his or her passion and present the chance for a fairly high payoff of work satisfaction.

■ **Think around your interests:** *How can they be put to practical use?*

Let's take a closer look at the four basic categories of interest and some of the activities that are found in each.

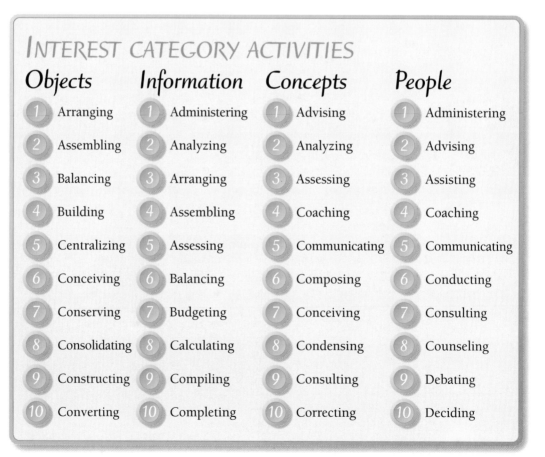

INTEREST CATEGORY ACTIVITIES

Objects	Information	Concepts	People
1. Arranging	1. Administering	1. Advising	1. Administering
2. Assembling	2. Analyzing	2. Analyzing	2. Advising
3. Balancing	3. Arranging	3. Assessing	3. Assisting
4. Building	4. Assembling	4. Coaching	4. Coaching
5. Centralizing	5. Assessing	5. Communicating	5. Communicating
6. Conceiving	6. Balancing	6. Composing	6. Conducting
7. Conserving	7. Budgeting	7. Conceiving	7. Consulting
8. Consolidating	8. Calculating	8. Condensing	8. Counseling
9. Constructing	9. Compiling	9. Consulting	9. Debating
10. Converting	10. Completing	10. Correcting	10. Deciding

Objects

- 11 Creating
- 12 Demonstrating
- 13 Designing
- 14 Determining
- 15 Developing

Information

- 11 Composing
- 12 Computing
- 13 Condensing
- 14 Coordinating
- 15 Correcting

Concepts

- 11 Counseling
- 12 Creating
- 13 Debating
- 14 Deciding
- 15 Defining

People

- 11 Delegating
- 12 Demonstrating
- 13 Determining
- 14 Directing
- 15 Discussing

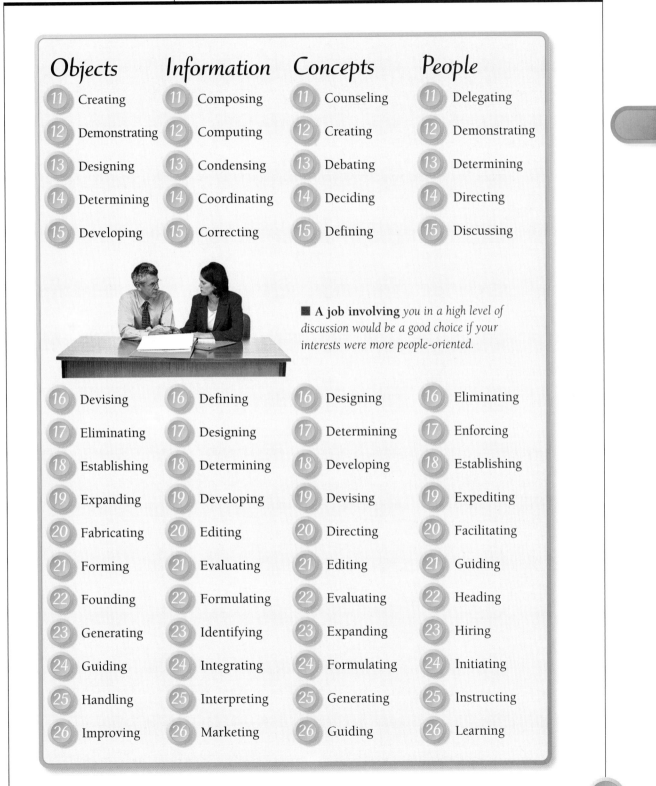

■ **A job involving** you in a high level of discussion would be a good choice if your interests were more people-oriented.

Objects

- 16 Devising
- 17 Eliminating
- 18 Establishing
- 19 Expanding
- 20 Fabricating
- 21 Forming
- 22 Founding
- 23 Generating
- 24 Guiding
- 25 Handling
- 26 Improving

Information

- 16 Defining
- 17 Designing
- 18 Determining
- 19 Developing
- 20 Editing
- 21 Evaluating
- 22 Formulating
- 23 Identifying
- 24 Integrating
- 25 Interpreting
- 26 Marketing

Concepts

- 16 Designing
- 17 Determining
- 18 Developing
- 19 Devising
- 20 Directing
- 21 Editing
- 22 Evaluating
- 23 Expanding
- 24 Formulating
- 25 Generating
- 26 Guiding

People

- 16 Eliminating
- 17 Enforcing
- 18 Establishing
- 19 Expediting
- 20 Facilitating
- 21 Guiding
- 22 Heading
- 23 Hiring
- 24 Initiating
- 25 Instructing
- 26 Learning

Objects

- (27) Innovating
- (28) Inspecting
- (29) Installing
- (30) Introducing
- (31) Inventing
- (32) Making
- (33) Modernizing

Information

- (27) Modifying
- (28) Organizing
- (29) Planning
- (30) Presenting
- (31) Processing
- (32) Promoting
- (33) Proving

Concepts

- (27) Identifying
- (28) Innovating
- (29) Instructing
- (30) Integrating
- (31) Interpreting
- (32) Inventing
- (33) Learning

People

- (27) Leading
- (28) Managing
- (29) Motivating
- (30) Negotiating
- (31) Operating
- (32) Organizing
- (33) Performing

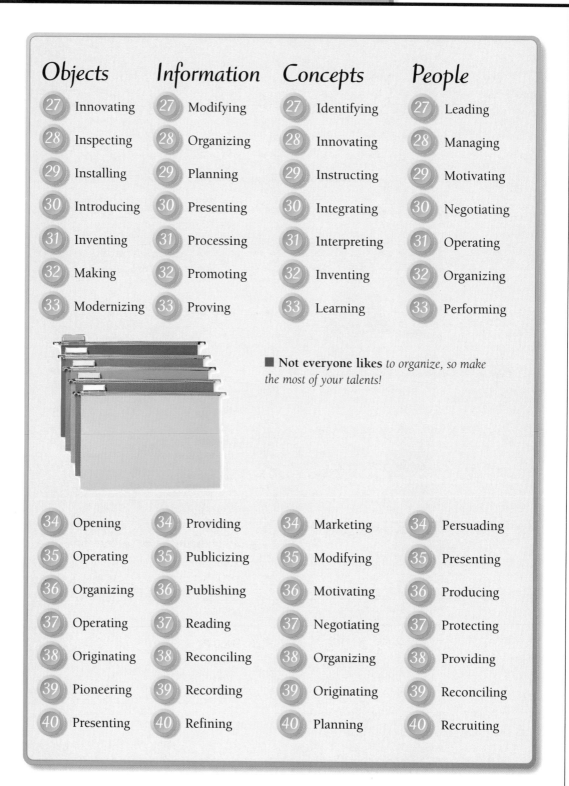

■ **Not everyone likes** *to organize, so make the most of your talents!*

Objects

- (34) Opening
- (35) Operating
- (36) Organizing
- (37) Operating
- (38) Originating
- (39) Pioneering
- (40) Presenting

Information

- (34) Providing
- (35) Publicizing
- (36) Publishing
- (37) Reading
- (38) Reconciling
- (39) Recording
- (40) Refining

Concepts

- (34) Marketing
- (35) Modifying
- (36) Motivating
- (37) Negotiating
- (38) Organizing
- (39) Originating
- (40) Planning

People

- (34) Persuading
- (35) Presenting
- (36) Producing
- (37) Protecting
- (38) Providing
- (39) Reconciling
- (40) Recruiting

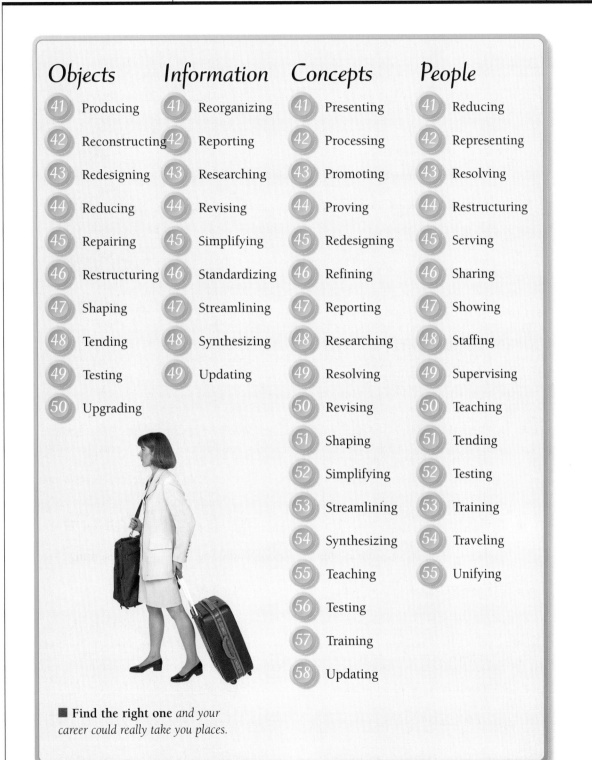

Objects

41 Producing

42 Reconstructing

43 Redesigning

44 Reducing

45 Repairing

46 Restructuring

47 Shaping

48 Tending

49 Testing

50 Upgrading

Information

41 Reorganizing

42 Reporting

43 Researching

44 Revising

45 Simplifying

46 Standardizing

47 Streamlining

48 Synthesizing

49 Updating

Concepts

41 Presenting

42 Processing

43 Promoting

44 Proving

45 Redesigning

46 Refining

47 Reporting

48 Researching

49 Resolving

50 Revising

51 Shaping

52 Simplifying

53 Streamlining

54 Synthesizing

55 Teaching

56 Testing

57 Training

58 Updating

People

41 Reducing

42 Representing

43 Resolving

44 Restructuring

45 Serving

46 Sharing

47 Showing

48 Staffing

49 Supervising

50 Teaching

51 Tending

52 Testing

53 Training

54 Traveling

55 Unifying

■ **Find the right one** *and your career could really take you places.*

99

Careers, like individuals, are complex

IT WOULD BE SIMPLE TO chart a career course if interests were all cut and dried and limited to one "world" of activity. But they're not. You're a complex individual, not one-dimensional, and there's a good chance that your interests extend in many directions.

Think of it this way: How often can you move toward your destination by heading only north, south, east, or west? Sometimes, but not frequently. More typically, you need to head in a direction that combines two basic points on the compass, such as northeast or southwest.

■ **Your career could** *involve more than one of your interests.*

Achieving satisfaction in your work involves the same principle.

Most work activities and environments involve two or more of the basic categories of interests.

Being a social worker, for instance, combines an interest in helping people with an interest in expressing concepts and theories. Being an editor combines an interest in organizing information with an interest in imaginative expression and communication of ideas. Being a customer service representative combines an interest in assisting people with an interest in being an authority on a particular product or service.

To choose work that will be satisfying to you, it's important to know which interest categories attract you the most and which attract you the least.

Can your basic interests change over time? It's possible, but if you're thinking about interests in big-picture terms, it's not probable. Chances are that if you hated math in grade school, you still hate it today. If you played with an erector set as a kid, rather than with watercolors, it's a good bet that you're drawn more easily as an adult to blueprints, not abstracts. If you just couldn't "get" chemistry in

YOU MAY HAVE ALWAYS BEEN DRAWN TO ONE PARTICULAR FIELD OF WORK high school, you probably don't fantasize about being a pharmacist.

In Chapter 11, you'll find a discussion of career change and choice. It presents an overview of a time-tested career theory, the Holland theory, which taps directly into a more detailed system of interest categories. The Holland system is designed to apply combinations of interest categories to specific occupations. It's helpful in developing possibilities for individuals who are looking to investigate career options. You might want to refer to it now to round out the assessment of your interests.

■ **Your love of reading** *and books could lead you down a whole new career path.*

A simple summary

✔ Smart career management is rooted in a process of self-assessment. A key to career success and satisfaction is congruence, a highly harmonious relationship between an individual's personal characteristics and those of a particular work situation.

✔ Career congruence is represented by an equation called the Job-Person Match, which outlines an ideal fit between an individual and his or her work situation.

✔ The self-assessment process typically begins with an inventory of work and leisure interests, since they point toward areas to which you feel connected.

✔ Interests typically can be broken down into four thematic categories: objects, information, concepts, and people. It's likely that your interests will gravitate toward at least two of them, but probably not all four.

✔ Various combinations of interest categories bring into focus work situations and career possibilities that may be worth pursuing.

Chapter 6

What Are You Good At?

NOW THAT YOU'VE CONSIDERED what might arouse your interest and hold your attention, it's time to shift your focus to skills – things that you do. More precisely, you're going to take stock of things you do well, either mental or physical, however large or small in scope and stature. Skills are mental and physical activities that you learn to do, with varying degrees of proficiency. Typically, skills can improve with application and practice. In the workplace, skills enable you to make contributions and add value. It's crucial to have a clear idea what skills you have to offer because it will help you describe your value to employers.

In this chapter...

✓ Actions speak loudest

✓ Identifying your skills

IT IS IMPORTANT TO GET A MEASURE ON WHAT YOU CAN DO BEST

Actions speak loudest

HOW WOULD YOU DESCRIBE *what it feels like to do something well? And when you are doing something well, is that activity the result of natural talent or practice?*

■ **When you are** *doing well at work, it shouldn't have to be broadcast.*

In the previous chapter, you learned about interests and some categories that they fall into. We agreed that interests are the areas that attract and pique your curiosity. Think of an interest as an aroma wafting through the air that arouses your senses and draws you toward it. But how do you follow it and ultimately capture it for added enjoyment? You have to pursue it by taking action.

In career management terms, the capabilities you bring into the workplace are called skills. It's important to remember that skills are activities that you do, not ideas that you think about, examine, or ponder.

Skills are the actions that enable you to help an employer reach goals. Simply put, skills are what you bring to the table in any work situation. There's a direct correlation between skills and goals: They are the actions that are the means to the ends.

VIP *Everyone has a multitude of skills. You may not agree, or you may not be able to identify readily what your skills are, so try thinking about skills in a way that's different from how you may have thought about them in the past.*

While it's natural to think of a skill as a high level of proficiency at a complex, difficult activity (such as "excellent management skill" or "sharp negotiating skill"), a simpler definition is more accurate and more useful: Skills are very basic activities that are one-dimensional and very focused. Sorting, for instance, is a skill. So is filing. And so is correcting. If you can see that skills are "micro-activities" that come into play in every work situation, you may be better able to identify the skills you have and those you may wish to develop.

■ **Your skill may be** *relatively new, or one that you have practiced many years.*

To illustrate the point about skills, let's refer back to chapter 5 and the discussion of interests. I drew a distinction between a natural inclination toward music (an interest) and the ability to actually make music. The creation of music involves distinct skills – like pressing the strings on the fretboard of a guitar, shaping the fingers to form chords on the keyboard of a piano, blowing through the mouthpiece of a trumpet, or keeping time with the foot pedal of a bass drum.

■ **Skills are activities** *that can be learned.*

Assessing your ability to make a difference

Another way to understand skills is to think of them as the basis for your paycheck. They are the activities you do to earn a living. Every occupation, every workplace role, requires a different mix of skills. It's important to know with certainty exactly what your skills are (and what skills you need to develop) so that you can speak with confidence about the ways in which you can make a difference to an organization.

One simple way to remember that skills are activities, not ideas, is to think of them in task-oriented terms.

In other words, whenever you write or speak of your skills, say organizing, not organization. Say instructing, not instruction. Take credit for revising, not revision. This technique will not only help you sort out the difference between skills and interests, but will provide you with a solid base of descriptive "power words" to use in developing your résumé and in describing your career accomplishments (see Chapter 16).

Skills are the activities that lead to the accomplishment of goals. Your skills are your tools for achieving two critical outcomes in any work situation:

 Your ability to make contributions

 Your ability to add value to the organization

You will need an accurate inventory of your skills so that you can carry out some of the fundamental activities of career management. For instance, your résumé must reflect your skills, along with the accomplishments they have enabled you to achieve. Similarly, you must be able to talk about your skills and demonstrate how you've used them so that interviewers and networking contacts can develop a clear and convincing portrait of what they might expect from you. In other words, you'll need to convey an accurate picture of your *marketable skills*.

Skills and talents

What's the difference between a skill and a talent, and why is it an important distinction to draw? The point is arguable, and for some people it boils down to a semantic difference. Think of it this way: A talent is an ability that's innate – typically you're born with it, and it usually doesn't go away. A skill is an ability that's learned – you attain a level of proficiency through practice and application. Skills can erode and disappear, but new ones can be cultivated and developed.

The distinction between skills and talents is important because skills can be developed (with, of course, the appropriate application and practice) but talents can only be cultivated. And the way you can cultivate a talent is to develop the skills that will enable it to blossom.

Consider the idea of "artistic talent," a term many people use to describe individuals who possess creative vision and an ability to express it through a visual medium. The creativity and expressive ability are innate. Individuals can often deepen innate abilities and traits by nourishing them, but to a large extent these are qualities that are inborn.

■ **Every job requires** *different skills and abilities.*

Many of the activities that are associated with artistic talent are actually skills that the individual develops. For a painter, they might consist of learning brushstrokes, mixing paints, choosing materials, and painting quickly. For a photographer, skills might include shooting film in low light, stopping fast action on film, using panoramic lenses, and printing on a variety of photographic papers.

INTERNET

www.careerpaths online.com

One site that can help you navigate a self-assessment is Career Paths Online. It features a ten-step career-planning guide, links to articles about careers, and other useful components. It even has a theme: "Life is a journey . . . enjoy the ride."

While some may argue that talents are more valuable and important than skills, one nonnegotiable key to effective career management is your ability to learn and apply new skills.

In today's world of work, where change and motion are the only constants, your ability to be flexible and open to skill building, rather than raw talent, is what will enable you to flourish.

Identifying your skills

WHEN ASKED TO IDENTIFY *and list their skills, many people draw a blank or freeze completely. Some typical responses are:*

(a) I don't have big, important skills.

(b) My skills are not what employers are looking for.

(c) I just show up and do my job.

(d) The things I do at work don't happen in other jobs.

(e) I haven't had the chance to develop any new skills.

(f) What I do all day doesn't involve skills of any kind.

(g) My skills are obsolete now.

(h) Other people have all the skills at my job.

■ **Don't sell yourself short:** *Every skill is valuable, no matter how insignificant you may regard it.*

Sorry, but none of these responses – or any others like them – is credible or acceptable. It's true that identifying your skills can be challenging. You may not be able to describe them readily, and in fact you may not be able to recognize the skills that you use every day. But that doesn't mean you don't have any – everyone has skills. Some people have a greater number of skills than others. Some have more highly developed skills than others.

Looking back at what you've done

Here's an exercise that will provide you with valuable insight and information about yourself. Many career counselors use it at the front end of their work with clients who are conducting career exploration or embarking on a job search to assess the client's *accomplishments*. It requires concentration, introspection, and a willingness to invest time, so don't expect to complete it in just a few minutes, or even in a single sitting. Rather, allow several days for completing the exercise, and on each of those days devote at least 45 to 60 minutes to it. You should be able to complete it fully within four to seven days.

DEFINITION

In career management terms, goals you attain or achievements you make are called accomplishments.

WHAT HAVE YOU ACHIEVED?

Look back over the course of your work life and personal life, and identify six to eight significant accomplishments you achieved in either. There are several important guidelines for selecting each accomplishment:

1

   a. It must be the achievement of a goal that involved you directly.

   b. It must be something you did well for which you received some recognition: praise, awards, compliments, or even just a pat on the back.

   c. It must be something that made you feel proud at the time and still does even as you think about it now.

   d. At least half of the accomplishments you identify must relate to some experience of work, from any part of your life or career.

Identifying accomplishments that fit these guidelines may happen quickly or, if you're like many people, may require a lot of brainstorming. That's why it's important to give yourself several days to complete this exercise. Don't rush through it, because the real "take away" of this exercise depends largely on which accomplishments you decide to focus on.

2

Write down as many details as you can recall about each of the six to eight important accomplishments. Recapture the background and setting of each accomplishment, and write about the activities you did to reach that outcome.

You can write in prose paragraph form or in the form of bulleted points. You can write in longhand or type your stories on a computer. If you're not comfortable with the act of writing, you can try speaking your stories into a tape recorder. Choose whatever method will help you piece together the story of each accomplishment and as many details as possible about it.

3

For each of your accomplishments, use the following list to take inventory of the activities you did that helped you achieve your significant accomplishments. Make checkmarks next to the activities for each of your accomplishments.

In case you haven't guessed, the words form a list of skills. It's not comprehensive, but it is fairly thorough. (If you did activities that are not included in my list, add yours to it.) You may wish to photocopy the following pages before you write on them.

SKILLS CHECKLIST FOR YOUR SIGNIFICANT ACCOMPLISHMENTS

☐ Administering	☐ Building	☐ Correcting	☐ Discussing
☐ Advising	☐ Calculating	☐ Counseling	☐ Editing
☐ Analyzing	☐ Centralizing		
☐ Arranging	☐ Coaching		
☐ Assembling	☐ Communicating		
☐ Assessing	☐ Compiling		
☐ Assisting	☐ Completing		

HOW ARE YOUR COMPUTER SKILLS?

☐ Balancing	☐ Composing	☐ Creating	☐ Eliminating
☐ Budgeting	☐ Computing	☐ Debating	☐ Enforcing
	☐ Conceiving	☐ Deciding	☐ Establishing
	☐ Condensing	☐ Defining	☐ Evaluating
	☐ Conducting	☐ Delegating	☐ Expanding
	☐ Conserving	☐ Demonstrating	☐ Expediting
	☐ Consolidating	☐ Designing	☐ Fabricating
	☐ Constructing	☐ Determining	☐ Facilitating
	☐ Consulting	☐ Developing	☐ Forming
	☐ Converting	☐ Devising	☐ Formulating
	☐ Coordinating	☐ Directing	☐ Founding

ARE YOU CREATIVE?

- [ ] Generating
- [ ] Guiding
- [ ] Handling
- [ ] Heading
- [ ] Hiring
- [ ] Identifying
- [ ] Improving
- [ ] Initiating
- [ ] Innovating
- [ ] Inspecting
- [ ] Installing
- [ ] Instructing
- [ ] Integrating
- [ ] Interpreting
- [ ] Introducing
- [ ] Inventing
- [ ] Leading
- [ ] Learning
- [ ] Making
- [ ] Managing

- [ ] Marketing
- [ ] Modernizing
- [ ] Modifying
- [ ] Motivating
- [ ] Negotiating
- [ ] Opening
- [ ] Operating
- [ ] Organizing

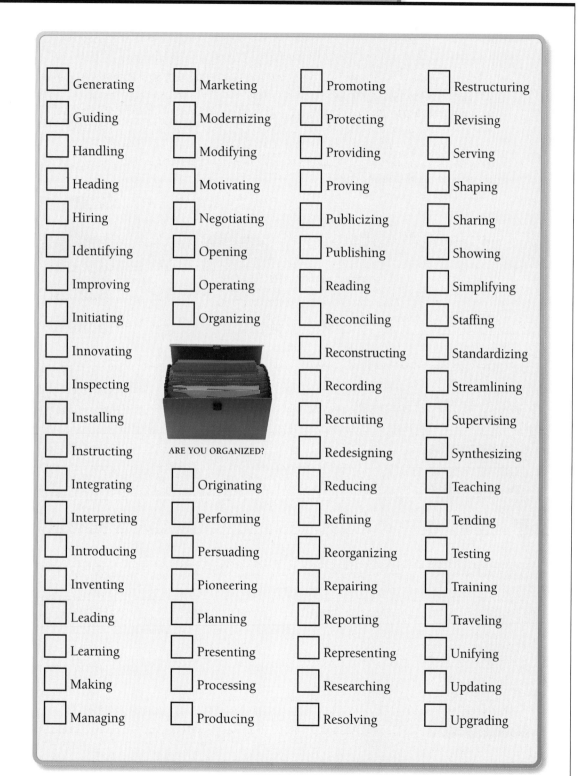

ARE YOU ORGANIZED?

- [ ] Originating
- [ ] Performing
- [ ] Persuading
- [ ] Pioneering
- [ ] Planning
- [ ] Presenting
- [ ] Processing
- [ ] Producing

- [ ] Promoting
- [ ] Protecting
- [ ] Providing
- [ ] Proving
- [ ] Publicizing
- [ ] Publishing
- [ ] Reading
- [ ] Reconciling
- [ ] Reconstructing
- [ ] Recording
- [ ] Recruiting
- [ ] Redesigning
- [ ] Reducing
- [ ] Refining
- [ ] Reorganizing
- [ ] Repairing
- [ ] Reporting
- [ ] Representing
- [ ] Researching
- [ ] Resolving

- [ ] Restructuring
- [ ] Revising
- [ ] Serving
- [ ] Shaping
- [ ] Sharing
- [ ] Showing
- [ ] Simplifying
- [ ] Staffing
- [ ] Standardizing
- [ ] Streamlining
- [ ] Supervising
- [ ] Synthesizing
- [ ] Teaching
- [ ] Tending
- [ ] Testing
- [ ] Training
- [ ] Traveling
- [ ] Unifying
- [ ] Updating
- [ ] Upgrading

4 Look at the inventories you just created and see if any patterns emerge. It's very likely that you used many of the same skills in each or most of your six to eight accomplishments. (Activities that you perform in a variety of personal and professional situations are called *frequently used skills*.) Use the following worksheet to list all the skills that appeared on your inventory. (Save the longer, checked list, since it shows all the skills you've used in the past, regardless of their frequency.)

Frequently used skills

_____   _____   _____

_____   _____   _____

_____   _____   _____

_____   _____   _____

_____   _____   _____

_____   _____   _____

_____   _____   _____

_____   _____   _____

_____   _____   _____

_____   _____   _____

_____   _____   _____

_____   _____   _____

_____   _____   _____

_____   _____   _____

_____   _____   _____

_____   _____   _____

Using your list of frequently used skills that you created on p. 111, choose the ten skills that you would not trade for any others – in other words, the ten that you most enjoy doing. These are your *motivated skills*. List them on the following worksheet.

■ **Once you have** *identified your motivated skills, you can put them to good use in the workplace.*

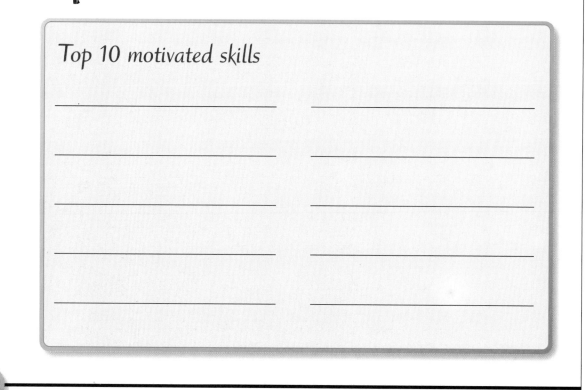

Top 10 motivated skills

_____ _____

_____ _____

_____ _____

_____ _____

_____ _____

Your motivated skills are the activities you must be able to perform and practice in a work setting in order to achieve congruence – an ideal fit. Also, describing your top-ten motivated skills to interviewers and networking contacts provides a basic outline of the strongest contributions you can make in a work situation.

Your top 10 motivated skills should be fresh in your mind at all times.

Naturally, the list will evolve as you develop new skills and leave others behind. Think of your list of motivated skills as your ready answer to the inevitable career question, "What are you good at?"

■ **Don't wait before** *using your skills – remember they are unique to you and should be used in as many work situations as possible.*

Linking skills with interest categories

You can gain another useful perspective on the activities you excel at by looking at your skills in relation to your basic interest categories (objects, information, concepts, and people) and the order in which you ranked those categories in Chapter 5. Each of those basic interest categories taps a different mix of skills, and many skills have application in two or more categories.

Using the inventory of skills you just completed, look through the following table and check off those same skills in each interest category. Check any other skills that you feel describe you, too. Be selective, but don't sell yourself short. Finally, consider your results here with the ranking of interest categories you did in Chapter 5.

■ **The range of skills** *you possess will most likely be spread over different categories.*

Skills by Interest Category

Objects

1. Arranging
2. Assembling
3. Balancing
4. Building
5. Centralizing
6. Conceiving
7. Conserving
8. Consolidating
9. Constructing
10. Converting
11. Creating
12. Demonstrating
13. Designing
14. Determining
15. Developing
16. Devising
17. Eliminating
18. Establishing
19. Expanding

Information

1. Administering
2. Analyzing
3. Arranging
4. Assembling
5. Assessing
6. Balancing
7. Budgeting
8. Calculating
9. Compiling
10. Completing
11. Composing
12. Computing
13. Condensing
14. Coordinating
15. Correcting
16. Defining
17. Designing
18. Determining
19. Developing

Concepts

1. Advising
2. Analyzing
3. Assessing
4. Coaching
5. Communicating
6. Composing
7. Conceiving
8. Condensing
9. Consulting
10. Correcting
11. Counseling
12. Creating
13. Debating
14. Deciding
15. Defining
16. Designing
17. Determining
18. Developing
19. Devising

People

1. Administering
2. Advising
3. Assisting
4. Coaching
5. Communicating
6. Conducting
7. Consulting
8. Counseling
9. Debating
10. Deciding
11. Delegating
12. Demonstrating
13. Determining
14. Directing
15. Discussing
16. Eliminating
17. Enforcing
18. Establishing
19. Expediting

Objects

20 Fabricating
21 Forming
22 Founding
23 Generating
24 Guiding
25 Handling
26 Improving
27 Innovating
28 Inspecting
29 Installing
30 Introducing
31 Inventing
32 Making
33 Modernizing
34 Opening
35 Operating

Information

20 Editing
21 Evaluating
22 Formulating
23 Identifying
24 Integrating
25 Interpreting
26 Marketing
27 Modifying
28 Organizing
29 Planning
30 Presenting
31 Processing
32 Promoting
33 Proving
34 Providing
35 Publicizing

Concepts

20 Directing
21 Editing
22 Evaluating
23 Expanding
24 Formulating
25 Generating
26 Guiding
27 Identifying
28 Innovating
29 Instructing
30 Integrating
31 Interpreting
32 Inventing
33 Learning
34 Marketing
35 Modifying

People

20 Facilitating
21 Guiding
22 Heading
23 Hiring
24 Initiating
25 Instructing
26 Learning
27 Leading
28 Managing
29 Motivating
30 Negotiating
31 Operating
32 Organizing
33 Performing
34 Persuading
35 Presenting

ARE YOU A GOOD COMMUNICATOR?

HOW IS YOUR TEAMWORK?

Objects

- 36 Organizing
- 37 Operating
- 38 Originating
- 39 Pioneering
- 40 Presenting
- 41 Producing
- 42 Reconstructing
- 43 Redesigning
- 44 Reducing
- 45 Repairing
- 46 Restructuring
- 47 Shaping
- 48 Tending
- 49 Testing
- 50 Upgrading

Information

- 36 Publishing
- 37 Reading
- 38 Reconciling
- 39 Recording
- 40 Refining
- 41 Reorganizing
- 42 Reporting
- 43 Researching
- 44 Revising
- 45 Simplifying
- 46 Standardizing
- 47 Streamlining
- 48 Synthesizing
- 49 Updating

Concepts

- 36 Motivating
- 37 Negotiating
- 38 Organizing
- 39 Originating
- 40 Planning
- 41 Presenting
- 42 Processing
- 43 Promoting
- 44 Proving
- 45 Redesigning
- 46 Refining
- 47 Reporting
- 48 Researching
- 49 Resolving
- 50 Revising
- 51 Shaping

People

- 36 Producing
- 37 Protecting
- 38 Providing
- 39 Reconciling
- 40 Recruiting
- 41 Reducing
- 42 Representing
- 43 Resolving
- 44 Restructuring
- 45 Serving
- 46 Sharing
- 47 Showing
- 48 Staffing
- 49 Supervising
- 50 Teaching
- 51 Tending

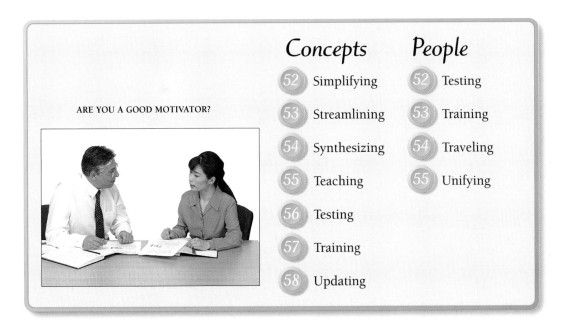

Concepts		People	
52	Simplifying	52	Testing
53	Streamlining	53	Training
54	Synthesizing	54	Traveling
55	Teaching	55	Unifying
56	Testing		
57	Training		
58	Updating		

ARE YOU A GOOD MOTIVATOR?

A simple summary

✓ Skills are actions and activities that you do. They represent what you bring to the workplace and what you accomplish in it.

✓ Skills describe abilities that are learned and involve various levels of proficiency. Typically, more application leads to higher proficiency ("Practice makes perfect").

✓ Skills are the things employers pay you to do. They are what enable you to make contributions and add value to work situations.

✓ Having a clear idea of your marketable skills is essential for managing your career effectively. It will help you assess what you have to offer in the workplace and describe your potential value to employers.

✓ You can take inventory of your skills with several different approaches, including a look back at important accomplishments – at work and in your personal life – that you did well and gave you a sense of pride.

117

Chapter 7

What Matters to You?

NOW YOU'VE TAKEN AN INVENTORY of your interests and skills, consider the qualities that influence decisions in your personal life as well as your work life. Your career values are powerful motivators – they represent the work ideals you cherish most. You'll see how career values can guide your career choices, and how and why values shift and evolve as your life does. You'll also reflect on your most important career values now and identify those that are present in and missing from your current work situation.

In this chapter...

✔ It's a living – and a lot more

✔ Ideals worth reaching for

✔ Sorting out your values

✔ Ease vs. effort

✔ Recipes for career values

✔ Finding other ways to live your career values

TAKE TIME TO THINK ABOUT YOUR PRIORITIES IN LIFE AND AT WORK

It's a living – and a lot more

WHAT DO YOU NEED *from your relationship with work? If you're like most people, the very first answer that comes to mind is, money. Let's face it, one of the biggest reasons we go to work is to earn a living. We all have to support ourselves and those who depend on us. But suppose that money was not an issue. Suppose you won the lottery and suddenly found yourself in the enviable position of not having to worry about earning an income. Would you still choose to work?*

■ **What would you** *do if you were to win a fortune?*

Whatever your immediate response might be, you would probably not end your career. You might decide to change your current work situation (in fact, you might quit your job in the blink of an eye!), or you might decide to take an open-ended vacation from work and the grind of earning a living. But it's a good bet that sooner or later, you'd want to do something more with your life than just lie on the beach. Chances are that what you'd want to do would become another chapter of your career.

Most people invest an awful lot in their careers. The ongoing activity of work carries the potential to offer them so much more than a paycheck. Some individuals allow their entire identity to be shaped by their work life. Others freely bring the dramas of their personal life into the workplace, and vice versa. Many people gauge success only in career-related terms. And many look to their jobs for friends, security, excitement, intimacy, romance, achievement, recognition, status, creativity, challenge, and a host of other life needs.

■ **Do you live** *to work, or work to live?*

Ideals worth reaching for

WHAT DO YOU THINK *of when you hear the word values? Do you think of purchases that save you money? Factors in mathematical equations? Guidelines that relate to morality and behavior?*

Values define what we cherish, what gives us a sense of purpose and meaning. Those things we hold closest to the heart – the things we value most – are what guide us in our decision-making, both in our personal life and in our career.

Think about it: Every day you reach crossroads that require decisions. Some crossroads are complex and consequential, with the potential to impact our lives in an enduring way. Fortunately, we don't face those every day. Other crossroads are simpler with modest, even inconsiderable consequences. Typically, we face dozens of those every day, without thinking too much about them. What helps us navigate these crossroads? What enables us to choose the right road? Our values do.

■ **We all have** *a different set of values that we use almost without thinking – try to identify yours.*

Values guide our choices and direct our decisions – at home, in our relationships with other people, and on the job. And when we see values as the ideals, beliefs, and conditions that we prize and cherish most, it's easy to understand that each of us has a unique mix that helps define who we are.

Each of us has a unique set of fingerprints, a unique DNA code, and a unique set of values. It's a highly personal mix of internal motivators.

But unlike fingerprints and DNA, values are invisible. They exist in the mind and in the heart. Yet they drive behaviors and decisions more powerfully than any other influences. And, unlike fingerprints and DNA, values can and do change over time.

A sense of direction

Values promote good, clear decision-making. When a person's ideals are well defined and strong, they become powerful influences on the process of reaching conclusive decisions. Think of a taxi driver getting from point A to point B by using a map to choose the straightest, most direct, and most efficient route.

But when ideals are not pronounced and well shaped, when a person feels indifferent or inconclusive, it's harder for him or her to follow their value map to a conclusive decision. Think of a taxi driver who travels from point A to point B by leaving the map in the glove box and wending his way down winding streets and back roads away from the main thoroughfares. Though he may eventually wind up at his destination, the journey there is indirect, inefficient, possibly confusing, and probably stressful.

Which taxi driver would you rather ride with?

What does all this have to do with managing your career? Simply this: Values are a powerful, highly active ingredient in your career. They exert a profound influence on the level of career satisfaction and success you will attain.

■ **Values give you** *a real sense of purpose and direction.*

Without values to guide you, your career decisions can become arbitrary and random. Reaching a conclusive career decision can be more difficult when the process lacks true direction. Values make for inspired career guidance.

Your values will influence the way you manage your career whether you're aware of them or not.

Obviously, it's better to be informed about what motivates you so that you can apply that knowledge carefully and purposefully to your important career decisions. So if you've never thought about career values or if you've never taken the time to figure out what you really need from your relationship to work, now's the time to start.

Your life and your career: destined to dance

Because you're about to think seriously about career values, this is a good place to remind you that your career and your life are intertwined. You can't separate one completely from the other. Sure, you can behave more formally on the job, and you can leave work behind you at the end of the day (which is a good practice to have), but you can't live in two different worlds.

What happens in your life profoundly affects your work and your career – like getting married, having a baby, or pursuing a graduate degree. And vice versa: What happens in your career affects your life significantly – like receiving a promotion or being transferred to a new geographic location.

So although it's a good thing to nourish your career and the other parts of your life with different initiatives, it's impossible to compartmentalize them totally. Don't even try. Your career and your life are like two dancers moving in unison, and values are the music they dance to – the ideals that shape your career and your life decisions.

■ **What happens at work** *has a knock-on effect on the rest of your life, and vice versa.*

Sorting out your values

SOME PEOPLE CAN RECITE *their top career values instantly and without hesitation, right off the top their heads. Others need some time to think and reflect about which values are most meaningful to their careers and to their lives.*

If you're like most people, a list might help you sort things out and trigger imaginative thinking. Sometimes it's important to see ideas expressed in print so that the words can guide your thinking. That's often the case when it comes to sorting out career values. And even if you think you're in touch with your values, you can still benefit from the doing exercises in this chapter. You'll may discover that you own values you weren't even aware of.

■ **Look on your list** *as a positive step toward identifying your values.*

Taking stock of your career values

This first exercise is to help you familiarize yourself with what career values actually are. Review the values in the following list. It is extensive but by no means comprehensive, so feel free to add whatever values you like on the blank lines (and add more if necessary).

Next, read through the list again and check off the values that are important to you in any way. Be as generous as you'd like – you'll whittle down the list later.

· *Tip: You may want to make several photocopies of the list before you mark it so that you can do these exercises again in the future.*

IMPORTANT CAREER VALUES

Review the following 50 values by substituting each of them in the appropriate place in this statement:

"At work, _____ is/are important to me."

☐ absence of tension

☐ achieving goals

☐ affiliating with a group or organization

☐ artistic creativity in my activities

☐ authenticity in management and coworkers

☐ authority

☐ autonomy in my approach to projects

☐ being innovative

☐ being of service to others

☐ being self-reliant

☐ competing with the performance of others

☐ conflict-free environment

☐ contributing to society

☐ deadline pressure

☐ desirable geographic location

☐ economic security

☐ esthetically appealing surroundings

☐ excitement and stimulation

☐ expressive creativity in my activities

☐ fast-paced workflow and environment

☐ feeling relatively secure in my job

☐ feeling satisfied by my work

DOES YOUR JOB GIVE YOU FULFILLMENT?

☐ feeling valued and appreciated

☐ financial security

IS FINANCIAL SECURITY IMPORTANT TO YOU?

☐ flexible working schedule

☐ friendly coworkers

☐ having my work evaluated by supervisors, peers, or customers

☐ high compensation

☐ high-precision activities

☐ holding high standards of quality

☐ influence over others' opinions

☐ intellectual challenge

☐ interacting with other people

☐ low-stress responsibilities

☐ making decisions about policies or procedures

☐ meaning and purpose

☐ moral fulfillment

☐ opportunities for advancement

☐ opportunities to take risks

☐ orderliness and organization

☐ physical exertion

☐ power

☐ pursuing deeper knowledge and understanding

☐ recognition for contributions

☐ recognition for intellectual abilities

☐ shared spirituality

☐ stable mix of activities

☐ supervising the work of others

☐ time alone for concentration and focus

☐ variety of activities

DO YOU VALUE THE OPINIONS OF OTHERS?

THINKING SERIOUSLY ABOUT YOURSELF

Values as moving targets

Take a look at the values you checked. First of all, are you surprised by the sheer number of values that you identified as important to you? Did you check off more of them than you thought you might, or fewer? Did you add any that did not appear on the list? If not, take this opportunity to do so, if you wish.

Now that you've made a rough-cut evaluation of the values that are important to you, you need to identify those that you prize and cherish most. But first, I need to introduce another key idea about career values.

If there's one rule to remember about values, it's this: They can change over time, and chances are that they will.

Some of your values may remain constant, but others will undoubtedly shift. Some that are important to you now may become less important over time. Others that are less important now might become more critical in the future. Depending on where you are in your life, your key career values are in perpetual flux. And in case you haven't guessed, that's proof that you're growing and developing as a person. So if you're noticing some discrepancies in what you've valued most at different points in your career and in your life, congratulations – you're a psychologically healthy adult!

■ **Allow your values to** *guide your career decisions.*

Core values

Let's try to narrow down your list of values to a manageable size. Refer to the values you checked as important in the first exercise, and transfer each of them to only one of the three categories in the following worksheet.

Tip: You may want to make several photocopies of this page before you mark it, so that you can do this exercise again in the future

MY CORE VALUES

I always value:	I sometimes value:	I seldom value:
_____	_____	_____
_____	_____	_____
_____	_____	_____
_____	_____	_____
_____	_____	_____
_____	_____	_____
_____	_____	_____
_____	_____	_____
_____	_____	_____
_____	_____	_____

The purpose of this exercise is to give you a clearer idea of which values are likely to remain constant over time and which are likely to change. The values in the "always" column are the most likely to stay constant, and the values in the "seldom" column are the most likely to change.

■ **Really get to grips** *with what you value and believe in.*

Now you're ready to determine your core values. Core values are the ideals you prize and cherish the most – the ones you absolutely, positively cannot compromise. Think of them as the ideals you'd go to the mat for, the things you'd insist on whenever given your choice.

In career management terms, core values are the things or conditions that are likeliest to promote job-person fit – and true career satisfaction.

From the three categories on the previous page, choose eight values you feel are nonnegotiable, that represent your most important ideals. Since we agreed that values will evolve over time, identify them as they exist right now. In the following worksheet, write today's month and year at the top of the first column, and write the eight values in the blanks provided.

Trivia...

Years ago, the most powerful and luxurious cars were built with engines that had eight cylinders. Think of your eight most important values as the cylinders that are powering your career engine.

Pull these from your "I always value" list as much as you can. If you need more, pull from your "I sometimes value" list. (Optional: Another way of identifying your most important values is to go back to the "Important Career Values" list on pages 124–5 and pull eight from the ones you checked.)

Why eight values? Why don't we settle on a top ten list or a top five? Because eight is a manageable number. If you absolutely must claim ten, then do it. But your work will be easier if you stay with eight.

■ **Use the lists you** *have just made to inform your career-management choices and decisions.*

MY TOP 8 CAREER VALUES

Month: _____   Month: _____   Month: _____   Month: _____

Year: _____   Year: _____   Year: _____   Year: _____

_____   _____   _____   _____

_____   _____   _____   _____

_____   _____   _____   _____

_____   _____   _____   _____

_____   _____   _____   _____

_____   _____   _____   _____

_____   _____   _____   _____

_____   _____   _____   _____

In six months, come back and re-do the exercise, and write your current top eight values in the second column. Do the exercise again six months after that, and write your top eight values in the third column, and so on. Each time, make note of the values that change – and the ones that remain the same – and assess what impact the changes have had or will have on your career.

■ **Discuss with someone** *how the values on your list have changed .*

Ease vs. effort

WHEN YOUR WORK SITUATION

provides you with the opportunity to enjoy or reach your most cherished ideals, all is right with the world. Going to work doesn't feel like work at all. Instead, when you're living your career values, you feel a sense of purpose and harmony, and it's relatively easy to be productive and efficient. There's a sense of effortlessness about going to work and managing your career. Success, both in big-picture terms and in small everyday ways, comes more naturally.

On the other hand, when you're working in a situation or an environment that conflicts with your prized values, going to work is a struggle. Individuals who don't have the opportunity to enjoy or reach their most cherished values are likely to experience a heightened level of tension and conflict in the workplace. These individuals experience work without the sense of harmony and meaning that is so critical to career satisfaction. What they experience instead is diminished energy, low motivation and productivity, burnout, and often depression. Rather than effortlessness, they experience a lack of ease – in fact, "dis-ease" in the purest sense of the term.

INTERNET

www.assessment.com

As you move through the process of self-assessment, you can visit the web site of the International Assessment Network. It's all about finding personal fit and fulfillment at work. The site offers specialized material for corporations, students, educators, and others. Membership enables you to take an assessment tool called MAPP (Motivational Appraisal of Personal Potential).

■ **Identifying your** *values may help you understand why you are unhappy at work.*

To dramatize the point, here's a compare-and-contrast exercise that will spotlight how values are a highly active ingredient in the career satisfaction equation.

YOUR BEST WORK EXPERIENCES

Think of the most satisfying work experience you've ever had. You can draw from any part of your career, as far back as you'd like. It can be the experience you had on the school newspaper, doing volunteer work, on your first job ever, or in a more recent work situation. The key criteria to use in selecting the experience is that it made you feel satisfied and purposeful. Once you've settled on the experience and you're visualizing it clearly, write down the career values that were present for you in that situation.

_____   _____

_____   _____

_____   _____

_____   _____

YOUR WORST WORK EXPERIENCES

Now think of the absolute worst work experience you've ever had – the situation from hell. Again, draw from any part of your career. The key criteria to use in selecting this experience is that it made you feel tense, out of sorts, and unhappy. You may have felt as if there was absolutely no "fit" at all, as if you were a square peg in a round hole, and its most memorable aspect is the torture it put you through. When you've recalled it and you're visualizing it clearly, write down the career values that were missing for you in that situation.

_____   _____

_____   _____

_____   _____

Look at the two lists of values. How do they relate? What patterns do you see? What conclusions can you draw about career values and about how they shift over time?

Your responses will reflect important information about what you value most in your relationship with work.

■ **You can get the** _best out of bad situations by identifying why you were unhappy – listen to yourself._

Life and work: experiences that add up to something big

Your career values result from the sum of your life and work experiences.

Being mindful of shifts and transformations in the mix of your values is essential to good career management. You can use informal evaluation exercises like the ones presented here, or you can complete a more detailed analysis using more intricate assessment instruments. Career counselors often use an instrument called "career anchors," set out in Edgar H. Schein's _Career Anchors_, to help clients sort out their most important values and understand their strongest needs.

Career Anchors sets out to help individuals think about how values relate to career choices. It presents a system of eight general categories (there's that magic number again!) that reflect distinctive orientations toward work, motives, ideals, and self-perceived talents. Through a careful review of work experiences and life events, the person using *Career Anchors* is encouraged to choose the category that most closely describes his or her priorities and work-related ideals. Unlike the results of interests and skills inventories, *Career Anchors* works toward identifying one general category – and one only – that acts as a guiding light in reaching important career decisions.

The most useful information that can come out of *Career Anchors* or any other review of work-related values is the ideas and conclusions you will reach during the process of recalling career experiences and life events. Whether you use a formal instrument to facilitate the process or not, it's important to complete a step-by-step, detailed review of the situations that have worked for you and those that have not.

■ **Taking time to look** *back on past situations can really help you in the future.*

Look back over the course of your life, including your educational history, and recall the transitions you have made. Think about the ones that were easy as well as the ones that were difficult. Ask yourself probing, analytical questions about those situations and transitions, and take notes. Work to reach meaningful conclusions about questions like the following:

a   Which transitions had the biggest impact on your life or career, and why?

b   What situations made you feel most contented and fulfilled?

c   What situations were most stressful and unsatisfying?

d   If you've ever declined to move into a job or a relationship, what were your reasons?

e   How have your goals and career ambitions evolved over the years?

f   What is the defining quality of your relationship with work right now?

g   What do you look forward to in your career in the future?

h   How does it feel to answer the question, "What do you do?"

Your career values: the real you

Your mix of most important career values is totally subjective and completely unique to you. What's essential is that you feel right about what they are. Think of the feeling you get when you see something that captures some quality of your personality. It could be a garment, a photographic image, a textual description, an abstract painting – whatever. If you see something of yourself in it, you'll think: "That's me!"

Career values work the same way. You need to see yourself in them. Your career values must be consistent with your self-concept. If they're not, you'll experience internal tension, conflict, and struggle. So, it's essential that you evaluate your ideals with complete honesty.

■ **When considering** *what your career values are, think about how you view yourself.*

Work to separate the values that you cherish absolutely from those that you think you should cherish. What's the difference? The absolutes result from your own thoughts and emotions; the shoulds result from outside influences.

We all experience battles with the shoulds in our careers and our lives. Typically, they represent advisements, guidelines, or boundaries that we could probably live without. Throughout life we have pictures of what we "should" do drawn for us by authority figures – parents, relatives, educators, clerics, and other influential people – who touch our lives in a lasting way. Usually these pictures are well-intentioned scenarios for us to follow. However, when the scenarios present standards or ideals that differ from those we naturally feel, there's potential for real inner turmoil. In defining your career values, there's no room for the infringement of outside influences. You have to think, and feel, for yourself. Once you're clear on what you need most in your relationship with work, you can begin the process of identifying the situation that will present the best opportunity for living your values.

Remember, don't expect to find perfection. The odds are against that you'll uncover a single career situation that can provide you with every bit of all the ideals you cherish.

But that doesn't mean you can't identify a situation that can provide you with the lion's share. Look for an ideal situation, not a perfect one. Thoroughly assess the qualities, demands, and challenges of each situation you investigate. Ask yourself if it's a job or an organization that's consistent with your career values as you know them now. If it is, there's potential in that situation for congruence, for a true fit. But if not, there's potential for true danger.

Recipes for career values

LET'S CONCLUDE THIS CHAPTER WITH *a look at the role*
of values in your current, or most recent, career situation.

Think about the everyday occurrences in your work life right now –
the typical day, as best as you can picture it. Drawing from your list of
Important Career Values, write down the ones that you have on the
following worksheet. (If you're currently unemployed or in transition,
think about the typical day in your most recent work situation, and
write the values that it enabled you to have.) Make the list as long as
you'd like.

IT'S TIME FOR
ANOTHER LIST!

Now draw up a wish list of the career values you'd like to have in your next job or work
situation. By all means transfer any values you wish to maintain as you move forward in
your career. This list should definitely reflect your top eight most important values as
you defined them earlier in this chapter, but it need not be limited to those eight.

CAREER VALUES PRESENT IN MY CURRENT WORK SITUATION

_____   _____   _____

_____   _____   _____

_____   _____   _____

_____   _____   _____

_____   _____   _____

_____   _____   _____

_____   _____   _____

CAREER VALUES I WANT TO HAVE IN MY NEXT WORK SITUATION

_____   _____   _____

_____   _____   _____

_____   _____   _____

_____   _____   _____

_____   _____   _____

Compare and contrast the two lists. Identify the values you need to concentrate on adding to your next work situation. Think of them as exotic ingredients that will make a recipe masterful and filled with subtle flavors. This list should be shorter than the previous two, since it represents key values to concentrate on as you make important decisions and target strategic career possibilities. In fact, the shorter this list is, the better off you are!

CAREER VALUES I PLAN TO ADD TO MY NEXT WORK SITUATION

_____   _____   _____

_____   _____   _____

_____   _____   _____

_____   _____   _____

Finding other ways to live your career values

BY NOW YOU'RE FAMILIAR with the golden rule about the job-person match: You can't expect to have all of your interests, skills, and values come into play in a single work situation. That might happen in a perfect world, but in the world of work you need identify the ideal situation.

There's a likelihood, then, that there'll be some leftover interests, skills, and values that won't be nourished by your everyday work situation. No one job can serve as the be-all and end-all for the entire scope of your unique qualities.

YOUR JOB MAY NOT PROVIDE YOU WITH ENOUGH STIMULATION

One of the great secrets of effective career management is finding other arenas in which to nurture and nourish the values that your work situation can't.

How can you do that when it comes to your most cherished career values? Think creatively and commit to doing a variety of activities. Here are eight examples that might add balance and fulfillment to your life and career. This is not an exhaustive list, but a model to spark your own imaginative thinking.

8 WAYS TO A MORE FULFILLING EXISTENCE

If this career value is missing:	Consider doing this:
Artistic creativity	Painting, drawing, writing, or practicing a musical instrument on at least two occasions per week
Intellectual challenge	Participating in regular meetings of a book discussion group
Contributing to society	Volunteering to facilitate community support groups for people in transition or recovering from personal loss

Precision work	Building intricate hobby models or pursuing a rigorous nutrition program
Aesthetically appealing surroundings	Decorating one or more rooms in your home strictly for visual appeal, not functionality
Financial security	Attending seminars on budgeting and investing money
Variety of activities	Scheduling a host of commitments in your leisure time to gain exposure to a breadth of ideas and environments
Physical exertion	Pursuing a formal exercise program that requires full participation at least three times per week

A simple summary

✓ Work provides you with a livelihood and much more. People typically seek (and often gain) far more from their careers than they're aware of, including friendship, security, challenge, recognition, and many other life needs.

✓ Values are the conditions and circumstances we cherish. They are ideals that instill a sense of purpose and meaning. Career values guide our choices and direct our decisions about the work we do and where we do it.

✓ Values are a powerful, highly active ingredient in your career management strategies. They exert an important influence on the level of career satisfaction and success you will attain.

✓ Your career values will shift and evolve as your life does. Your top career priority at one point in your life may not head the list at a later point. Values are moving targets.

✓ It's rare that a single career situation will provide the opportunity to live all of your most important values. You can pursue those that are missing from work in your leisure activities.

Chapter 8

What's Your Style?

THIS CHAPTER CONCLUDES the section on self-assessment by addressing the most subjective information that relates to the Job-Person Match: style. As you'll see, your style characteristics are what set you apart from other individuals. Personal style is what makes you distinctive. It has a great impact on your career, how you go about making decisions and carrying them out, and it will influence how others see and think about you at work.

In this chapter...

✓ The way you do the things you do

✓ Taking stock of your personal style qualities

✓ Measuring personal style formally

✓ Charting personality types

✓ Developing a comfortable MBTI profile

✓ The last word on style (for now)

IT'S IMPORTANT TO UNDERSTAND THE IMAGE THAT YOU PROJECT TO OTHERS

The way you do the things you do

WHAT DO YOU THINK *of when you hear the word style? Do you think of fashion trends? Rules for expressing written material? Patterns in decorative arts? Each of these would be accurate within their respective context. But here, we're talking about you. What exactly is personal style, anyway, and how can you describe yours?*

■ **What do you think** *is the best way to create an impression – by what you wear or by how you are with colleagues?*

The little things that people do, and the manner in which they do them, are behaviors that can be either endearing or off-putting to others. They are the tendencies, the acts, the habits, and the patterns that define personality. In so many ways, these style qualities are the things that cause people to fall in (and out of) love with each other. And, by the same token, they are the things that cause employers and employees to fall in (and out of) favor with each other. The sum of the qualities that make you unique is known as personal style. Consciously or unconsciously, each of us uses personal style – in our dress, home décor, use of language, and countless other ways – to distinguish ourselves from others.

Painting the big picture

The qualities of personal style are rarely meaningful as isolated behaviors. (So what if someone wears a hat at an odd angle?) But when they are seen and experienced in a larger context, they become especially vivid and telling. ("The guy wears suede shoes, a droopy overcoat that's never buttoned, a scarf thrown over his shoulder, and a hat that he pulls so low it hides his eyes.") Style qualities add color, shading, and texture to a big picture.

No two people have the same style, although they often share many style qualities. Do people need to share a majority of style qualities to get along? Not necessarily. Some of the best relationships, at work and in life, are shared by individuals who are stylistic opposites.

Trivia...

When Levittown, New York, was built during the years following World War II, the developer's original intention was to create a community in which all homes looked alike. They were appalled when some homebuyers began to customize their residences by changing the color scheme, adding decoration or landscaping, and constructing extra rooms. In fact, the buyers were simply following a very human tendency - adding their own personal style to set themselves apart from others.

What's style got to do with it?

Your personal style has a lot to do with how you present yourself to the world and how people perceive and experience you. It can have profound influence on your successes and setbacks in the workplace. There's an old tongue-in-cheek career management adage that holds a good measure of deep truth: People get hired for what they can do and fired for who they are. Let's expand on the idea of the job-person match.

There's an important difference between the "hard" and "soft" qualities of the job-person match.

You encountered the "hard" qualities of the equation when you learned about interests and skills as defining traits in your personal profile – the elements you need for success and satisfaction in the workplace. These qualities draw the clear outline of your "career contours." .

YOUR STYLE WILL AFFECT HOW OTHERS ACT TOWARDS YOU

Then, as you saw in the previous chapter, adding your career values to the picture filled in some of the details of your personal profile with nuances of tone and texture. To complete the picture, you need to add style qualities, which introduce more shadings, subtleties, and complexities. You can think of values and style traits as the "soft" qualities of the equation, those that serve as counterpoints to skills and interests.

Consider these questions about how you relate and behave in the workplace:

a) Do you like to work alone or with others?

b) Do you prefer to dress casually or more formally?

c) What kind of pace do you like in your workday: fast or relaxed?

d) Are you comfortable being open and friendly with others, or do you prefer to be reserved and keep some distance?

e) Can you "be yourself" on the job, or are you more comfortable showing only certain facets of yourself?

f) Do you finish tasks quickly, or do you need deadline pressure to get you moving?

■ **Are you more comfortable** *in casual clothes, or do you prefer the more formal look of a business suit?*

These are just a few of the questions that relate to personal style – the way you do the things you do. It's what gives you distinction – in life and in the workplace. Think of personal style as the aggregate of your personality traits, your good and bad habits, your idiosyncrasies, your strengths and vulnerabilities, your beauty marks, and your blemishes.

When it comes to personal style, the bottom line is this: Being aware of the personal style you bring into the workplace will help you make more intelligent, informed decisions about your career.

In the context of the job-person match, style is just as important as interests, skills, and values in determining what makes you tick and what rounds out the you side of the match.

■ **Your style is a** *vital part of what makes you the person you are.*

Taking stock of your personal style qualities

THERE ARE MANY TOOLS THAT *can help you take a look at your personal style qualities. Career counselors use a variety of informal and formal instruments to measure style, some of which describe distinct categories of personality type. You'll get a look at the most widely used of those in just a little bit, but first let's perform a more fundamental exercise to identify your personal style qualities.*

The following worksheet is a wide-ranging inventory of personality traits that come into play in many situations at work. There's no way that all – or even most – of these will describe you, but you will find many that do apply to you. And so will your friends and colleagues. Read on.

Tip: Before you mark the worksheet, make several photocopies.

1. Check all the traits you are confident describe you well. Check as many as you wish, but make sure you really feel that you "own" each trait you check.

2. After you've finished the rough-cut selection, go back to the top of the list and narrow down the traits you've chosen to the 12 that describe you best. Circle them.

3. Using photocopies of the list, have other people check off the traits that they think apply to you. Have each person do a rough cut, and then have them circle the 12 traits that describe you best.

4. Compare the rough-cut lists and the top-12 lists. What are the similarities and differences between the ways you see yourself and the ways in which others see you? Make notes and discuss your ideas with the others who completed the exercise.

100 QUIRKS AND CHARACTERISTICS OF PERSONAL STYLE

Accommodating	Charming		Easygoing	Firm
Accurate	Competent		Efficient	Flexible
Adaptable	Competitive		Emotional	Forceful
Adventurous	Confident		Empathic	Formal
Aggressive	Conscientious		Energetic	Frank
Alert	Conservative	CAPABLE	Enterprising	Friendly
Ambitious	Considerate	Dependable	Fair-minded	Gentle
Calm	Cool	Detail-minded		
Capable	Cooperative	Determined		
Careful	Curious	Direct		
Cerebral	Deliberate	Discreet		
		Dominant	EFFICIENT	

Helpful	Meticulous	Quiet		Trusting
Honest	Moderate	Rational		Unaffected
Idealistic	Open-minded	Realistic		Unflappable
Imaginative	Optimistic	Reflective		Uninhibited
Informal	Organized	Relaxed		Versatile
Insightful	Original	Reliable	Spontaneous	Visionary
Intelligent	Outgoing	Reserved	Steady	Warm
Inventive	Painstaking	Resourceful	Strong-minded	
Laid back	Persevering	Responsible	Sympathetic	
Likeable	Persistent	Savvy	Tactful	
Logical	Persuasive	Sensitive	Tenacious	
Loyal	Poised	Serious	Thorough	
Mature	Practical	Sharp	Tolerant	
Methodical	Precise	Sociable	Tough	

PRECISE

RATIONAL

Measuring personal style formally

NOW THAT YOU'VE BEGUN to think about some of the qualities that add up to your own personal style, let's take a look at how you can deepen your knowledge. Career counselors and human resources professionals often use formal *assessment instruments* to measure and categorize personality styles and behaviors.

DEFINITION

Inventories or information tools that measure personality traits, aptitudes, skills, and interests are called assessment instruments. Most people think of these as tests. However, since there are no right or wrong answers, they are more accurately described as measurement instruments.

There are dozens of tools that claim to measure personality traits, and they range from simple inventories to complex diagnostic instruments that draw in-depth psychological profiles. A trained career counselor can guide you through the jungle of personality instruments and help you make the best use of one or two that will work well for you. To keep you moving on your mission of self-assessment, I describe one of the most commonly used tools in the following section.

Charting personality types

ONE INSTRUMENT THAT MEASURES *personal style and shows how it relates to career choice, workplace situations, and communication style is the Myers-Briggs Type Indicator (MBTI). It is used widely in organizational, educational, and counseling settings.*

Found in classrooms, in human resources departments, in a raft of books and web sites devoted to its interpretation and applications, the MBTI is literally all over the place. It's good that it's so accessible, because it can help you develop a valuable awareness of your personal style. It can also help you understand and appreciate other styles, and cultivate some important ways to work, communicate, and coexist with individuals who do things differently from you.

■ **Many books**
apply MBTI theory to career issues.

The MBTI sorts information about behaviors and preferences, and relates it to 16 distinct personality profiles. This is not to say that there are only 16 ways of being in the world, because each one of us is unique. But the MBTI does suggest that the 16 profiles can serve to help us understand more about how we learn, make decisions, and relate to other people and the environment around us. The better you understand your preferences in each of those key areas, the easier it will be for you to identify compatible career pathways and work environments and make informed, smart decisions about them.

Let's get acquainted with the MBTI so that you know some of its basic concepts and can relate them to your thinking about career management. There are many resources that will enable you to learn more about the instrument and the 16 profiles it describes (see the appendix), but a top-line look at its central ideas will enhance your awareness of personal style and its importance to the job-person match.

INTERNET

www.typelogic.com

Here's a web site devoted to MBTI resources (the instrument itself is not available online). You can access links to articles and information about the MBTI and its origins, history, interpretation, and uses.

The MBTI is rooted in the work of Carl Jung, a Swiss psychologist who pioneered important work in personality theory. His early work was expanded and reinterpreted by two American women, Katherine Briggs and her daughter, Isabel Briggs Myers. These women and their colleagues, who were not psychologists, devoted many years to the process of making Jung's work understandable and meaningful to general audiences. The system of 16 personality types and the abundance of type theory that explains it is the result of their efforts. In basic terms, the MBTI identifies an individual's preferences in four areas of activity.

The term preference in MBTI context refers to what comes naturally, without forethought or effort.

To see what that means, try writing your signature first with your "normal" hand, and then with the other hand. Or, step into your favorite jeans as you always do, and then step into them with the other foot first. Most people describe the feeling of doing things in different ways from their natural tendencies as awkward, uncomfortable, or difficult – like "going against the grain" or "swimming into the tide."

The MBTI measures what comes naturally to you regarding interacting with people, gathering information, making decisions, and relating to the external environment. Each of these four areas is presented as a scale of preference between two opposite ways of

Behavior	Scale of Preference	
Interacting with people	Extroversion	Introversion
Gathering information	Sensing	Intuition
Making decisions	Thinking	Feeling
Relating to environment	Judging	Perceiving

being. Type theory suggests that most individuals have either one natural preference or the other on each scale. The four pairs of preferences on the scale are as follows:

Some of the descriptors in MBTI language may seem imprecise, and the decision-making scale presents the most striking example. A preference for Thinking does not mean that a person lacks emotionality. By the same token, a preference for Feeling does not signify an absence of intellectual activity. They are just two different but equivalent ways of being in the world – like the difference between brown eyes and blue.

A preference for Judging does not mean that the person is "judgmental," which is generally not considered a positive quality. The two terms are not interchangeable.

Although most people tend to approach the MBTI by looking at one scale at a time – a natural way to reach a fundamental understanding of type theory – the richness of the MBTI happens in the very exotic stew it cooks up by combining an individual's preferences on each of the four scales. In other words, the MBTI preferences are not independent, they are interdependent.

Your four preferences work with and influence one another in a dynamic interaction.

And that's how the system presents a total of 16 personality profiles: combinations of the eight different preferences – that is, four times four – equals 16. But I'm going to keep things simple for you in this chapter and just talk about the four scales and their opposite preferences. That will give you a general overview of personality type and style. As you read on, think about your own natural tendencies for each area because you'll eventually need to write them down.

Collaborate or concentrate?

The first of the four MBTI preference scales measures how you are energized. The opposite style preferences that serve as sources of energy are called Extroversion and Introversion.

If you feel comfortable and stimulated by a lot of interaction with other people, you may have a natural preference for Extroversion. People who prefer the extroverted style like lots of variety and action, and they like to involve people in as many of their experiences as possible. Extroverts are great in brainstorming sessions and in large meetings, where ideas and conversation abound. Often, extroverts communicate by "thinking out loud," without necessarily planning or settling on what they intend to say. They tend to be drawn in many directions. You might say that Extroverts are attracted to breadth.

The opposite way of being energized has less to do with personal interaction and more to do with reflection and careful thought. If you're more comfortable thinking things through before you speak, and don't mind spending time alone or with only one or two other people, you may have a natural preference for Introversion. Individuals who prefer the introverted style like quiet for concentration and enjoy intellectual activities like reading, writing, deliberating, and even daydreaming. They tend to be less comfortable in large gatherings and more at ease relating to smaller groups or one person at a time. Introverts tend to communicate by thinking about what they're going to say, then saying it, and then thinking about what they've said. Typically they are pulled in fewer directions, but they go deeply into each of them. You might say that Introverts are attracted to depth.

In American culture there's a slight negative stereotype associated with the term Introvert, but in MBTI parlance a tendency toward Introversion is no less preferable or valuable than a tendency toward Extroversion. Introverts are sometimes shy, but they are not necessarily wallflowers.

Bottom line or down the line?

The second of the four MBTI preferences measures how you learn about things and the kind of information you naturally notice and remember. The style preferences that describe opposite ways of taking in information are called Sensing and Intuition.

If you're very detail-oriented and feel comfortable focusing on facts, concrete information, and hard evidence, you may have a preference for Sensing. Individuals who lean toward the Sensing preference are very attuned to information that comes to them through the five senses: touch, taste, sight, smell, and hearing. Sensing types learn by taking in concrete information, and they focus on the immediate significance of things. They're adept at zeroing in on the fine points of any situation, and they place a high value on the learning they gained through past experiences. Sensing types are typically concerned with the "net-net" or the "bottom line" in any problem or situation.

The opposite way of taking in information relies less on the five senses and more on abstractions and patterns of meaning. If you're comfortable paying attention to information that isn't necessarily factual, but rather more suggestive and abstract, you may have a natural preference for Intuition. People who prefer Intuition typically form impressions about things by using ideas and nonfactual information, such as hunches. Intuitive types learn by assembling information that is not necessarily concrete, and they focus on implications and consequences. They tend to be oriented toward future possibilities and alternative ways of doing things. Intuitive types like to think about situations not necessarily as they are, but as they might be.

Stylistic differences between preferences for Sensing and Intuition can lead to major communication conflict.

The two types view the world in completely different terms. It's like the difference between seeing things in black and white or in shades of gray.

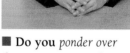

■ **Do you** *ponder over things, or act upon them?*

Tough-minded or tenderhearted?

The third of the four MBTI preferences measures how you arrive at conclusions and make decisions. The style preferences that describe opposite ways of making decisions are called Thinking and Feeling.

If you tend to use logical and impersonal analysis to reach a conclusion about a particular issue or situation, you may have a natural preference for Thinking. People who prefer Thinking typically look at issues as observers and reach conclusions by adopting an objective perspective. In other words, Thinking types tend to take themselves out of a situation, evaluate it logically and impersonally, and then form a conclusion about it. Thinking types typically approach problems with an analytical, detached involvement.

The opposite way of reaching conclusions relies less on head work and more on heart work. If you tend to make decisions by trusting your gut values or what you perceive are other people's values, you may have a natural preference for Feeling. Individuals who tend to make decisions by using a preference for Feeling typically look at situations as participants and form conclusions by getting a subjective read on the issues involved. Unlike Thinking types, people who prefer Feeling tend to throw themselves into a situation, evaluate

■ **Some people instinctively** *make decisions based on a gut feeling.*

their visceral reaction to it, and reach a conclusion based on the comfort level that results from their reaction. Feeling types tend to approach problems with a heartfelt, self-inclusive involvement.

Check off or chill out?

The last of the four MBTI preferences measures how you like to live your life and move through your days. The opposite style preferences that describe different ways of being attuned to the external environment are called Judging and Perceiving.

If you're comfortable having things settled and decided, with no uncertainty hanging over your head, you may have a preference for Judging. People who prefer the Judging style tend to be highly organized and like a lot of structure and scheduling in their lives. Judging types enjoy keeping to-do lists and gain great satisfaction from checking off goals as they accomplish them. They like to do lots of planning, and they tend to be very methodical in their approach to almost everything. In short, Judging types are driven by a need for closure in situations and activities.

The opposite way of navigating daily experience puts organization on hold and tunes in instead to flexibility and open-endedness. If you're comfortable moving through your days by staying in the moment and addressing situations as they develop, you may have a preference for Perceiving. Individuals who prefer the Perceiving style generally attune to their environments by responding to it, rather than controlling it. Instead of moving to get things settled and decided, Perceiving types will go out of their way to keep options open. They like lots of spontaneity in their lives and tend to take things as they come. Perceiving types don't hesitate to change their minds about things, even after decisions are made. Unlike their counterparts on this preference scale, Perceiving types are driven by a need to keep things open-ended.

Developing a comfortable MBTI profile

NOW THAT YOU'VE HAD A BRIEF exposure to the MBTI preference scales *and the opposite ways of being each describes, you should be able to decide where you fall on each scale.*

Although the actual MBTI permits ties, you should commit to one preference or the other for this exercise. This is not the real MBTI, nor is it an official cut-down version of it. It is an extremely simple method of giving you a way to think about personality type and style so that you can proceed on your self-assessment journey.

THE MBTI PREFERENCE SCALES

Behavior	Preference
How I'm energized	Extroversion – I like lots of interaction and conversation with people.
	Introversion – I like lots of calm and quiet time to relax and think about things.
How I gather information	Sensing – I look at facts, details and concrete evidence.
	Intuition – I look at abstractions, hunches and patterns of meaning.
How I make decisions	Thinking – I use logic, impersonal analysis, and tough-mindedness to decide.
	Feeling – I trust my values and instincts, and let my emotions help me decide.
How I like to live my days	Judging – I'm most comfortable when things are structured, organized and settled.
	Perceiving – I'm most comfortable when my options are open and I can be spontaneous and flexible.

Using MBTI to find viable job-person matches

So what does all this have to with managing your career? Plenty. In order to choose career pathways and work environments that are compatible with the person you are, you need to understand your fundamental personality traits and what will (and won't) complement them. Pursuing the MBTI is one of many things you can do to develop a portrait of your style.

The MBTI has attracted an abundance of attention over the course of many decades. Because it allows for deeper learning about behaviors and tendencies, it has been given a wealth of different applications. Many books have been written to apply MBTI theory to the subject of career choice and workplace behavior. Among the most outstanding are:

1. *Do What You Are*, by Paul D. Tieger & Barbara Barron-Tieger, Little, Brown, 1995.

2. *Type Talk: The 16 Personality Types That Determine How We Live, Love, and Work*, by Otto Kroeger and Janet M. Thuesen, Delta, 1989.

3. *Work Types*, by Jean M. Kummerow, Nancy J. Barger, and Linda K. Kirby, Warner Books, 1997.

The last word on style (for now)

PEOPLE OFTEN ARGUE THAT *they behave differently at work than they do at home. This may be true to a certain extent, but you don't leave your personality at the doorstep when you show up for work each day. You bring it with you, however well (or poorly) disguised it may be. For that reason, effective career management means being thoughtful about matching your style qualities with those of your job and your workplace environment.*

INTERNET

www.keirsey.com

www.temperament.com

These two web sites focus on a different kind of personal-style theory: character and temperament types. Related to (but distinct from) the MBTI, temperament theory also seeks to trace and celebrate differences among individuals. You'll find more detailed explanation, along with links to many other related resources.

Here's a quick exercise to get you up to speed on personal style in the context of workplace style.

25 FIT FACTORS OF WORKPLACE STYLE

Review each of these 25 workplace characteristics. Determine which statement about each best describes what you'd prefer to have in your ideal work situation, and put a check next to it. If your preference falls in the middle, put a check next to "Balance." To arrive at a clear, sharply focused understanding of your desired workplace style characteristics, limit the number of times you choose "Balance" to five.

Absorbing work

☐ I like thinking about work on my own time and taking work home.

☐ I prefer to leave my work in the workplace and keep my home life free.

☐ Balance

Attention to detail

☐ I like work that requires me to concentrate on details.

☐ I prefer work that enables me to keep clear of details.

☐ Balance

ARE YOU COMFORTABLE IN FORMAL SITUTATIONS?

Compensation structure

☐ I prefer steady, regular compensation for my contributions.

☐ I'm comfortable with variable compensation that's linked to my performance.

☐ Balance

Contact with customers or clients

☐ I like lots of contact with customers, clients, vendors, and suppliers.

☐ I prefer minimal contact with customers, clients, vendors, and suppliers.

☐ Balance

Decision process

☐ I prefer to reach decisions on a consensual basis.

☐ I'm comfortable when decisions come down through the ranks.

☐ Balance

Decision responsibility

☐ I prefer having major responsibility for making important decisions.

☐ I prefer having minimal responsibility for making important decisions.

☐ Balance

Dress code

☐ I'm comfortable with a casual wardrobe and workplace atmosphere.

☐ I prefer a more traditional business wardrobe and workplace atmosphere.

☐ Balance

Focus of skills

☐ I prefer working in situations that require specialized skill sets.

☐ I like working in situations that use generalized skills.

☐ Balance

Innovation

☐ I like bringing creativity and innovation to the workplace.

☐ I prefer bringing minimal creativity and innovation to the workplace.

☐ Balance

Internal communication mode

☐ I prefer communicating with management and coworkers by phone or in person.

☐ I prefer communicating with management and coworkers through memos and e-mail.

☐ Balance

SOME PEOPLE PREFER DIRECT COMMUNICATION

Job structure

☐ I'm most comfortable when project goals and procedures are set by others.

☐ I'm most comfortable when I can set my own project goals and procedures.

☐ Balance

Managing others

☐ I like managing other people and teams.

☐ I prefer working alone or participating on teams.

☐ Balance

DO YOU ENJOY HIGH-PRESSURE SITUATIONS?

Pace of workflow

☐ I thrive in a fast-paced, results-oriented environment with many deadlines.

☐ I prefer an evenly paced, process-oriented environment with few deadlines.

☐ Balance

Performance evaluation

☐ I like lots of feedback to help me know exactly how I'm doing at all times.

☐ I prefer minimal feedback that is typically general in scope.

☐ Balance

Procedural guidelines

☐ I'm most comfortable when there are established guidelines and procedures.

☐ I like lots of "rope" to get things done however possible.

☐ Balance

Project length

☐ I prefer short-term projects, variety, and lots of new activity.

☐ I prefer longer-term projects, focus, and minimal new activity.

☐ Balance

Promoting your ideas

☐ I like getting others to support and "buy into" my ideas.

☐ I prefer acting on my own ideas without having to promote them to others.

☐ Balance

Quantitative work

☐ I like working with numbers, data, and statistics.

☐ I prefer minimal work with numbers, data, and statistics.

☐ Balance

ARE YOU A GOOD TEAM PLAYER?

Relation to coworkers

☐ I like to get things done by collaborating with others on teams.

☐ I prefer to get things done by working independently.

☐ Balance

Risk

☐ I'm comfortable when there's considerable risk and the stakes are high.

☐ I prefer low risk with minimal chance of loss or failure.

☐ Balance

Schedule flexibility

☐ I prefer the routine of a work schedule that doesn't vary.

☐ I'm comfortable working flexible hours that may change from time to time.

☐ Balance

Supervision

☐ I like close supervision and direction from management.

☐ I prefer to work in a self-directed manner with little supervision and direction from management.

☐ Balance

MANY PEOPLE LIKE TO TRAVEL FOR WORK

Travel

☐ I like a good amount of work-related travel and time away from home.

☐ I prefer minimal travel and remaining close to home.

☐ Balance

Upward communication

☐ I like being in close, frequent contact with my boss or manager.

☐ I prefer infrequent contact with my boss or manager.

☐ Balance

Visibility of contributions

☐ I like my work to have a high profile, to be seen and acknowledged by top management.

☐ I prefer my work to have a low profile, to be seen and acknowledged by my department or my customers rather than top management.

☐ Balance

When you've finished, examine your choices carefully. How would you summarize your personal style and the workplace style you'd like to have in your ideal job? Make notes, and refer back to them as you consider your important career decisions. And, as with each component of your job-person match profile, be sure to update the list periodically.

A simple summary

✓ Your personal style is what makes you unique. It refers not so much to what you do, but how you do it.

✓ Personal style has important influences on what work situations and environments align well with you.

✓ The better you understand your personal style and what nourishes it most in the workplace, the better equipped you'll be to make smart, sound decisions about your career.

✓ Many tools and instruments are available to help you measure and inventory your personality traits and stylistic preferences. The Myers-Briggs Type Indicator is among the most popular and useful.

✓ Style characteristics also describe work situations and environments. An understanding about which traits are among your strongest needs will guide you through important career management decisions.

PART THREE

SUCCESS CAN FOLLOW A LEAP INTO THE UNKNOWN

PLANNING YOUR NEXT STEPS

Now that you've learned about the world of work and about yourself, it's time to begin plotting some career action points. This section of the book will give you what you need to put what you've learned into action.

First, you'll examine your main options. If you're in transition, there are five career *configurations* that can help you identify where you are and where you need to go in the short term and the long term. If you already are employed in an organization that works for you, you'll learn about several possible courses of career action to take.

If you're considering a major career *overhaul,* you'll need to organize your thinking by learning how to develop occupational possibilities. You'll see what being an entrepreneur entails: Starting or acquiring a business, franchising, and ways of working independently.

Finally, you'll make a strategic career action plan: This plan will be your blueprint for progress in your career – and success.

Chapter 9

Choosing the Career Shape That Works Best for You

I F YOU ARE IN CAREER transition or are anticipating a transition in the near future, you must decide now what you want your career to look like. This chapter describes five different career configurations, or shapes, and explains why it's important for you to commit to one now – and in the future. You can make a choice that will serve you on an interim basis or a permanent one. Or, you can make choices that will serve you both ways. Are you ready to chart your course?

In this chapter...
✓ The career crossroads

✓ The five career configurations

DON'T JUST THROW YOURSELF INTO THE FRAY – THINK FIRST!

The career crossroads

IF YOU'RE IN A CAREER TRANSITION, it's a good bet that you're at a crossroads. Maybe your most recent job ended – expectedly or unexpectedly – and you're transitioning from one work situation to the next, however slight or large the difference may be. Or, maybe you're coming into the workforce for the first time. If so, it's likely that you're transitioning from student life to "working" life and wondering how to accomplish that successfully.

Or, you may be planning to re-enter the workforce after a long time away from it. Perhaps you took a sabbatical or another kind of "career break." Perhaps you devoted time to your family or a long project that has been especially meaningful to you. Now you're ready to "get back into it" and pick up where you left off – or head in a different direction altogether.

Whatever your situation, and however you're thinking about your relationship with work, you have important career choices to make. One of the most fundamental of these has to do with career configurations.

You must be able to level with yourself and decide what you want your career to look like – now and in the future. The vision that will influence your decisions most immediately will be, of course, the one that defines the shape of your career right now. But the vision of the future shape of your career will also be highly influential, since the decisions you make this year will set you up for the career choices you have in years to come.

INTERNET

www.careers.org

Here's a panoramic web site that presents itself as "the Web's directory of career directories." It offers information on learning resources, career services, regional career and leisure resources, employer directories, jobs on the web, and top career web sites. You'll find guidance and direction no matter what career shape you're in, including working solo and running your own business.

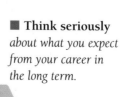

■ **Think seriously** *about what you expect from your career in the long term.*

Trivia...

The boundaries of an individual's work life form what is called a career configuration. It defines the shape of your career within the greater context of your life experience.

The five career configurations

IN AN ARTICLE THAT ORIGINALLY appeared *in* The Five O'Clock News *and subsequently in Kate Wendleton's* Targeting the Job You Want, *Betsy Jaffe, Ph.D., outlined new shapes for careers. She suggested that there are five distinctive career configurations. Think of these as shapes for the sum of your work experiences at any given point in time. For our purposes in this chapter, these configurations can be described as:*

1. New traditional

2. Fixed focus

3. Dual axis

4. Patchwork quilt

5. Conditional

As you read about each of the five configurations, keep in mind what you learned about yourself in the earlier self-assessment chapters of the book. Ask yourself which of these career configurations best suits you and provides what you need from your relationship with work.

■ **Which way of working suits** *you best? In today's career landscape you have more opportunity to choose.*

New traditional

Progressing through a series of workplace experiences as an employee of one or more organizations is called maintaining a new traditional career. This isn't a contradiction in terms; it's an acknowledgment of workplace realities in the early 21st century.

As you saw in Part One, the workplace today is a far different planet from the one your parents lived on. It bears almost no resemblance to the work planet their parents lived on. What you can count on most in the workplace today is change – lots of it, moving at astonishing speed.

Organizations will continue to reshape and restructure in response to change. That means that old ways of succeeding – by climbing up through the ranks one notch at a time – won't work anymore. The trend of eliminating hierarchies and ladders will continue to gain momentum as organizations strive for less bureaucracy and less "fat," and greater efficiency and productivity.

■ **Our grandparents'** *generation would not recognize the world in which we work today.*

Does that necessarily mean you can't plant your feet inside an organization and plan to stay there as long as you want? No, it certainly does not. If you identify an organization that works for you on many different levels, by all means work for it. However, if you choose this career route at present, you will need to keep in mind two overarching new-century ground rules about working for organizations.

The first key ground rule, which you explored in Part One, is that no work situation lasts forever. Under the "new" work contract, employers and employees owe each other very little.

If you take a job with an organization, think of it as an arena in which to play out as many of your career interests, skills, values, and style qualities as possible.

Be aware that as your personal qualities shift and evolve, the arena you've been working in may lose its appeal and usefulness. When it does, you'll need to find a new one. If at that point you're still organization-minded, your career strategy should be to identify another organizational situation that works for you on as many levels as possible.

If you can appreciate the new-century truth that no work situation lasts forever, you may also appreciate the idea that it's usually better to turn the page on an organization before it turns the page on you. In other words, it's preferable to leave on your terms than on theirs.

Why? If you choose to leave, chances are that your choice is a part or a result of a larger plan. That means you're exercising control. On the other hand, if you're asked to leave, chances are that you didn't see the end of the relationship coming or were otherwise unprepared for its demise. That means you're not in control – or, at best, you have less control over your career predicament than you would if you had initiated the parting of the ways. Which way of closing out a work situation seems more appealing?

■ **It's best to make a decision** *after careful thought rather than as an emotional response to a situation.*

The second key ground rule about working for organizations is that success is yours to define.

As organizations continue to flatten and refine, the traditional, highly visible signposts of success are disappearing. As you've seen, gone are the days when careers progressed sequentially from one station to another within an organization and with commensurate salary increases along the way.

Today organizations are asking (and requiring) their employees to stay longer at a particular professional level and to identify ways to enrich their jobs themselves and take on new challenges. (Options for career movement posed by this reality are covered in the next section, "Fixed Focus.")

What this means is that the signposts of success have largely been dismantled. You'll need to learn how to experience the sense of success from your own internal feeling of accomplishment, rather than from external indicators and trappings. The good news is that, for many people, experiencing success within themselves can be far more gratifying than experiencing success that other people define for them.

■ **While you may not climb** *the ladder at work in the traditional sense, your role may expand and diversify in other ways.*

The new traditional career places accountability squarely on your shoulders. It also places you in charge of what happens to you.

Typically, people who feel nervous or anxious about the new relationships between organizations and individuals do not want to assume responsibility for managing their own careers. Basically, it's your car to drive.

Organizations remain at the heart of the new traditional career. The fact that the ground rules have changed isn't a truth to be afraid of, but rather one to be energized by. Despite the collapse and disappearance of hierarchies, ladders, and the militaristic corporate structures of old, organizations still provide viable arenas in which to play out your career. They can nourish it, promote it, and advance it as well as they can stifle, squeeze, and quash it. Usually, the scenario that takes effect depends on just what you, the individual, bring to the stage.

Fixed focus

A career that revolves around a concentration of knowledge or expertise, or around a single product or service, is called a fixed focus career. As its name implies, a fixed focus career has a single emphasis, which typically does not change over time.

For example, if you were a professional writer, the fixed focus career configuration would mean that all of the work you do involves writing. You may start out by writing advertising copy, magazine articles, and web site content. You may then decide to start a small business partnership that provides writing services to corporate clients. Later you could launch a newsletter that capitalizes on your skills as a wordsmith. All of your work activities still relate to writing regardless of whatever else changes.

■ **Your job may** *be based around the preparing and giving of presentations.*

■ **Do you find that** *people look to you for expert advice?*

Consider another example. If you have a deep expertise in a particular area, you may wish to leverage your knowledge and experience by consulting to business or other organizations.

Independent consulting requires many lifestyle adjustments (you'll get a closer look at some of these in Chapter 12). However, many people value the relative freedom that being a consultant carries. In theory, they can say no to an assignment any time they want to! (But in fact, many consultants are motivated by the lure of money to tackle any assignment they can get.)

Dual axis

A career that provides two sources of work activity simultaneously is called a dual axis career. When an individual pursues two separate career efforts at the same time, he or she has a dual axis career. Typically (but not always), a dual axis career involves a full-time job and another endeavor or two. It also involves a lot of dedication, resolve, and perseverance.

There are many ready examples of a dual axis career. For instance, in addition to your day job you may have a regular commitment to do volunteer work twice a week at a local community center. Or to generate extra income, you may work a night or two at a nearby bookstore or other retail shop. Or to pursue a growing career interest, you may carve out two or three sittings a week to do freelance writing or designing.

If you're considering, planning, or implementing a major career change, the dual axis phase is almost a necessity – at least for awhile. Perhaps your change involves returning to school for a degree or some professional retraining. If you want to accomplish this while remaining in your current work situation, you will – for a period of time, at least – fit your career into the dual axis configuration.

If your career strategy involves choosing a new industry or profession, you will very likely need to acquire some related experience before you can leave your current situation behind completely.

This related experience could be done at night or on weekends, as your current job allows. If you do, you'll need to reconfigure your career to a dual axis one for a time.

The dual axis career is very demanding. Those who choose to pursue it are usually opting for the career high road. In other words, having two major career activities going on at once is an arrangement that is typically purposeful, not accidental. It gets you closer to your ultimate career goal. The dual axis career is very demanding, but it is usually a prerequisite for a major change. The good news is that you won't have to keep it up forever. A dual axis career is almost always temporary in nature.

■ **Much of the time** *you may feel like your fixed-focus career resembles a dual-axis one!*

Patchwork quilt

Stitching together a variety of work situations for interest and income is called pursuing a patchwork quilt career. If you're imagining many pieces of cloth sewn together to form a large whole, you've got the right picture.

Patchwork quilt careers aren't necessarily crazy quilts. Many individuals progress through their entire careers without ever moving away from the patchwork quilt configuration. For them, the sheer variety of work situations produces a level of satisfaction that is just not attainable by sticking with a single organization or situation (or even two).

If your relationship with work consists of earning income from several different sources, you're maintaining a patchwork quilt career configuration. Let's say you're a substitute teacher with four classes a week to carry. That situation

■ **One person's** *way of working may not suit all . . ..*

by itself will probably not provide you with enough income, gratification, and opportunity to sustain your career. You may need to pursue other opportunities to enhance your career vitality. For example, you may decide to run workshops at a church or community center, teach a continuing-education course at another school, write an article or two for a professional journal, and work a day a week as an information specialist at a library.

The work activities comprising a patchwork quilt career do not necessarily have to be related. Think of the actor who survives long spells between parts by pursuing voiceovers (related to performing), modeling (also related to performing), and waiting tables (not related to performing, although some waiters and diners alike argue that there's a definite connection).

Patchwork quilt career activities are replaceable pieces of a larger whole. As one situation wears out or loses its appeal, it is replaced by a new – and perhaps altogether different – activity. Perhaps all of the activities are strategically related and designed to move an individual closer to a unified goal. The beauty of the patchwork quilt career lies in its tailorable, totally individual nature.

■ **Some are** *happier making their own rules.*

■ **You may** *want to become a florist.*

Though the patchwork quilt career has its undeniable appeal, it presents a few aspects that aren't necessarily appealing.

First, most individuals will have to constantly renew their effort to unify the work activities into a larger career cloth. It's essential to ask constantly whether or not each activity is helping you move ahead or just allowing you to tread water. Though it's ideal for all work activities to relate to and advance a primary pursuit, such as acting or photography, in reality that situation is not always attainable. That's when jobs like waiter and receptionist become means to an end.

A potential drawback is the lack of continuity the patchwork quilt career imposes. It's a constant procession of situational beginnings and endings. You may have the personality that thrives on that kind of continuing transformation, but you may not.

It's important to understand that pursuing a number of different work activities requires an ongoing investment of energy and dedication.

To keep a patchwork quilt career viable, you can't afford to ease up on an aggressive pursuit of new opportunities.

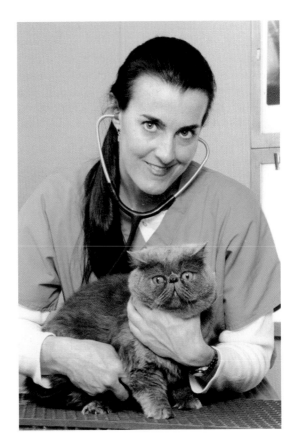

■ **What about becoming** *a veterinarian?*

Conditional

The final type of career configuration is one that arises out of distinct conditions and provides time-limited opportunities for income and career experience. Taking advantage of work situations that are temporary is called maintaining a conditional career phase.

The conditional career phase revolves around work situations that are typically not predictable or open-ended. Sometimes conditional work will fill a very specific need, especially one that is determined by distinct time limitations.

■ **If you are looking** *for a steady source of income, conditional work may not be your best bet.*

In the conditional career configuration, you go where the work is. For example, some people run bed-and-breakfast lodgings during vacation seasons. Artisans sell their crafts at fairs that are held at certain times of the year. Stunt actors get the call only when spectacular feats are being filmed. And construction workers go where buildings are being erected and stay on site until the work is finished.

Conditional career work includes any employment situation that is limited to time limitations. Some examples are project assignments, interim positions, temporary work, and seasonal jobs. Each of these has its place and could work to your benefit at certain points in your career. However, if you're in the habit of relying on conditional work to define your career, you may want to ask yourself if that's in your best interest over the long haul.

Typically, conditional work is suitable for the present and the immediate future. But, like renting your home, it's probably not the best long-term investment.

■ **You may be thinking** *about entering a new field, in which case, taking a temporary position in a relevant company is a good way to see if it suits you, and vice versa.*

■ **You may take a while** *to decide what it is you*
really want to do, and so pursue other jobs in the meantime.

A simple summary

✓ Managing your career successfully requires taking steps to build forward momentum into your work life.

✓ If you're in a career transition or are anticipating one, it's essential to decide how you want your career to be shaped, now and in the future.

✓ There are five career configurations: new traditional, fixed focus, dual axis, patchwork quilt, and conditional.

✓ Each career configuration holds a unique set of appeals and cautions.

✓ Deciding on and committing to a career configuration is not a one-time event. Settling on one configuration while you work toward another can be a smart career strategy.

Chapter 10

Moving Forward from Where You Are

THE LEAST EFFECTIVE WAY TO MANAGE YOUR CAREER is to do nothing at all, yet many people who have made a considerable investment in an organization are plagued by a feeling that there is nothing they can do. They wait until the organization provides a new assignment, a promotion, or a termination. In short, many people wait until someone or something moves it forward for them.

If that career management strategy is unacceptable to you, then you're in the right place. This chapter describes six career moves that begin with your current work situation.

No matter how long you've been in a particular job or employed by particular organization, you always have options for career growth and moves. Are you ready to count the ways?

In this chapter...

✓ Career vitality demands change

✓ Growing your career from here: six career moves you can make

TEACHING OTHERS OFTEN HELPS US LEARN MORE ABOUT OURSELVES

Career vitality demands change

EVEN IF YOU'RE EMPLOYED, *it's a good bet that you're not entirely satisfied with your career right now, or you wouldn't be reading this book. Maybe your career has been on the stable side up to this point. In fact, maybe that's the problem – it's been too stable. If you've made a substantial career investment in a particular organization, you may be thinking of making an important move. Maybe you're feeling bored or unchallenged in your job, or maybe you no longer find it appealing. Maybe your skills have developed beyond the job you currently hold.*

If you're like most other people who have stayed put for a long time, the people around you have probably come and gone over time. Maybe you don't feel the professional kinship with your current set of coworkers that you did with others. Maybe you no longer feel like you belong where you are – if you ever did in the first place.

It's natural to want to change. Usually, change is healthy. In fact, for true career vitality, it's necessary. But, if you're like most career-minded individuals, you wonder about the degree of change to undertake – and about the options that are available to you.

Often we are faced with the urgency of change in the context of a work situation that seems nonnegotiable. You may think that change is unrealistic and improbable, or even impossible, because too much of your life and career is bound into the organization that employs you. If you do, then think again.

VIP *No matter how untenable your career situation may seem, you always have options for change.*

There are other options, not equally attractive or palatable, but which present you with alternatives and flip sides to your present career picture.

■ **If your heart's desire** *is to work outdoors, it's not too late to change your career direction.*

While managing your career, it's crucial to keep sight of an overarching theme that can serve as a beacon for your decisions.

Bring change into your career before change comes to you.

If you do nothing, involuntary change is likely to invade your career and throw your life into turmoil. Taking command of change, embracing it, and introducing it into your career, will heighten the satisfaction and sense of success work can offer you.

Growing your career from here: six career moves you can make

IN THINKING ABOUT CAREER *options and alternatives, begin with where you are and what you have. Undertaking a radical change (like quitting your job) is not the only solution to a stale and unpleasant work situation. Nor is it necessarily practical, given the obligations and responsibilities you may have.*

INTERNET

www.careermag.com

Click onto the web site of Career Magazine for an archive of articles by Caela Farren and other career development experts.

Career development consultant Caela Farren has written extensively about options for career movement that can proceed from your current employment situation. Whether happily or unhappily employed, there are six basic career moves you can make. On the career game board, all of them begin at square one – where you are right now – and move forward from there in different directions.

The six basic types of career moves you can make are:

- Sliding across
- Firming up
- Climbing high
- Scaling back
- Branching out
- Moving on

■ **If you're close** *to pulling your hair out, perhaps it's time for a change!*

The following sections describe each of these moves in detail, as well as some considerations that may facilitate your decisions and choices if you find yourself sitting on the fence, unsure of what move you should make.

It's important to note that each of the options detailed here is portrayed as a strategic, not tactical, career move — that is, a choice that will enrich and enhance your career over the long haul, not just in the immediate future.

Sliding across

Making a lateral, or horizontal, move within your current organization is called *sliding across*. Typically a lateral, or horizontal, move is accomplished without changing the level of responsibility, status, or compensation that you have now. It is simply a relocation to a different functional area, division, or location.

Why would you want to opt to change your work situation by sliding across? There are many reasons. Chief among them is that sliding across enables you to learn and apply new skills and develop new areas of expertise – without compromising or sacrificing the investments in your current organization that you have made to date. In many ways, sliding across makes you more valuable both internally and externally, since it enables you to expand your portfolio of skills and your network of professional contacts.

Other benefits of sliding across include gaining familiarity with different work styles within the same organization and establishing your reputation in areas that extend beyond your current situation. You'll also become more visible.

If you're on the fence about whether to make such a lateral move, consider the following:

1. Pinpoint your real motivation for wanting to make a career move. Is it overall dissatisfaction with your organization or just with your current situation within that organization?

2. Identify at least three of your strongest skills that you could apply in the new area.

3. Decide how sliding across will influence your future within the organization. Do a reality check with co-workers or a mentor.

■ **Think about why** *you want to be a chef rather than a clerk.*

Firming up

Expanding and shifting the emphasis of your responsibilities in your current job is called *firming up*. This career move is one that people typically overlook. Firming up means expanding and reconfiguring your responsibilities in your current job without changing the key circumstances that surround it. It means doing more and taking on new and different challenges. Think of it as conditioning your body. You can improve your health by going beyond the minimum activities typically required for keeping fit. Through vigorous exercise and dedication, you can add tone and new definition to your muscles.

Firming up in your current job is sometimes the only option that's available – for the moment. Remember, there is always an alternative to the situation you're in, even if it's only to change your attitude about what you do.

Firming up can help you find benefits in a work situation that may not suit you well, and play the situation for what it's worth until you can change it.

Often the greatest rewards of firming up are intrinsic and not measurable in financial terms. That means that you elect to take on more responsibilities and challenges not necessarily because you'll earn more income, but because meeting them can produce a great sense of accomplishment and satisfaction.

You'll also gain depth of experience and strengthen your repertoire of skills – which will enhance your suitability for future jobs within (or outside of) your current organization. An investment in your career future, choosing to firm up in your current work situation requires great discipline and self-motivation.

If you're on the fence about expanding and shifting the emphasis of your responsibilities in your current job:

1 Challenge yourself to find ways to grow professionally without making an external change.

2 Identify at least three skills you could develop and apply in your current situation.

3 Seek new projects, tasks, or roles that will enable you to push past your comfort zone.

■ **A project** *that evokes enthusiasm and needs dedication may keep you glued to your chair.*

Trivia...

A client once described an epiphany that transformed his work life. He had been terribly unhappy in his job, but was not yet sure about how he wanted to initiate change. He could find no alternative to sticking out his situation for at least another six to 12 months. When he explained this to a mentor and confided that the prospect made him feel discouraged and depressed, the mentor replied: "For as long as you have it, make your job magical." He did, simply by changing the way he viewed his role on the job. And in less than a year, he gained the clarity he needed to begin pursuing a major career change.

Climbing high

Working your way through the ranks of an organization to its upper management level is called *climbing high*. This is the move that's most often associated with the stereotypical climb up the organizational ladder. Climbing high involves advancing methodically within your organization until you get to the top – or as high as you're going to go.

■ **If your aim** *is to sit at the top table, be aware that there are fewer seats than ever before.*

■ **Employers often prefer** *to utilize their staff's creative abilities rather than offer them managerial positions.*

Many career-minded individuals still choose to manage their workplace behaviors according to this old-model strategy. It can still work, but organizations are typically eliminating ladders and levels now, not adding them. Thus employees are left with far fewer rungs to climb – and fewer chairs at the top management levels. Also, many organizations are realizing (to their great benefit) that their most talented employees can add the greatest value as individual contributors, not top managers.

The benefits of reaching the top of an organization are well known. The payoff comes in the form of status, prestige, power, financial reward, and influence – or a combination of all of these. The journey to the top, however, is often perilous.

If you're on the fence about working your way through the ranks of an organization to its upper management level:

1 Look carefully at your current organization, and decide how much potential for upward mobility it offers. Consider your total investment in the organization to date and whether or not it has positioned you for further advancement.

2 Consult with a mentor who knows and understands your organization's culture. Together, assess whether or not you have the "equipment" to reach the top.

Trivia...

As organizations become flatter and opportunities for advancement rarer, just how does a career-minded individual exercise the option of climbing high? One professional took on an additional set of managerial responsibilities without relinquishing any of those that were written into his job description. Eventually he asked for a new title that would reflect the enlarged scope of his job to his peers. He received it, along with a substantial bonus for contributing to the vitality of the firm. The following year, he requested yet another set of additional responsibilities.

Scaling back

Paring down your responsibilities in your current job or choosing another job at a lower level within the organization is called *scaling back*. Scaling back can be the most liberating choice an individual might make because it enables him or her to invest more time in other areas of life, including home and family and, yes, career planning for the future.

There are a number of circumstances in which scaling back represents the most viable of all career move options. If you require more flexible scheduling, for instance, or a rebudgeting of your time, you'll need to consider scaling back before you look at other options. If your department (or your organization) is being restructured, scaling back can be the option that enables you to remain grounded while you plan and implement a fresh career management strategy.

If you've been elevated to a level of responsibility that just does not align with your interests, skills, values, or style qualities, you may choose to scale back in order to regain a work situation that is congenial and fulfilling. Top-performing salespeople, for instance, are often rewarded with promotions to the ranks of sales management. But effective management requires different skill sets than effective salesmanship, and they are not necessarily interchangeable. The sales manager who elects to scale back to frontline sales work may be opting for the work that suits him or her best – and produces the most meaningful and notable personal successes.

Think of scaling back as simplifying. It may mean that you'll earn less income for your contributions, but if you elect to scale back as part of a larger career strategy, a pay cut can be a worthwhile investment.

Often, scaling back is the option that allows you to have your cake and eat it, too.

If you're on the fence about paring down your responsibilities in your current job or choosing another job at a lower level within the organization:

1. Consider the pros and cons of scaling back. Look at trade-offs through short- and long-term lenses.

2. Consult with a trusted peer, preferably within your organization, who has opted to scale back. Have him or her describe the benefits and drawbacks of the choice in personal terms.

3. Decide whether you'll be comfortable with the changes in status and earnings that scaling back is likely to incur. Ask yourself if it represents a truly viable option for you at this point in your career. Consider the trade-offs carefully.

■ **Seeking advice** *about scaling back needn't be embarrassing. Simply ask a friendly colleague.*

Branching out

Investigating alternative career options both in and out of your organization is called branching out. For many workers, branching out represents the safest career move.

Often individuals who are experiencing the first pangs of career restlessness choose to branch out simply to gain a breath of fresh air. For anyone who has hit a point of career stagnation, branching out is the first choice to make. The activities of branching out will not only yield new information, but also acquaint you with an exhilarating feeling of progress.

Think of branching out as detective work. At first, you have only a circumstance to deal with – your career restlessness, which is kind of like the crime situation that a clueless detective is faced with solving. Through a process of careful investigation, clues fall into place. When you assemble enough of them, you may be able to clarify a vision of the career alternatives that are realistic for you, whether they are within your organization or not. You may even be able to design a strategy of career next-steps, which can free you from the trap of focusing only on your discontent.

■ **Don't be afraid** *if you are thinking of branching out. That is often a good career option.*

Branching out is a healthy choice for everyone, regardless of your level of career satisfaction and success.

There's an old tongue-in-cheek saying that you can never be too rich or too thin. Whether or not you agree, it's a sure thing that you can never know enough about what else is out there.

If you're on the fence about investigating alternative career options both in and out of your organization:

1. Conduct a variety of information-gathering interviews. Talk to professionals in and outside of your field about what they do.

2. Identify other industries and functional areas to which you could transfer your skills. Research them carefully.

3. Read newspapers, trade journals, newsletters, and other periodicals that cover your industry and others. Become familiar with workplace environments beyond your own.

Moving on

Ending your employment with a particular organization and directing your career to another work situation is called moving on. Sometimes (although rarely), there is simply no viable career alternative but to make a clean break and a fresh start. If that's your case, then moving on is the option you need to choose.

If you conclude, after long and careful evaluation, that your organization does not provide what you need from your relationship with work – and is not likely to provide it in the future – you may elect to end your employment there. Of course, you understand that leaving an organization is a very momentous act, right up there in importance with graduating from school and landing your first real job. It is not something to be done lightly.

Moving on is the career move you make only when no others are feasible.

If you're on the fence about ending your employment with a particular organization and directing your career to another work situation:

1. Never make a decision to leave your organization right after a negative experience. Allow some time to pass to see if your perspective changes.

2. Identify ways to use your experience with the organization you're leaving to advantage during your career move. Decide how you will take advantage of your association there as you move ahead in your career.

A simple summary

✓ Career vitality requires change and movement. If you're experiencing restlessness or dissatisfaction in your career, you need to move forward.

✓ A substantial investment of time in an organization may make movement seem unlikely or impossible. Options for change and movement are available.

✓ A key to managing your career effectively is to initiate change before change comes to you.

✓ Each of the six career moves has distinct career benefits. Each may represent a good strategy at different points in your career.

✓ There are six basic career moves you can make: sliding across, firming up, climbing high, scaling back, branching out, or moving on. Each begins in relation to the organization you're currently employed by.

Chapter 11

Plotting a Major Career Change

IF YOU ARE CONSIDERING ALTERNATIVE career pathways at any stage of your career, then this chapter is for you.

In this chapter...

✓ Where to?   ✓ A time-tested career theory

✓ Realistic: getting down to brass tacks

✓ Investigative: thinking things through

✓ Artistic: getting it out there

✓ Social: lending a helping hand

✓ Enterprising: taking the lead

✓ Conventional: keeping things right

✓ Matching interests with career choice

✓ More about Holland's theory

EVEN GLAMOROUS CAREERS ARE THE PRODUCTS OF YEARS OF DEDICATION AND HARD WORK

Where to?

IF YOU'RE THINKING OF *pursuing a major change in your career, you need a sense of direction. Whether you're entering the workforce for the first time, at midcareer and dreaming of doing something different, or in late career and looking for alternatives to the work you've done up to now, you'll want to focus on the most viable career possibilities, and this chapter will help you create your short list of options.*

■ **If you're** *falling asleep at work, it's time that you started thinking of a career change.*

■ **If you want** *to be an artist, your dream can come true but do some research before you jump in.*

The four basic interest categories outlined in Chapter 5 – objects, information, concepts, and people – are useful for identifying the fundamental directions of your interests, and it's essential to take stock of your interests, skills, values, and style qualities before you can identify career options that will be realistic and satisfying. If you haven't completed the self-assessment in Part Two, do so now. With your results in hand, you'll be prepared to relate these interests with potential career paths.

INTERNET

www.jobweb.org

The web site of the National Association of Colleges and Employers (NACE) features employment information and an e-zine on job choices. Students transitioning into the workforce may find this site especially useful.

In this chapter you'll learn about a more detailed system of classifying interests, which taps directly into specific occupational roles. Some of them may present you with fascinating career options for more thorough investigation.

■ **If you want** *to reach the top, start planning now!*

A time-tested career theory

IN WORKING with clients who need a sense of direction, many career counselors use a system of interest categories designed by prominent career theorist John Holland. The Holland system forms the foundation of a sound career theory that has helped millions of individuals think more clearly about their careers and explore occupational options that tie into their interests.

■ **Don't waste time** – *try John Holland's career theory!*

Holland's career theory is fairly straightforward. It presents five main ideas:

1. Individuals can be broadly described using six basic categories of interests and attitudes that capture the spirit of the individuals they profile: Realistic, Investigative, Artistic, Social, Enterprising, and Conventional.

2. Individuals are seldom represented by one category alone. Most people's interests fall into two or more. The categories that best represent an individual's interests are the result of many influences, including family, upbringing, cultural environment, educational opportunities, early work experiences and a host of other factors.

3. Careers, and the series of occupations that form them, can be described using the same six basic categories.

4. Particular work environments can also be described using six basic categories.

5. Individuals who work in occupations and environments that show a profile of interests similar to their own are more likely to feel comfortable with their work and satisfied with their careers.

■ **It's easy** *to recognize those who are satisfied with their work. Your aim is to be this happy too!*

Holland's theory is useful for many reasons. First, each category has a "personality" all its own. Second, the theory allows individuals to relate to characteristics from each of the categories, not just one.

The Holland system encourages individuals to think of themselves (and their careers) generally in terms of two or three main categories of interest.

Let's take a look at each of the six Holland categories to see where your interests fall. The following table shows which interest directions comprise each Holland category.

	Interest Directions			
Holland Category	Objects	Information	Concepts	People
Realistic	X			
Investigative		X	X	
Artistic			X	X
Social				X
Enterprising		X		X
Conventional		X		

As you read through the detailed descriptions of the categories in the following sections, you'll probably identify with some elements of each one, which is just fine because individuals are complex beings and often embody contradictory traits. However, it's likely that one, two, or possibly three categories will capture more of you than the others and will just feel "right" to you. Make a note of those you most identify with.

INTERNET

www.self-directed-search.com

Access this site for a detailed explanation of the Holland career system and the Self-Directed Search. Click on "What is the SDS?"; "Find a Career Counselor"; and, if you like, "Take the Test."

■ **Take some time** *to think about your interests and how they relate to the career you would like to pursue.*

Realistic: getting down to brass tacks

Are you the kind of person who:

- Wants to get where you're going quickly?
- Likes to see the results of your work?
- Prefers immediate gratification?
- Enjoys making things work?
- Prefers simplicity to complexity?
- Takes a hands-on approach to work?

If so, you may identify with the Realistic type.

■ **If you are** *the Realistic type yet don't feel this content in the office, get out of those office clothes and work outdoors!*

The Realistic type describes people who are oriented toward tangible objects and physical activities. Realistic types like working with machines and tools, and typically don't mind working alone. They are often drawn to the outdoors. Typically, Realistic types are "doers" who enjoy taking decisive action, without a lot of pondering or intellectualizing. They prefer to take a concrete approach to problem solving rather than an abstract, theoretical approach.

The Realistic type corresponds to the basic interest category of Objects, since it is oriented toward the world of tangible things.

12 likes and dislikes of Realistic individuals

Likes

- Mechanical and athletic activities
- Working outdoors
- Building things with tools
- Operating machines
- Working with plants and animals
- Spending leisure time on boats, trailers, cycles, and so on

Dislikes

- Mingling socially
- Expressing themselves with words
- Educational activities
- Working with people
- Abstract ideas
- Cultural activities

■ **Business meetings** *can be a bit intimidating for the Realistic type.*

The Realistic personality

■ **Realistic types** *are happy doing business both indoors and outdoors.*

Often, people who identify with the Realistic type are practical, robust individuals who favor traditional values like honesty and loyalty. They're solid, steady individuals who typically steer clear of unconventional politics. Realistic types are usually not drawn to the arts, but may be interested in science or mechanical activities. They'd probably rather go bowling than visit a museum. They like to dress very casually and communicate with simple and direct language.

At work, Realistic types prefer a good deal of structure, clearly specified goals, and a pronounced line of authority. They tend to be practical and task-oriented and usually enjoy work that enables them to produce tangible results or allows them to operate equipment.

12 typical career paths for Realistic individuals

- Architect
- Athlete
- Broadcast technician
- Carpenter
- Construction worker
- Electrician
- Engineer
- Medical technician
- Pilot
- Police officer
- Tape librarian
- Veterinarian

■ **Working as a pilot** *could be the ideal job for the Realistic type.*

Investigative: thinking things through

Are you the kind of person who:

- Wants to know how something works?
- Likes to analyze situations and things?
- Is thrilled by new discoveries?
- Places importance on research?
- Needs to know the whys and wherefores of any situation?
- Prefers an intellectual approach to work?

If so, you may identify with the Investigative type.

If you're interested *in analyzing facts and figures, you could be the Investigative type.*

The Investigative type describes people who are oriented toward intellectual, and particularly analytical, activities. Investigative types are drawn to the world of the abstract, especially as it relates to mathematics and science. As the name implies, Investigative types value the process and results of investigation. They enjoy observation and theory, prefer thought to action, and are energized by the challenge of solving problems with innovative, creative theoretical thinking.

The Investigative type corresponds to the basic interest categories of Information and Concepts, since it is oriented toward the worlds of facts, figures and ideas.

If you enjoy *analytical and intellectual pursuits you may be the Investigative type.*

12 likes and dislikes of Investigative individuals

Likes

- Abstract problems and challenges
- Scientific inquiry
- Working independently
- Complete absorption in projects or tasks
- Thinking problems through
- Unstructured work situations

Dislikes

- Repetitive activities
- Rules and regulations
- Formal socializing and small talk
- Conventional viewpoints
- Assertive behavior
- Tasks that are unambiguous and predictable

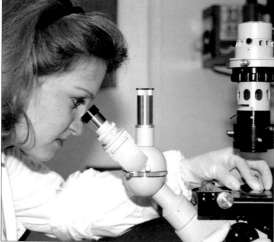

■ **If your likes are** *of an Investigative nature, a career in science could be right for you.*

■ **If you have the capability** *to be this absorbed in your work, you may do well within the scientific and scholarly professions.*

The Investigative personality

People who identify with the Investigative type are often introspective, reserved, and intellectually oriented. They're curious and ingenious individuals who value original thinking and innovative attitudes. They love to analyze both information and concepts, and they can often lose themselves in thought. Investigative types are typically inclined toward mathematics. They tend to be observant, thoughtful individuals who take pains to explain their ideas with a great deal of care and complexity.

Investigative types are attracted to work that is analytical and oriented toward research and theory. They typically enjoy work that is complex, scholarly, or scientific and that provides them with plenty of opportunities to solve problems.

12 typical career paths for Investigative individuals

- Biologist
- Chemist
- College professor
- Information system programmer
- Inventor
- Market research analyst
- Physician
- Psychologist
- Research and development manager
- Scientist
- Statistician
- Systems analyst

■ **If you want to** *climb your way to the top, develop a career that suits your character.*

■ **If you have** *an Investigative personality, why not consider a career in market research?*

Artistic: getting it out there

Are you the kind of person who:

- Likes to use your imagination?
- Trusts your intuition?
- Has a degree of artistic talent?
- Enjoys daydreaming?
- Is comfortable being expressive?
- Looks for creative ways to get things done?

If so, you may identify with the Artistic type.

The Artistic type describes people who are oriented toward creativity and who value human expression. Artistic types are drawn to the world of ideas and abstractions, but with a strong emotional connection. They rely on their own self-expression to connect with other individuals, and they value the expression of emotion by others. Artistic types frequently enjoy being or working alone. They can be deeply dedicated to one or more method of expression, such as writing, painting, acting, singing, or dancing. But the Artistic type extends well beyond the performing arts. It describes many creative individuals who have a need to be self-expressive and original.

The Artistic type corresponds to the basic interest categories of Concepts and People, since it is oriented toward ideas and expression, as well as interaction and exchange with others.

12 likes and dislikes of Artistic individuals

Likes

- Art, drama, music, performing arts
- Conceptual thinking
- Unstructured work situations
- Working alone or in small groups
- Appreciating esthetic qualities
- Taking risks to try new things

- **If you have an Artistic personality,** *risk-taking may feel more comfortable for you than for many other people.*

Dislikes

- Rules and regulations
- Conventional dress
- Predictable solutions to problems
- Physical work not connected to an expressive medium
- Being assertive about their own abilities
- Conformist attitudes

The Artistic personality

Typically, Artistic types are complex, free-spirited individuals who value creativity and individuality. They are characteristically intuitive, idealistic, and emotional, and they often are extremely sensitive to criticism. They can be impulsive and highly nonconformist, but not all Artistic types are rebels. Self-expression is the strongest trait of the Artistic type and is the driving force in virtually all individuals who fall into this classification. Artistic types value culture and the arts but include among their ranks many types of people with a need for individualistic expression.

Artistic types gravitate toward work environments that are flexible, unstructured, creative, and expressive. They typically enjoy work that enables them to compose or design or to articulate their own impressions and perspectives. They usually don't mind functioning independently and often feel different or special in their approach to work.

12 typical career paths of Artistic individuals

- Actor
- Advertising executive
- Announcer
- Composer
- Corporate trainer
- Editor
- Fashion designer
- Graphic artist
- Interior decorator
- Musician
- Public relations director
- Reporter

If you strive *for success but still want to be able to express your creative abilities, why not consider a career in advertising?*

Social: lending a helping hand

Are you the kind of person who:

■ Likes to talk with people about their feelings?
■ Prefers harmony to contention?
■ Enjoys teaching or advising others?
■ Tends to think about others' needs?
■ Likes making people feel comfortable?
■ Feels gratified by helping out?

If so, you may identify with the Social type.

The Social type describes individuals who enjoy assisting other people, often in a teaching or developmental capacity. Social types are "people" persons in the sense that they often place others' interests before their own. They're typically warm, friendly individuals who communicate and interact well with others. Because they're concerned with emotions, Social types can achieve a deep level of intimacy with other individuals. They derive gratification from touching other people's lives in an assertive, positive way.

The Social type corresponds to the basic interest category of People, since it is oriented toward supportive interaction with other individuals.

■ **If you enjoy** *teaching new skills to others in the office, consider using this talent as a professional teacher.*

12 likes and dislikes of Social individuals

Likes

- Working in groups
- Informing, training, and developing others
- Using verbal and interpersonal skills
- Putting people at ease
- Having the attention of others
- Academic environments

Dislikes

- Physical exertion and manual labor
- Highly structured work situations
- Working alone
- Intellectual, rather than emotional, conversation
- Working with tools or equipment
- Scientific or overly methodical approaches to problem solving

- **If you love talking**, *make the most of your communication skills. They could just get you the job of your dreams.*

- **If you're a Social individual**, *working all day at a computer may not be for you.*

The Social personality

Social types are characteristically congenial, gregarious, and generous. They are caring individuals who value harmony and cooperation with other people. Social types are naturally concerned with the welfare of others and go out of their way to be responsible and helpful. They are humanistic and idealistic in their orientation toward life. In general, social types experience a sense of meaning when they enable other individuals – by working through problems, by teaching or training, or by assisting with physical needs, such as home care.

At work, Social types value an environment that is more casual than formal, one in which people feel relaxed and comfortable. They usually welcome a certain amount of structure, but not to a confining degree. Social types place great importance on recognition for their contributions. They value authenticity in people and have a natural aversion to infighting and disagreement.

12 typical career paths for Social individuals

- Caterer
- Child care provider
- Flight attendant
- Guidance counselor
- Human resources manager
- Marriage counselor
- Minister
- Nurse
- School administrator
- Social worker
- Speech pathologist
- Teacher

Enterprising: taking the lead

Are you the kind of person who:

- Feels comfortable being in charge?
- Likes to influence or persuade others?
- Has a lot of energy and drive?
- Enjoys symbols of status and prestige?
- Likes to make deals?
- Feels comfortable in the spotlight?

If so, you may identify with the Enterprising type.

■ If everyone *around the table is listening to you, then perhaps you may be a born leader.*

The Enterprising type describes people who are natural leaders. They are typically confident, assertive individuals who are drawn toward the public eye and roles of influence. Enterprising types are driven by challenges and a need to conquer them. They often succeed in entrepreneurial ventures. Enterprising types tend to be highly communicative individuals who use their verbal skills to persuade and motivate others. They thrive in the business environment and value what the world recognizes as the trappings of success.

The Enterprising type corresponds to the basic interest categories of People and Information, since it is oriented toward persuasive interaction with other individuals and toward factual data.

12 likes and dislikes of Enterprising individuals

Likes

- ■ Making things happen
- ■ Attaining organizational goals
- ■ Being at the center of attention
- ■ Speaking or presenting in public
- ■ Motivating others
- ■ Material goods that signify status and prestige

■ If you are *the Enterprising type, you will probably enjoy giving presentations or speaking in public.*

Dislikes

- Concentrated intellectual work
- Scientific or systematic thinking and activity
- Postponing conclusions
- Aversion to risk
- Routine
- Taking direction

The Enterprising personality

Enterprising types are typically assertive, self-confident, sociable individuals with high standards for achievement and success. They are driven by a need to lead – to influence and motivate other people. Enterprising types are often risk takers, although they take calculated risks at least as often as reckless ones. They are characteristically ambitious individuals who gravitate toward power and status. Enterprising types typically set their sights high and find a way to get what they want and need.

At work, Enterprising types flourish in a fast-paced, high-energy environment that is oriented toward accomplishment and achievement. They tend to be on the fast track and often demonstrate impatience when progress doesn't happen as rapidly as they'd like. Enterprising types are often attracted to corporate environments, which they view as arenas for competition and success. However, they are hard-driving individuals in almost any environment.

12 typical careers paths for Enterprising individuals

- Advertising account executive
- Elected public official
- Financial planner
- Fund raiser
- Insurance agent
- Marketing executive
- Operations manager
- Real estate agent
- Sales representative
- Small business owner
- Stockbroker
- University business manager

- **For all you** *Enterprising types, remember that patience is a virtue!*

Conventional: keeping things right

Are you the kind of person who:

- Prefers to be highly organized?
- Values being reliable and steady?
- Keeps a meticulous checkbook?
- Feels comfortable with numbers and statistics?
- Likes things to run efficiently?
- Prefers practical to idealistic solutions?

If so, then you may identify with the Conventional type.

The Conventional type describes individuals who feel comfortable following well-defined rules, guidelines, and traditions, and who enjoy work that involves organization and routine. Conventional types tend to be very orderly. They place a high value on neatness and efficiency, and are generally oriented toward detail and precision. Conventional types tend to have excellent ability with numbers and clerical tasks, both of which require a high level of structure and orderliness. They usually don't mind working alone and frequently prefer to be self-reliant in their approach to problem solving.

The Conventional type corresponds to the basic interest category of Information, since it is oriented toward the world of facts and figures.

■ **Conventional types** *who are highly organized and meticulous can be an asset to any company.*

12 likes and dislikes of Conventional individuals

Likes

- Systematic verbal and numerical work
- Paying attention to details
- Controlling and planning finances
- Highly structured environments and situations
- Well-defined tasks
- Conservative, traditional lifestyle

Dislikes

- Ambiguous situations
- Abstract, rather than concrete, thinking
- Leading other people
- Untested solutions to problems
- Involvement with emotional conflict
- Nonconformist behavior

■ **If you are a** *Conventional individual, you probably have a knack for keeping processes organized.*

■ **Explaining exactly** *what is required from the Conventional type helps everyone achieve better results.*

The Conventional personality

Individuals who identify with the Conventional type are typically solid, dependable, and disciplined people who place a high importance on practicality. They tend to be highly oriented to details and take pride in keeping track of them. Conventional types are very orderly and efficient, and appear to the world as possessing a great deal of calm and inner strength. They are typically conscientious, persistent, and reliable. Conventional types are not attracted to extreme forms of thought or behavior, and they usually prefer to stick with a trusty middle-of-the-road approach to living.

At work, Conventional types are comfortable responding to clearly defined guidelines, boundaries, and policies. They are characteristically systematic, and they usually enjoy work that enables them to organize data or keep records and schedules. They place high importance on accuracy and value a reputation for steadiness.

12 typical career paths for Conventional individuals

- Accountant
- Auditor
- Bookkeeper
- Collection investigator
- Credit manager
- Data entry clerk
- Dental assistant
- Office administrator
- Paralegal
- Payroll officer
- Secretary
- Securities trader

■ **Having a Conventional type** *as a bookkeeper is a good way to feel certain that accounts will always balance.*

Matching interests with career choice

As you read through the descriptions, which of the six types seemed to capture more of your traits than the others? It's a good bet that you identified strongly with two or even three types. If you did, consider yourself lucky – because jobs seldom call for traits that fall into only one thematic category.

The overwhelming number of jobs, as the Holland system demonstrates, tap into characteristics of two or more of the six types. Once you have a sense of which types describe you best, you'll want to look at the occupations that correspond to your personal combination of types and basic interest categories.

The Holland system is actually depicted as the six sides of a hexagon. The hexagon is meant to show that there are meaningful relationships between the sides that are contiguous – the categories that are adjacent to one another.

For example, the combination of the Artistic and Social themes has elements in common – namely, interests that extend toward people and the act of expression. This combination of basic interest categories presents a great number of occupational possibilities.

■ **The Realistic** *type is definitely not a people person.*

On the other hand, interest categories that lie in opposite positions on the hexagon refer to conditions and characteristics that are not typically compatible. The Realistic type, for instance, describes people who like to work alone in the world of hands-on activity. Directly opposite on the hexagon is the Social type, which describes people who thrive on interpersonal exchange and an emotional focus on life. This combination of interest categories presents a very limited number of occupational possibilities.

■ **If you identify** *with more than one particular type, you're probably the ideal candidate for a variety of jobs.*

More about Holland's theory

THERE ARE SEVERAL WAYS *you can access Holland's theory and its application to occupational pathways. As its name implies, you can navigate through the Self-Directed Search on your own or with a career counselor as a guide. It's available in a printed form (consult a career counselor) and online (at www.self-directed-search.com). In addition, you can take the more intricate Strong Interest Inventory (SII), which also ties into Holland's system of six main interest categories. Be aware that the SII must be administered and interpreted by a qualified career professional. Both instruments forge connections to clear and distinct career possibilities based on your patterns of interest.*

■ **If your interests tend** *toward unusual themes, you may have a smaller pool of potentially satisfying jobs.*

Using Holland to find good job-person matches

Once you know which of Holland's categories best describe your interests, the following four reference guides will help you explore matching career possibilities:

1. *The Dictionary of Holland Occupational Codes* (Psychological Assessment Resources) lists jobs by combinations of the Realistic, Investigative, Artistic, Social, Enterprising, and Conventional categories (and assigns each one a numeric code, similar to the familiar Dewey Decimal System used in libraries).

2. *The O*NET Dictionary of Occupational Titles* (JIST Works) is arranged according to a newly designed numeric classification system, the Occupational Information Network. The O*NET provides descriptions of more than 1,200 jobs, which cover most of the labor market.

3. *The Complete Guide for Occupational Exploration* (GOE) (JIST Works) classifies jobs into 12 different interest areas that easily relate to the Realistic, Investigative, Artistic, Social, Enterprising, and Conventional categories, and references more than 12,000 job titles.

4. *The Occupational Outlook Handbook* (OOH), published bi-annually by the U.S. Department of Labor, provides more detailed descriptions of jobs and job categories. Here you'll find information on representative work settings; typical work conditions; required education, training, and other qualifications; typical earnings; and the outlook for employment. The OOH is also very helpful in fostering an understanding of the differences among related but distinct occupational roles, such as Book Editor, Features Editor, Copy Editor, and Managing Editor; or Clinical Psychologist, Counseling Psychologist, Developmental Psychologist, and Child Psychologist.

INTERNET

www.bls.gov

The U.S. Department of Labor's Bureau of Labor Statistics makes its valuable Occupational Outlook Handbook (OOH) available online here.

■ **No-one wants** *to be this bored. Consult* The Occupational Outlook Handbook *to find out more about your dream job.*

Each of these is a standard reference work that employs a system of interest categories and relates it to real-world occupational pathways.

*You can cross-reference The Dictionary of Holland Occupational Codes with the listings and descriptions in the O*NET Dictionary of Occupational Titles if you wish. The GOE and the OOH can be referenced in tandem or independently.*

When you've identified some occupational possibilities, you're ready to explore each of them further. Library research – delving into books, periodicals, and software – is critical, but you'll need information that goes beyond that. You'll need human perspective. So, once you've completed a hefty amount of library and online research, conduct interviews with people who are in, or close to, the occupational roles you're considering. The information and insights you gather there will go a long way in helping you to make smart career choices and decisions.

A simple summary

✔ If you're thinking of pursuing a major change in your career, you need a sense of direction.

✔ John Holland's time-tested career theory outlines a system of classifying interests – and corresponding workplace profiles – into to six categories: Realistic, Investigative, Artistic, Social, Enterprising, and Conventional. Individuals, and jobs, typically relate to two or more categories.

✔ Individuals who work in occupations and environments that are compatible with their own profiles of interests are more likely to feel comfortable with their work and satisfied with their careers.

✔ You can explore career and occupational options using references available in print and online. Personal interviews will round out your research with an invaluable human perspective.

Chapter 12

Working on Your Own

NOWADAYS IT SEEMS to be everybody's career dream to be an entrepreneur. Here, you'll find out why self-employment is becoming attractive to more people and what it takes to succeed.

In this chapter...

✓ The entrepreneurial trend

✓ Do you have what it takes?

✓ Five keys to entrepreneurial success

✓ Six ways to work on your own

✓ Developing and launching a new business

✓ Acquiring an existing business ✓ Franchising

✓ Consulting ✓ Independent contracting

✓ Temping ✓ Researching early and thoroughly

YOU CAN TURN ALMOST ANY HOBBY OR INTEREST INTO A PROFITABLE BUSINESS THAT'S RIGHT FOR YOU

The entrepreneurial trend

IF YOU'RE LIKE MOST other people, you've thought at one time or another about working on your own. During these earliest years of the 21st century, more and more people are choosing to go the entrepreneurial route.

There are many reasons for this rising trend in entrepreneurship, including several key cultural and economic trends:

- The reshaping of the workforce and the "new" employment contract between employers and employees (see Chapter 1)
- The increasing emphasis on the balance one's work life and personal life
- Technology that enables telecommuting and promotes global communications
- The panoramic range of business opportunities presented by the Internet
- Longer life expectancy and its impact on family living and responsibilities
- The demeanor and disposition of post-Baby Boom generations toward large organizations

While each of these has been cited often as partly responsible for the upward trend in entrepreneurship, none is by itself a good enough reason to elect to reconfigure your career into one where you're working on your own. There are many important points to consider before committing to a career option as momentous as going solo, regardless of the mode of self-employment you're considering.

■ **Many are attracted** *to entrepeneurism because of the success lure of money.*

INTERNET

www.workingtoday.org
www.workingsolo.com

Working Today is a national nonprofit membership organization that promotes the interests of people who work independently.

Visit Working Solo for a trove of information and resources "for the self-employed, home-based business owners, e-lancers, telecommuters, consultants and other independent professionals."

■ **Thanks to computers** *and the advancement of technology we can communicate with each other no matter where we are in the world.*

Do you have what it takes?

THERE ARE TWO OVERARCHING *considerations about working on your own.*

First, if you have "the right stuff," entrepreneurship is a good career option for you. What's the right stuff? It's a recipe that varies from person to person, but it usually calls for a blend of suitable personality attributes, helpful external resources, and favorable circumstances.

Second, if you decide to go the entrepreneurial route, you must look before you leap. Look to the left, to the right, and then up and down. It may seem like overkill, but being thorough is crucial to making the right career move.

Posing difficult questions for yourself

As you dream your dream and consider turning it into reality, you should ask yourself the following two questions and answer them honestly:

1. Can I shift gears without losing ground on my long-term career path?

2. Do I have the qualities to be as thorough as I need to be – both before and after I go out on my own?

■ **Make sure** *your plan has been finely tuned, for example, before starting your own digital music business.*

Assessing your entrepreneurship quotient

The first thing you need to do is evaluate your ability to succeed as an entrepreneur. This is not something you can do in an hour, or even a day. You need to carefully consider your ability to accomplish each of the following phases of an entrepreneurial endeavor:

1. Assessment (evaluating whether or not you're self-directed)

2. Planning (researching possible business pathways and options)

3. Financing (calculating the monetary resources needed to launch and sustain your business)

4. Startup (establishing yourself in the marketplace)

5. Marketing (promoting your product or service to the right customers)

6. Follow-through (delivering on the promises and commitments you set)

7. Maintenance (keeping your endeavor successful)

8. Growth (taking your business to new levels of success as your life and career evolve)

■ **Always think ahead**
and plan carefully to achieve success as an entrepreneur.

Tip: If you can't be painstaking with this exercise, or if you're starting to lose interest, consider developing other career options.

While it's natural that some of these phases will be more appealing and suitable to your personality than others, you will need to apply your resources, vision, and talents to all of them before (and after) committing to the career of the solo worker. If you can't imagine applying yourself to each phase with dedication and resolve, think about pursuing career options that may offer more structure and support.

■ **Marketing is vital**
if you want your business to be a success – don't hesitate, get on that phone!

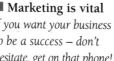

Five keys to entrepreneurial success

SINCE YOU'RE STILL READING, *it means you're still tantalized by the idea of working on your own. Okay, then start thinking of yourself as an entrepreneur, and read on. If you have always thought of entrepreneurs only as impossibly clever, driven people who'll stop at nothing to succeed in business, think again. It isn't quite as simple as that.*

There are many qualities that go into making an entrepreneur successful, but five in particular are essential:

1. Visionary thinking – You'll need to think big, long-term, and positively.

2. Ability to deliver no matter what – You must be able to come through for your customers. If you don't, they'll give their business to someone who can.

3. Competitive instinct – You'll probably be going up against others who can provide similar products or services. You'll need to distinguish yours from theirs – memorably.

4. Perseverance – Chances are that your business venture will not be an overnight success. You will need to weather long periods of uncertainty and ambiguity.

5. Thoroughness – The details of running your own operation are endless. If continually attending to the small things is not your strong suit, you're at a disadvantage.

■ **Persistently pestering** *future customers will not make your business successful. Instead follow our five useful tips.*

■ **Don't give up if** *your business isn't everything that you expected – it pays to persevere.*

Six ways to work on your own

THERE IS MORE THAN ONE WAY *to be an entrepreneur. Out of the basic six, you're sure to find at least one that suits your needs and personality.*

The basic six are:

1. Developing and launching a new business

2. Acquiring an existing business

3. Operating a franchise

4. Working as a consultant

5. Working freelance (independent contracting)

6. Working as a temp

Like all work situations, each of these options has advantages and disadvantages that you should consider. The following six sections describe each entrepreneurial option.

■ **If thought out** *properly, entrepreneurism doesn't need to be a gamble.*

■ **If you think** *that others could benefit from your knowledge and experience, consultancy could be the job for you.*

Developing and launching a new business

ALTHOUGH MORE PEOPLE ARE *choosing the entrepreneurial route now than ever before, the success-to-failure ratio has not improved as the number of new entrepreneurs has soared. In fact, four out of every five new businesses fail within their first five years of operation. Those are daunting odds. To make sure your venture falls within the healthy part of the equation, follow the big-picture guidelines presented in this section.*

Prepare a business plan

This is the backbone of any enterprise. Without it, you will not succeed. A business plan is the detailed map of your venture, and it's the closest you will come to ensuring vitality. Joseph Anthony, author of *Working for Yourself*, outlines these essential components of any business plan:

1. Concept – A summary of your business idea, your "mission statement," along with a thumbnail description of where your business fits in the marketplace and why it will succeed.

2. Detail – A thorough description of your business, with an in-depth explanation of the product or service you plan to bring to market and its benefits to those who will buy and/or use it.

3. Market profile – A complete description of your customers, your competitors, the need for your product or service, and the health and vitality of the marketplace. This is not guesswork. It must be based on careful, reliable research.

4. Strategy – Your detailed plan for bringing your product or service to market. This includes what you will name your business, how you will protect it, what pricing structure you will establish, and your estimated sales projections.

5. Operation/Production – A thorough discussion of the process of bringing your product or service to market, including office space, production schedules, inventories, supplies, suppliers, licenses, insurance, and meeting any existing business regulations.

■ **There is no excuse** *for not preparing a business plan. If you don't do it your business will fail.*

6 Structure and personnel – How your enterprise will be organized (sole proprietorship, partnership, limited-liability corporation, or other status) and who, besides yourself, will be involved.

7 Financial plan – A detailed picture of your finances: how much money you have, how much you'll need, where you'll secure it, projected revenues, and a timeline for anticipated profits.

Secure adequate capital

The strongest business idea will not get off the ground without sufficient funding. What's more, most businesses wind up requiring a far greater startup investment than their entrepreneurial owners typically forecast. The bottom-line questions you need to answer about startup capital are:

- How much money is required up front?
- How much money needs to be borrowed?
- How will the money be paid back?
- How will you know your business is profitable?

■ **Discussing the future** *of your business with someone else will help cement your plans.*

Examine your motivations carefully

It is essential for you to be honest with yourself about why you're thinking along entrepreneurial lines. Maybe you've been downsized, or maybe you have a hunch you'll never be able to find the "right" employer to work for. Maybe you think you're just ready to try something new and different in your career. Starting a business is not for everyone, and it may not be for you. Only you can know; be sure that you take the time to find out.

■ **No matter** *how fantastic your business idea is, you'll always need money to back it up.*

Project yourself into the lifestyle of the startup-business owner

Take a good hard look at the consequences of the necessary commitment of the time, energy, and resources that will be required of you as an entrepreneur. Don't think that health considerations aren't relevant: You need stamina, as well as mental and emotional resilience. Don't think that your family and friends will automatically adjust their relationships to fit your new startup-business lifestyle. Nearly all of your relationships will change – some for the better, some for the worse. Are you flexible enough to adjust to those changes?

Acquiring an existing business

IF YOU DON'T LIKE YOUR ODDS for success in starting your own business but you're still attracted to the lifestyle of the business entrepreneur, you might consider buying an existing business. In contrast to the dismal failure rate of startups, about 50 percent of all existing businesses that are sold to new owners survive for an additional five years or more. Although still pretty far from a guarantee for success, it's significantly less risky than a startup.

Many of the rules for operating your own business still apply if you're looking to buy one. Don't make the mistake of believing that the original owners have done all the thinking for you.

If you identify an existing business you think you'd like to acquire, then the real work begins. The planning process requires you to be at least as thorough as if you were starting your own enterprise, with a few added twists.

First, be sure you have the skills necessary to acquire and operate an existing business. Size up your expertise in the areas of finance, marketing, sales, and operations. Then, do your detective work: learn about the business up one side and down the other.

You can't have too much information about an existing business, its history, or its owners.

Finally, research the market thoroughly before you commit to a purchase. Find out exactly why the owners are selling and whether or not their decision is a response to changing market conditions.

■ **It's vital** *that you research your chosen company thoroughly before you even think of acquiring it.*

Franchising

IF YOU KNOW YOU'D LIKE *to work for yourself but you don't want the headaches of starting or acquiring a business, the franchising option might be right for you.*

However, bear in mind that franchising may not provide the complete independence you're seeking, because you won't be able to do everything your own way.

Operating a branch of an established enterprise within a framework of guidelines established by the owner or owners is called franchising a business. Basically, franchising involves running one outlet in a chain according to a shared code of operating principles.

Is franchising worth it?

There's a wealth of opportunities in the world of franchising, ranging from tax-preparation businesses to monolithic fast-food chains. For an initial investment in any of them, you'll need anywhere from $5,000 to more than $1 million, depending on the size of the business, its history, the number of franchises it offers, and the location of the one you're considering. Thereafter, you'll have to fork over 5 to 10 percent of your business revenues in rolling royalty payments to the franchiser. On top of that, you'll need to think about cooperative advertising costs that can eat up another 3 or 4 percent of revenues.

If those things don't turn you off, think hard about the necessary commitment of time. Many franchisees put in 12 to 18 hours a day, often for six-day or even seven-day work weeks, just to keep their business close to the expected success level. It's definitely not a road to quick riches.

■ **Think hard:** *Are you prepared to work 18 hours a day?*

INTERNET

www.franchise1.com

This site promotes itself as "the #1 franchise destination on the Internet." You'll find a directory of franchise opportunities, profiles of featured franchises, and a list of worldwide franchise associations.

INTERNET

www.franinfo.com

"A world of information about franchising," this site provides links that pertain to buying a business and franchising your business.

Going to the source

As with any career venture, franchising calls for you to seek the advice and guidance of people who have experience in the area you wish to pursue. Talk to franchisees. Ask them about their work. Ask them if it's giving them what they need in their careers. Tell them you're thinking of operating a franchise of your own, and ask them what they would do if they were in your shoes. Listen carefully to their career stories, and let their experiences inform your decision.

■ **Be aware** – *the franchising option leaves very little time for rest.*

Trivia...

Believe it or not, most franchisees take home less than $35,000 in annual income. There are titans who exceed that amount by far. There are also "newbies" who fall far short of it.

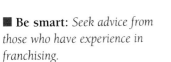

■ **Be smart:** *Seek advice from those who have experience in franchising.*

Consulting

HERE'S THE CAREER OPTION EVERYONE
*with experience fantasizes about: being paid to give advice
and offer guidance. That's what* consultants *are about,
and it's the career avenue of choice for many professionals
who opt to work on their own.*

Why are consultants hired?

Consultants are typically hired to provide an expertise that's missing from a particular business environment. Some consultants assume responsibility for implementing the recommendations they develop. Others are hired to investigate a business situation, formulate a vision for change and improvement, make a formal presentation of their conclusions that may include advice or counsel, and then leave the implementation to the organization without any further obligation or responsibility.

*Consultants are hired to provide the objective "outsider" perspective
that many organizations need – the breath of fresh air that can
revitalize a stagnant enterprise.*

Another reason organizations hire consultants is inadequate staffing. The organization may not have employees with the necessary skills or depth of knowledge required to complete a project as quickly or as well as management envisions.

How do consultants work?

Working as a consultant can take many forms. Some major corporations, like Andersen, McKinsey & Co., and Deloitte & Touche, provide a full range of consulting services to organizations around the world. The consultants they employ tend to be specialists with varying degrees of firsthand experience in their area of specialty. These professionals travel a great deal in order to serve the clients of their firm. Often, their schedules consist of 50 percent travel or more. Other consulting firms operate on a much smaller scale. There are many partnerships that serve clients in specialized areas of expertise and limit their operations to a defined geographic area.

Typically, they function in the same manner that "boutique" agencies do, providing personalized, go-the-extra-mile service to the clients that hire them.

Then, there are the independent consultants, who are typically specialists with significant experience and a proven track record in a specific area. Some offer their services exclusively as solo contractors, while others hook up on a project basis and work as a team.

What's not to like?

To many employed professionals, the consulting life sounds like an American dream come true: minimal startup costs, no set schedule, no bosses, no politics, and no nitpicky work, but with lots of prestige, recognition, freedom, and, of course, money. But dreams do not a reality make.

■ **Being your own boss** *may make you smile, but don't forget you have clients who are even more demanding than a boss.*

Independent consultants need to worry at least as much as organizational employees about time, reporting, details, and results.

What's more, consultants are often hired to carry out assignments within unreasonably tight schedules – the kind that may not be realistic for staff employees to meet. When all is said and done, independent consultants are usually held to higher standards.

Most independent consultants would tell you that they don't think of themselves as their own boss. They think of their boss as the client for whom they're working at the moment. And since consultants with a healthy practice typically have numerous clients, it follows that really successful consultants have numerous bosses.

If independent consulting holds a strong appeal as a career next-step for you, make sure you investigate it thoroughly before you present yourself to the work world as an expert at large. In many ways, establishing your own consultancy is just like establishing a startup business, except that the product being brought to market is you. You'll need expert guidance from other professionals who consult in the same field you're considering.

■ **Consultancy is far** *from easy. It has the same stresses and strains as running any other type of business.*

Independent contracting

SOMETIMES CALLED *independent contracting, freelancing is often chosen as an interim career stop by professionals who are considering a major change or by people who may find themselves suddenly and unexpectedly unemployed.*

The difference between freelancing and consulting

On the surface, working as a freelancer is similar to working as a consultant, but there are important differences.

Consultants are usually hired to formulate and provide business recommendations and counsel, whereas freelancers are usually hired to carry out specific work tasks, such as text editing, graphic design, or proofreading.

Another way of looking at the difference is this: Consultants are often regarded as strategists, while freelancers are typically thought of as specialists. Another distinction has to do with compensation. Consultants are typically paid to complete lengthy projects, and they take payment on a project basis. Freelancers are typically paid to work on shorter projects (which they sometimes call "small jobs"), and they're usually paid at an hourly rate they negotiate up front. Consultants and freelancers are both paid directly by their clients.

There is plenty of overlap between the work situations of consultants and freelancers. In general, freelancers usually work on very focused, time-limited projects, while consultants typically take on more long-term, wide-ranging assignments. Many consultants work only with particular clients, sometimes just one. But one of the predictable parts of the freelance life (and one that holds a charm or

■ **Graphic designers** *often choose to do freelance work because it is more flexible and sometimes more lucrative.*

carries a curse) is making your expertise and services available in as many settings as possible – and to as many clients. Freelancing is truly, in the purest and most literal sense of the term, independent contracting.

Finding work

Freelance work abounds in the communications, entertainment, and media industries and especially in publishing, television, advertising, and public relations. Many professional roles are suitable to freelance situations, regardless of the industry, including:

- Accountants
- Copywriters
- Desktop publishers
- Electronics repair specialists
- Food service providers
- Housekeepers
- Illustrators
- Interior decorators
- Musicians
- Office services managers
- Personal fitness instructors
- Proofreaders
- Translators
- Wedding planners
- Woodworkers

■ **Even trumpeters**
can do freelance work!

The trend toward outsourcing has favored freelancers by creating a wider range of industry opportunities and a greater variety of projects, both short- and long-term. In fact, entire organizational functions are being outsourced; payroll services and human resources are typical examples.

Developing your pool of clients

Some freelancers start out with an existing pool of business contacts on whom they can rely (at least temporarily) for a steady stream of work and income. Even with a startup base of clients, however, it's important to cultivate new clients – and a big bunch of them at that.

■ **Copywriters can often** *get freelance work from newspapers, magazines, and journals.*

Freelancers can't count on receiving a paycheck with any kind of regularity, so when the work from your most benevolent clients dries up, you must be able to turn to others for income. If you're not prepared to deal with a certain measure of ambiguity and uncertainty in your career, you should carefully reconsider whether freelancing is right for you.

Your biggest challenge as a freelancer will be marketing your services.

Keep in mind that organizations make decisions and commitments slowly, except of course, when they're up against ridiculous project deadlines. That's when they call in freelancers to bail them out, and that's when your name needs to be on the tip of their tongues.

Networking is by far the most effective way for freelance professionals to learn about prospective projects and for broadening and deepening your client base. Your network should include client contacts as well as other freelancers. (For pointers on networking for career vitality, see Chapter 21.)

INTERNET

www.freeagent.com

Click on this information hub for freelancers, consultants, and independent contractors to locate work and connect with other "free agents."

No organization will assign you projects unless they know with certainty three key facts about you:

■ You're out there
■ You're available
■ You're reliable

■ **When tight deadlines** *have to be met, hide your frustration or the company may not employ you again!*

It's up to you to cultivate that awareness and promote it. Freelancers need to spend almost as much time marketing their services as carrying out their assignments.

Rounding out your research

Talk with other freelancers to find out how they market their services. Do some research on the Internet, and read some of the excellent guidebooks on succeeding as a freelancer. Two noteworthy titles are:

✔ *The Complete Idiot's Guide to Making Money in Freelancing* by Christy Heady and Janet Bernstel
✔ *Successful Freelancing: The Complete Guide to Establishing and Running Any Kind of Freelance Business* by Marian Faux.

■ **The information** *that can be found on the Internet now is vast and often well-researched.*

WORKING FROM HOME

An important trend in the workplace today is telecommuting, that is working out of a home office and interacting with coworkers, customers, or clients via phone, fax, and e-mail rather than in person. Telecommuting provides benefits to entrepreneurs, employees, and employers alike – and a few important drawbacks.

Chief among the benefits is flexibility. Simply put, telecommuting enables people to do a variety of work tasks at any hour of the day (or night), instead of just the traditional workday window of 9 a.m. to 5 p.m.

Flexibility also benefits individuals who have to balance child and elder care with the pursuit of a career. Even for people whose lives are not complicated by family issues, the idea of working from home can be alluring.

Telecommuting can save precious time. If you work from home, you don't spend valuable workday hours commuting. For employers, telecommuting represents a way to attract and retain talented employees without incurring the "headcount" costs of permanent employees.

There can be some steep downsides to telecommuting, too. Working from home means spending lots of time alone. That may sound great at first, but a surprising number of people who opt to work at home at least part-time come to experience a sense of isolation. And, organizations face distinct challenges that relate to having employees out of sight. Telecommuting increases the difficulty not only of monitoring worker performance, but evaluating it. If they do not have a formal policy on telecommuting, they must negotiate different sets of terms and expectations with any employees who opt to work from home, which can be a drain on organizational time, money, and efficiency.

Working from home requires a healthy measure of entrepreneurial spirit. You'll need special qualities to make a work-at-home situation work well. Most of all, you'll need discipline. The vast majority of people really don't appreciate how many distractions there are at home until they try to separate from them. Before you take the plunge into working from home, give it a test run by devoting chunks of time on Saturdays, Sundays, and off-days to some work-related activities you'd like to get done. Gauge your effectiveness – and your comfort level. There's just no substitute for firsthand experience. For additional perspectives, check out *101 Tips for Telecommuters* by Debra A. Dinnocenzo.

Temping

DEFINITION

Working in a situation that is officially recognized as interim by employer and employee alike is called temping – short for working on a temporary, rather than permanently employed, basis.

MANY INDIVIDUALS TAKE *on temporary work, referred to as* temping, *to supplement their regular income or to work on an interim basis while in a career transition. In this time of fast-paced change in the work world, agencies that specialize in placing temps are cropping up all over the country to fill the temporary needs of organizations "in progress."*

Working with an agency

Unlike consultants and freelancers, who are hired and paid as independent contractors directly by the organization. Temps, on the other hand, do not have a direct business relationship with the organization buying their services. They are typically placed and paid by an agency, which is retained by the hiring organization. And, unlike the work done by consultants and freelancers, temporary work is almost always done at the location of the hiring organization. So, if you decide to take on temporary work, chances are your paycheck will not be cut by the organization where you spend your working hours.

INTERNET

www.temp24-7.com

This is an informative e-zine for workers pursuing or holding temporary jobs.

Check the help-wanted ads in your local newspaper. Many temp agencies place ads regularly, and these can give you a sense of what types of jobs they fill. You can check your local phone book for additional listings.

Never pay a placement fee to any employment agency, including those that specialize in temporary work.

■ **Sometimes with temping** *you have to do the work that no-one else wants to do.*

Performing seasonal work

Work that is seasonal almost always counts as temporary work. Retail establishments typically need extra hands around the holidays. Gardeners and landscapers usually find they need to increase their work schedules during warm-weather months. And cruise ships employ huge staffs to enrich the vacation experiences of travelers during peak sailing months.

While it's not always a good strategy to rely on seasonal work for all of your income, many entrepreneurial types do. It simply requires adjusting your work and personal life balance to accommodate long stretches of time when your work is out of season.

■ **During the summer months,** *farmers or landscapers usually seek temporary workers.*

Researching early and thoroughly

REGARDLESS OF WHICH TYPE *of entrepreneur you choose to be, early in the planning stage you should tap into the resources offered by various national, state, and local organizations.*

INTERNET

www.sba.gov

The Small Business Association provides a panorama of information and guidance on starting and maintaining a small business. If you're serious about launching yours, this site is indispensable.

The Small Business Association (SBA)

The Small Business Association (SBA), a federal agency that provides loans, guarantees, and other forms of financial assistance. The SBA assists many state and local government programs that are designed to support small business ownership. It also offers a host of consulting services, training programs, and informational periodicals, which are available at nominal cost.

The SBA also sponsors a variety of small business funding programs. Some are designed exclusively to support minority-group entrepreneurs. Others work in conjunction with banks, corporations, community groups, and other government agencies to provide assistance to individuals with clear economic and social needs. Also, check the SBA for special loan programs that may make financing available to individuals who are unable to obtain adequate startup capital in the credit marketplace.

The Service Core of Retired Executives and the Active Corps of Executives

Two other valuable resources to take advantage of are the Service Core of Retired Executives (SCORE) and the Active Corps of Executives (ACE), both organizations affiliated with the SBA.

You can tap into the experience and knowledge of experienced businesspeople for guidance on entrepreneurial issues and topics, including developing a business plan and conducting market research.

SCORE counselors can help you assess whether or not you have the right resources and commitment to make your enterprise succeed. Individual counseling sessions with SCORE consultants are typically free of charge.

SCORE also sponsors a program of business-planning workshops that you can attend for a modest investment (typically $25 to $35, depending on your location). For more information on SCORE, call its national office toll-free at (800) 634-0245.

Tapping into other resources

INTERNET

www.score.org

The Service Core of Retired Executives (SCORE) hosts this site to provide expert advice to individuals pursuing self-employed business options.

You should also investigate other organizations and resources available to help entrepreneurs plan and launch small businesses. There may be state or local government programs in your area, or your local library might be able to help, or you could look for seminars and conferences that offer training and retraining programs that can provide grounding in what it takes to become self-employed.

Finally, consider looking into small business research programs that tap into the resources of government agencies such as the Department of Defense (www.defenselink.mil), Health and Human Services (www.hhs.gov), and the Department of Energy (www.doe.gov).

INTERNET

www.sbdc.org

For valuable information and counseling on planning and launching a small business, check out the Small Business Development Center, a cooperative venture between the SBA and community businesses.

Cracking the books

If you sense that you'd like to pursue this option further, one noteworthy title that can help you take steps is *Mind Your Own Business! Getting Started as an Entrepreneur*, by LaVerne Ludden, Ed.D. and Bonnie Maitlen, Ed.D. Another valuable resource is written by David Lord, a marketing consultant who wrote the *National Business Employment Weekly's Guide to Self-Employment*,

Lord urges you to consider the questions he pondered before establishing himself independently:

 1   What specifically would be the scope and focus of your service?

2   Who would represent the market (customers) for your service?

3   What revenue projections can you make for the short-term and long-term future?

4   What startup and maintenance resources would you require, and how much would they cost?

5   How will your decision affect and shape your career – now and down the line?

INTERNET

www.nase.org

Sponsored by the National Association for the Self-Employed in Washington, D.C., this site offers articles and news on self-employment. You can also pose queries and search for links to a host of related resources and information.

A simple summary

✓ Self-employment is a career option you may wish to consider now or at some point in the future. A number of important trends in the work world continue to make self-employment increasingly attractive to many professionals.

✓ Working on your own requires a congenial combination of suitable personality attributes, external resources, and favorable circumstances.

✓ If you're considering self-employment, you'll need to assess your ability to succeed as an entrepreneur throughout the various stages of a business enterprise.

✓ There are six basic entrepreneurial options for self-employment. Three typically involve other people, and three are typically solo-focused.

✓ Choosing any of the six basic options as a career pursuit requires careful planning, commitment, and the benefit of expertise and resources that are readily available.

Chapter 13

Developing Your Career Action Plan

WHILE YOU MAY NOT BE ABLE to look into a career crystal ball, you can draw a roadmap that will help you reach your career destination, which is what this chapter will help you do. The basis for any effective plan is a vision – a mental picture of a hoped-for outcome. In this chapter you'll learn how to form a vision and allow it to produce goals, both long- and short-term, and evaluate their feasibility and vitality. Your career action plan is your roadmap for success. Got your ruler and pencils?

In this chapter...

✓ Anticipating what's down the line

✓ Seeing what you want

✓ What you see is what you can get

✓ Developing your career action plan

✓ Setting goals the SMART way

229

Anticipating what's down the line

IN PART ONE, YOU SAW HOW *a career is like life itself – an ongoing series of experiences that build upon and interrelate with one another. At virtually any point in your career, you have a past, present, and future, and where you have been in the past exerts great influence on where you are now.*

■ **If you have children** *of your own, perhaps you would find working in a kindergarten enjoyable.*

The work experiences of your past inform the experience of work that you're having now, for better or worse.

And what you learned from previous work situations has a great influence on what you need from your relationship with work at this point in your career. If you're about to enter the workforce for the first time, or re-enter after a long absence, think about recent life experiences that may have prepared you for this event.

Just as your career today is a by-product of your career yesterday, your career tomorrow will unfold from where you are right now. You have a choice in how that will happen. You can make some effort to influence and control where your career will go, or you can hang back and ride with it wherever it takes you. Guess which option is more difficult? Then guess which one is more rewarding?

Here's an important early step in managing your career. Decide that letting your career happen to you is not good enough.

Decide to take charge of your career and do whatever you can to make it what you want it to be.

Commit to the high road, with all its struggles, setbacks, and sweat, and to the idea that what you put into your career will be the best predictor of what you'll get out of it. You've heard the expression, what goes around comes around? It applies double in the world of career management.

■ **If you dream** *of being an astronaut, plan what you need to do and do it!*

Seeing what you want

OKAY, SO YOU'RE WORKING ON YOUR RESOLVE. *What about your direction? Where are you headed, anyway? If you don't have a clue, you need to get one (or several) – fast! Here's a visualization exercise that might help.*

You can do this exercise anywhere, but it's best to do it while you're sitting quietly in your favorite room. (If you're not in your favorite room, part of the exercise is to imagine that you are.) Have a pencil and some paper nearby. Get into a comfortable, seated position that you'll be able to hold without moving for at least five or six minutes.

Looking within

Close your eyes, and think about your life today. Begin by reminding yourself of your age right now. Then think quietly about state of mind, your level of contentment, your accomplishments, your family, your relatives, your home, your work, your frustrations, and your joys. What does your life look like right now? What does it feel like?

■ **Concentrate and think,** *are you satisfied with your life right now?*

Looking back

When you've completed the mental picture of your life at present and you've gotten in touch with your emotional reaction to it, change direction. Keep your eyes closed, and let your mind take you back five years. Tell yourself what year it is and how old you are at that time. Then begin to look at your life as it was then.

What were your major concerns at the time? What were you worried about and happy about? What were you apprehensive about, and what were you anticipating anxiously? Ask yourself the same questions that defined the picture of your life at present. Picture, five years ago, your accomplishments, your family, your relatives, your home, your work. Complete the picture in your mind's eye.

Looking ahead

Now comes the hardest part of the exercise. Stay seated and stay focused. Keep your eyes closed and now do a fast-forward to five years in the future. Tell yourself what year it is and how old you are that year. It's important to hear yourself saying those words.

Picture your life as you would like to have it at that time and at that age. What do you see? What do you look like? How are you feeling? Who is around you? Who is no longer there? What are your concerns? What are your accomplishments? What does your work situation look like, and how does it compare with earlier situations?

If you have trouble visualizing the future, try imagining what you will look like five years from now. Then visualize your surroundings, which may or may not be completely different from those you're used to. Stay focused, and flesh out the picture with details of your life as you'd like it to be in five years. Stay with that vision, and let it linger for several minutes. Now, with your vision in hand – uh, mind – it's back to reality!

Comparing images with reality

So far you've done the equivalent of taking three snapshots: views of your life as it's shaped now, five years ago, and, to the best of your imaginative ability, five years from now. Now pick up that paper and pencil and jot down some notes.

■ **Back to reality –** *you can stop dreaming right now!*

First, compare your snapshot of the present with that of your past. What are the major similarities and differences? What were the important events that influenced and gave shape to your life today? Write down as many thoughts and observations as you can.

Second, compare your snapshot of the present with that of your future, as best as you could envision it. What are the major similarities and differences? Be as explicit and detailed as you possibly can be. Keep writing until you capture all the ideas and observations you can think of.

Getting from here to there

Now here's the challenging part of the exercise. Identify the gaps that exist between your life now and your life five years from now. Ask yourself the following questions:

What separates me now from where I want to be in five years, and what do I need to do to get there from here?

■ **Get your pen** *and paper ready to make those notes!*

In what ways do my life goals involve my career and, more specifically, what must my career look like in order for me to reach and achieve those goals?

Write down more notes. List specific characteristics of your career vision for the future. What kind of work will you be doing? What income level will you need? What combination of job conditions will provide you with a good measure of career satisfaction: working closely with people? Earning a high salary? Feeling a sense of security? Working in an environment that fosters creativity? Enjoying a variety of roles and responsibilities? Working steadily in and perfecting a single function? Working with minimal supervision? (For help in prioritizing your career values, see Chapter 7.)

What you see is what you can get

THE LIST AND NOTES YOU DEVELOP *as a result of the visualization exercise will provide you with the foundation for a career action plan. This plan is a roadmap that can guide you from one career point to the next. And, to be sure, you do need a plan. Setting off on a driving trip with a destination in mind but no roadmap undoubtedly will mean wrong turns, lost time, and just plain getting lost. Your career action plan – your roadmap – will help you chart your course effectively and, quite probably, offer alternative routes that will lead you to the same destination.*

Your roadmap to the future

No matter where you are in your career, you can take charge of your career by drawing up an action plan that represents a roadmap to the future.

The most effective career action plan lists specific goals and then breaks each one down into small steps that move you closer toward attaining it.

For example, if your goal were to complete a professional certification program that may enhance your standing in a particular field, one step that you could immediately take toward that goal would be to obtain the program bulletin that outlines courses and requirements. Another step would be to identify and contact a graduate of the program for an interview to learn specifically how he or she is using the training and with what measures of success.

Handling the curves

No matter how detailed and precise your career action plan is, chances are that you will revise it many times before you fully achieve your goals. It fact, it's inevitable that you will – and that's a good thing. Why? Because you can't anticipate everything that will happen along the way. Some of your plans may not turn out in quite the way you imagined. Life may place some unexpected events in your path that will require your immediate – and perhaps full – attention.

■ **There is often** *more than one road to take when aiming for the sky. But don't worry because that means you may find a better way of doing it!*

Think, for example, about how you would handle a sudden health crisis – your own or a loved one's. Or, how would you respond to an unanticipated need for significant financial resources – let's say for some emergency household repairs? Any of these, and other unanticipated events, would surely require you to adjust your career action plan. So design your plan to be flexible.

Also, don't lose sight of the happy fact that once in awhile serendipity comes along. It's not only bad news that you can't always anticipate – good stuff happens, too! In fact, you'll probably find that when you're primed and poised for success, good fortune and happy coincidences come to you more readily than when you're not as open and receptive to change. They'll also add color and texture to the big picture of your career action plan. Surprises sometimes occur, and so do setbacks. Build on your experiences, and let them help you revise and reshape your goals.

■ **Don't worry** *if you have to revise your career plan. Simply tear off the page and write it again.*

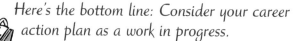

Here's the bottom line: Consider your career action plan as a work in progress.

Don't feel completely locked into an action plan. When you're writing it, use a pencil rather than a pen, or use word-processing software. Both will enable you to make as many revisions as you'd like along the way.

Follow the plan as long as it works for you. As you move ahead and your values or goals evolve, you can refine the design. If your career action plan moves you forward, it has done its job. More precisely, you have done the job – by creating and committing to a roadmap for success in managing your career.

■ **If your plan** *isn't working, the solution is simple: change it!*

Trivia...

Here's an example of how serendipity can enhance and enlarge career movement. A midcareer professional enrolled in a degree program to achieve a major career change from the world of business to the world of mental health. Along the way, an educator encouraged him to lead workshops on the topic of career transition. He did, and found over time that he felt comfortable and gratified as a group facilitator. As a result of that early, unexpected opportunity, he now supplements his work as a counselor with teaching assignments at a major university.

Developing your career action plan

WHEN YOU'RE PREPARING FOR A LONG TRIP, *you probably don't just throw a map in the car and hit the road. Well, maybe you do, but that won't work for your career. For your career action plan to take you where you want to go, you must always have on hand the following things:*

- Long-term goals
- Short-term goals
- Action steps
- Available resources
- Success indicators

A worksheet is provided at the end of this chapter for you to photocopy and use during this exercise. Fill out one copy for every long-term goal that you have. Until you actually get started, creating your career action plan may sound like an awful lot of work. But when you do get started, you'll find that the sections connect in a very fluid way. Your thoughts will gain momentum and you'll have a career action plan in no time – and don't leave home without it.

Setting goals the SMART way

TO REACH ULTIMATE SUCCESS, *you need to be smart about the goal-setting process for the long and short term, and the following simple guidelines will enhance your chances of achieving what's most important to you. They'll be easy to remember because the names of the five guidelines create the appropriate acronym SMART – Specific Measurable Attainable Relevant Timed. With these under your belt, setting your goals will go much more smoothly.*

Specific

As you've seen, generalities don't work in terms of goal-setting – they set you up to fail. The more well-defined and detailed your goals are, the better you're set up for success.

Here are some examples of vague and useless goals:

- Be successful
- Become a good leader
- Be a great communicator
- Become happier in my work
- Be more popular on the job
- Feel better about my contributions

- **If you define** *your goals, success will soon follow!*

Consider how would some of these goals would look if they were better defined:

- Develop leadership skills to become director of regional sales force
- Refine public speaking skills to achieve responsibility for regular presentations to key clients
- Achieve increased career satisfaction that I can sense each week
- Enhance my interpersonal skills to have smoother workplace relationships
- Develop increased confidence in the value I add to the organization

Each goal is clear, concise; and complete. Be sure to follow these examples when you write your own goals.

Measurable

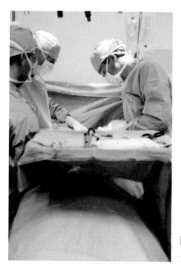

Ask yourself how you will know you are making progress. What will be the yardsticks that measure your movement toward your goal? You'll need these indicators to help you understand whether or not you're on track.

Yardsticks can be applied by you or by others. Your own journal, or random notes, could serve over time as a narrative of your progress. Formal measurement instruments, such as grades or credits that are attached to a course, also provide indications of progress.

- **If your goal** *is to become a surgeon you will have to set yourself numerous yardsticks – the ultimate being your first operation!*

Feedback from other people can be a valuable (and often highly reliable) indicator of your progress. Feedback can be formal (for example, annual or semi-annual performance reviews) or informal (casual opinions expressed by friends and coworkers). Take responsibility for initiating feedback of both kinds.

Attainable

Ask yourself whether or not your goal is truly within your reach. In other words, do you have a realistic chance of achieving it? To help clarify matters, you might want to think about all of the influences that are favoring the process of reaching your goal and those that are impeding the process.

Earlier in the book, you met Stan, the early-thirties professional who was musing about a career change to baseball. Ultimately he was not able to settle on "become a professional baseball player" as a long-term goal because, realistically, this outcome was not attainable for him at his age.

Whether or not a goal is attainable is usually easy to determine. If it's not, don't commit the goal to your career action plan until you believe it is possible to attain it.

Relevant

This goal-setting guideline is tricky, but critically important. You need to ask yourself how your goal fits into a larger context – your career, your avocation, your personal fulfillment. Basically, determining how a goal is relevant involves viewing it as part of a larger whole, a detail in a bigger picture.

This is the place to ask yourself why you really want to reach a particular goal. What are the real reasons for setting this goal? And, assuming you reach it, how will it serve you? Where will it get you? What will it do for you?

Timed

Setting a target accomplishment date is essential to the process of attaining a goal. Without one, you can spin your wheels forever. Don't do it. Give yourself a time frame that is reasonable and considerate of everything else that's going on in your life and career. Decide on a deadline that you can realistically commit to.

It's a good idea to give yourself permission to extend the deadline if you need to, but don't cross that bridge until you come to it.

■ **Before you ask** *anyone else, think how you can actually achieve your goals.*

Ready to define your long-term and short-term goals with confidence and clarity?

Long-term goals

Think of long-term goals as the images in the snapshot of your visualized future. They are definitely big-picture goals. Achieving them requires a strategic pursuit.

VIP *Long-term goals are basically the things you want to attain over roughly the next two to five years, or beyond.*

Identifying long-term goals well is not as simple as it sounds. For example, the long-term goal "to be successful" is far too vague to be useful. And because it's a goal that has no real shape or definition, you'd be setting yourself up to fail to reach it.

On the other hand, the long-term goal "to be successful as the line manager of the marketing department in my current firm" would better set you up for achieving it because it has a fairly detailed definition. Because you can see your destination more clearly, it will be easier to know what you need to do to reach it.

■ **If you want** *to be a veterinarian, you'll need to make a plan to cover the next five years of your life.*

Use the SMART guidelines to develop a set of long-term goals for your career action plan.

Short-term goals

VIP Think of short-term goals as objectives that will get you closer to the long-term goals you've already set. They are goals that bridge the present to the future.

Your short-term goals define what you'd like to attain in a period of about one month to two years.

Short-term goals relate both to the big picture and to the "micro view" of managing your career. They differ from long-term goals in that short-term goals are usually smaller – and easier to reach. Suppose that a long-term goal is "to earn an MBA in Finance by the year 2006." Some examples of short-term goals that relate to that would be:

- Complete two core courses in each of the next four semesters
- Lead a research team to prepare for thesis
- Apply my learning in a mentoring role in my organization
- Take responsibility for a departmental project that taps my learning
- Investigate the possibility of transferring to a department more closely aligned with my learning

For each long-term goal you set, you'll want to identify at least three short-term goals that will carry you forward. Apply the SMART guidelines to these short-term goals as well.

■ **How far** *up the career ladder will you be in two years' time?*

Keep in mind the differences between strategic and tactical approaches to achieving goals. Achieving long-term goals requires a wider variety of actions and behaviors – a bigger-picture pursuit. Achieving short-term goals demands a more concentrated cluster of actions and behaviors – a more focused pursuit that typically demands fewer initiatives.

Remember that short-term goals relate to the present day as well as the far future. What does that mean in the context of managing your career? Simply this: Short-term goals take into account where you are in your career today and bridge that situation with the snapshot of where you want to be in five years and beyond (your long-term goals).

■ **If you plan on becoming** *a florist, one of your first short-term goals should be completing a course in flower arranging.*

Action steps

This section of your career action plan is the "kick start" part, because it serves as a constant reminder that you can get moving right away. And that's why it's so critical.

Action steps are essentially tasks that you can complete within a time span of one minute to about one month.

Think of action steps as "small behaviors" – like making a phone call or arranging to have a networking meeting (and then having the meeting). Action steps can be either "micro" or "macro," meaning that they can more closely resemble major initiatives.

Don't confuse action steps with an intricate sequence of events that you must complete in order to reach a goal. Action steps are small tasks that move you forward.

■ **Get on the phone** *and put your action plan to work!*

Whenever you're thinking about a goal, ask yourself what you can do right away to move just one step closer to it. You might come up with a very short list, or you might able to put together a long list of things to do. Use your imagination. Be creative in pulling together your list. Remember, thinking about your action steps is not the same as plotting every move you need to make between now and the time you reach your goal: Action steps are the behaviors you can do just to get moving in the right direction.

For each goal you set, short-term and long-term, identify three to five action steps that might have an impact on how you reach the goal.

Available resources

Even though your career action plan is your own, you won't be able to do everything yourself. You should find and use every resource at your disposal at all times: people, tools, conditions – even yourself. Anything that can facilitate the process of reaching your goals should be considered available resources. These are an extremely important component of your career action plan. For each long- and short-term goal you set, list the people, tools, and conditions that will make it easier for you to achieve it.

■ **If one of** *your qualities is the ability to concentrate, use it in an appropriate profession.*

Your list of people resources can include mentors, advisors, colleagues, supervisors, former teachers, counselors, clergy, and other individuals who take a personal interest in your success. Taking a personal interest is not the same as getting you to the destination of success, or even giving you the figurative boost. Think of an individual who takes a personal interest as one who would be pleased if you succeed in your pursuits.

When putting together a list of people resources, ask yourself "Who would be genuinely happy to know that I've successfully reached my goal?"

Tools are things you can leverage to move yourself forward. Your list of tool resources can include books, periodicals, Web sites, training experiences, seminars, courses, or anything else that will contribute to the process of reaching your goal. You could also include financial resources on your list.

Conditions also are resources that can facilitate your success. For instance, it's easier and safer for a jet to take off in clear weather than in a storm. Your list of condition resources might include some existing or impending conditions that will make it easier for you to succeed, such as "summer approaching – more daylight hours available for networking golf games" or "kids at camp – more time to complete comprehensive career assessment."

Finally, available resources should include some of your own personal qualities and attributes that you will tap into as you work toward your goals. Forexample,motivation, perseverance, flexibility, and ingenuity are all qualities that will serve you well as you pursue goals. What others do you have?

Success indicators

Here is the most beautiful part of your action plan. Basically, this is the place where you give success an identifiable shape. To do so, ask yourself: "How will I know I've succeeded?" "What will the picture look like when I've achieved my goal?"

■ **If you are dedicated** *to your job, you are probably both good at it and a valued member of the staff.*

Think of success indicators as the reassurances you need along the way to be sure you're on the right track. Success indicators are most constructively applied to your short-term goals, since those represent the bridge from your present to the vision of your future.

Success indicators in the process of reaching a goal are the equivalent of flag signals on a racecourse: They tell you very clearly whether or not you're headed for your destination with maximum effectiveness.

To help you determine your success indicators, think of measurements. Ask yourself "How can I measure my success? What are the factors or conditions I need to achieve that will let me know I'm there?"

We've agreed that a workable career action plan has five distinct sections to develop, and we've looked at what kind of information ought to comprise each one. Until you actually get started, creating your career action plan may sound like an awful lot of work. When you do get started, though, you'll find that the sections connect in a very fluid way. Your thoughts will gain momentum!

Keep in mind that a well-crafted career action plan is like a set of blueprints for success: You really can't build a lasting structure without them. So, now that you've done the learning, do the plan!

■ **Once you have** *achieved your first success you can relax, smile, and congratulate yourself.*

THE SMART GOAL GUIDELINES

S – Specific
M – Measurable
A – Attainable
R – Relevant
T – Timed

Career Action Plan

Date written: _____

✓ Long-term goal _____
_____

✓ Short-term goal (1) _____
_____

✓ Short-term goal (2) _____
_____

✓ Short-term goal (3) _____
_____

✓ Action steps _____
_____

✓ Available resources _____
_____

✓ Success indicators _____
_____

A simple summary

✓ All your work experiences influence how you think about work and your approach to it.

✓ Visualization exercises are valuable tools in the process of setting and reaching goals. If you do the exercises well, they can help you envision the hoped-for outcomes that are the basis of goals worth pursuing.

✓ A career action plan is an essential tool. It will enable you to set short- and long-term goals, take action, measure your progress, use resources, and evaluate your success.

✓ Use the SMART guidelines to facilitate the goal-setting process and provide you with an indication of goal vitality.

✓ Be flexible in pursuing your career action plan. Allow life, luck, and serendipity to exert their due influence.

PART FOUR

MANAGE YOUR JOB-SEARCH CAMPAIGN TO SUCCEED

MANAGING YOUR JOB SEARCH CAMPAIGN

THE NEXT PART COVERS A PROCESS that almost no one enjoys, and everyone endures: looking for a job. You'll probably go through a job search several times throughout your career. This part will provide tips and training that will enable you to *manage* the process effectively – now and in the future.

I'll start by putting the big picture of a job search into perspective. Then you'll learn how to construct a solid, sure-footed foundation for an efficient job search campaign. I'll explain how to sharpen the *strategic* edge of your campaign by tapping critical research resources, and how to develop an effective self-marketing plan that will serve as a blueprint for your search.

This part also takes the mystery and the dread out of writing your resume and managing interviews. It really is simple when you have a set of guidelines.

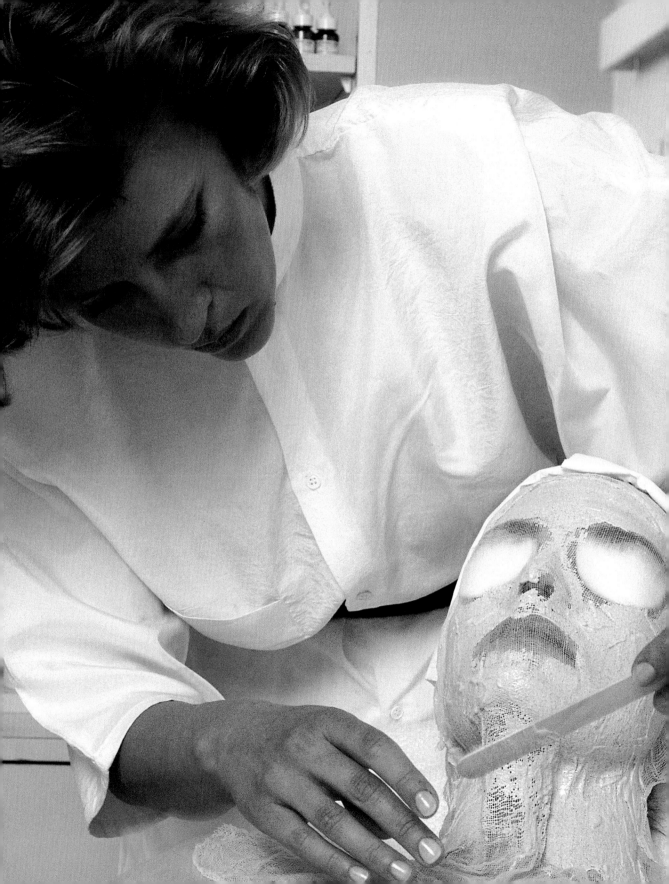

Chapter 14

Getting a Handle on the Job Search

A BIG PART OF MANAGING YOUR CAREER is hunting down a series of suitable work situations. That means looking for a job is an activity you'll likely engage in not just once, but many times during your career. Does that idea excite you, or exhaust you? Searching for a job doesn't have to be agonizing. Nearly everyone has to look for work at some point in his or her career – and usually several times. We'll look at a job search from a big-picture perspective and draw some conclusions that will be useful as you navigate toward your ultimate goal. Then you'll get acquainted with ten key concepts about job search – the big ideas you'll need to know and remember to get where you're going more effectively.

In this chapter...

✓ Keeping it in perspective

✓ Ten concepts you need to know

GIVE YOUR CAREER A FACELIFT BY LEARNING TIPS FOR MANAGING IT MORE EFFECTIVELY

Keeping it in perspective

NO ONE RANKS *looking for a job at the top of his or her list of favorite things to do in life. Finding a job that pays well can be difficult and challenging. Finding a job that taps into your talents, pays well and provides real satisfaction is usually considered, even by the most experienced and sophisticated career-minded people, daunting.*

Although most people do not enjoy looking for a job, the process doesn't have to be as agonizing as it may seem. To be sure, a job search can be stressful, but believe it or not, it can also be an enriching experience. It can stretch you in a number of positive directions, and help you grow psychologically and emotionally. And yes, it can even be fun. How successfully you'll rise to the challenges of a job search depends to a large extent on how you choose to approach it.

What's your situation?

There are six basic job situations that prompt career-minded people to begin a job search. You may be in one of these situations right now:

1. Employed and looking to move within your organization

2. Employed and looking to leave your organization

3. Not employed and entering the workforce for the first time

4. Not employed and re-entering the workforce after a lengthy absence

5. Soon to be unemployed and anticipating a transition

6. Recently unemployed and unexpectedly in transition

■ **If you are happy** *in your place of employment, why not go for promotion?*

If you're really serious about landing a new job, consider the search your top priority.

If you're unemployed, your search is your job until you find work that is acceptable. When you begin to experience the myriad demands of conducting an effective job search, you will learn firsthand that, for most people, looking for a job is a full-time job in itself.

Is one better than the others?

Are any of these situations better than any other? Does any pose greater handicaps than others? It depends. Certainly, each of these career situations carries its own mix of upsides and downsides. People who are employed when they embark on a job search typically experience less internal pressure to resolve their career situation than people who are unemployed. Also, employed individuals have more time to proceed through the foundational stages of a job search more deliberately. That's because employment provides a sense of financial security.

■ **Having money** in the bank means you can take as long as you need to find your ideal job.

However, the demands of holding down a job and meeting your responsibilities can get in the way of conducting an effective job search. You can't always be available for meetings and interviews, and communicating with job-search contacts and prospective employers can be a risky, secretive activity when it's done from your existing workplace. And, most important of all, the job you're holding is likely to be a highly efficient distraction – which means it's extremely tough to keep a focus on searching for a new job with any kind of momentum.

The possible exception is if you're looking to make a move your organization. In that case, simply doing your job every day provides proximity to a potential new situation. In short, you're closer to the destination you've set for yourself. Also, it's easier for your reputation to travel within the walls of an organization than across the terrain of the whole job search landscape. It's easier for the people you may be working for to learn, for better or worse, about who you are and how you work.

Isn't it better to be working?

Many career-minded people are indoctrinated to the idea that it's easier to land a job while you're holding a job, because employment demonstrates that you're a valued commodity. Smarter people know better.

In today's world, given the pace of change and advancement in the workplace, career transitions are commonplace. In fact, people who have not navigated at least one work-related transition are the exception, not the rule. Many people weather multiple transitions, and come to view them as par for the course in managing their career. The good news is this:

Because of the shape of today's work world, the pace of change that drives it, and the new work contract between employers and employees, the stigma that was once attached to being out of work is largely gone.

Today, what's more important than telling prospective employers that you have a job is telling them what you understand about yourself and your career, about their business needs and about all the ways those worlds align. Believe it or not, employers are generally less interested in your past than in your future – because that's what may involve them. Of course it's important to demonstrate your talents, your career accomplishments and your work ethic, and so you'll need to be forceful and persuasive about describing your career focus and past work experiences. But bear in mind that prospective employers are focusing on one overarching question that may be spoken or unspoken: What can you do for me?

NOTABLE JOB-SEARCH BOOKS

- *The Complete Job-Search Handbook* (Third Edition), by Howard Figler, Ph.D. (Henry Holt, 1999)
- *Job Hunting in the 21st Century*, by Carol A. Hacker (St. Lucie Press, 1999)
- *Job Search Secrets*, by Kate Wendleton (Five O'Clock Books, 1997)
- *What Color Is Your Parachute?* by Richard Nelson Bolles (Ten Speed Press, 2000)
  This is the granddaddy of all job search books. It is revised and updated annually.

Tips and tricks of the trade

When it comes to a job search, tips, tricks, and techniques abound. There are thousands of books and web sites that offer advice on everything from résumé writing and interview skills to networking strategies and negotiation techniques. Many of these can be valuable resources. Many others are totally useless. It's a good idea to tap a variety of tools to facilitate your search, but it's best to be selective. Find those that work best for you and your personal style, and go with them.

INTERNET

www.jobhunters bible.com

This web site is sponsored by Dick Bolles, author of What Color Is Your Parachute?, *and is designed as a supplement to that seminal book on career change and job search.*

You'll find other references throughout these pages, but there's no substitute for discovering your own resources in libraries, bookstores and on web sites.

- **Get organized** *by keeping a record of all your job applications.*

Ten concepts you need to know

BECAUSE SO MUCH of a job search campaign is focused on details and nuances, it's useful to take a step back and view the big picture. There are ten key concepts to understand about the process of finding and securing work. While it's not necessary to memorize them, it is important to be thoughtful about each of these key concepts. Together, these ten will help you develop and keep a positive, productive perspective on job search.

1. There's no magic formula for finding work

It would be simple if an effective job search was a predictable series of exercises to perform. That's not the case. Different strategies work for different people, in different combinations. There are well-defined steps to the typical job search, which are covered in the rest of this chapter, but every individual approaches them uniquely. Think of a job search as a system of initiatives for you to take. How you take them depends on your own unique personality.

Don't ever believe that there's just a single, scientific way to carry out an effective job search.

Rather, an effective job search involves being engaged in a strategic variety of activities and pursuits simultaneously.

2. A job search is a process, not an event

When you need work, or when you're yearning for a different kind of work, you want to find it as quickly as possible. But when you're looking for a job things are rarely settled as quickly as you'd like. That's because there are many factors involved, and you can only control some of them.

Think of job search as a process. Plan to pursue it over a significant span of time, not just a week or a month. Keep the process open-ended, and try not to be badgered by self-imposed deadlines. If you like, think of your search as a journey that will take you on many turns and detours as you move toward your destination. Keep sight of your goal – the new job itself – rather than the calendar.

■ **Be patient** – *job searching takes time!*

TAMING YOUR STRESS

There's no question that looking for the right work situation can be a tough grind physically, mentally and emotionally, especially if you are pressed for income. One big reason for the stress of a job search is that it requires you to live with ambiguity. Many job hunters feel extremely uncomfortable with the uncertainty of the process. They say it reduces them to a sense of powerlessness over what happens to them.

One career management tip that can go a long way toward taming some of the stress of a search is this:

If you manage every factor that's available to you to manage, you're doing everything you can do.

There will always be factors that are beyond your control. yourself to be stressed by them is not a productive use of your mental and emotional energy. And you need to conserve as much as possible!

Anticipate an emotional roller coaster ride as you move through the process of search. You can expect to be tantalized by leads and prospects, and deflated by setbacks and disappointments. You can also expect uncomfortably long dry spells, when nothing seems to be moving forward except your impatience.

3. There's no reason to conduct your search in isolation

Help is out there, in many different and valuable forms. You'd be foolish not to take advantage of it. If you can, get a career

■ **Don't rule out** *professional advice – many careers counselors are relatively inexpensive.*

counselor or coach who can be your co-pilot in developing job search strategies and techniques. Professional counseling services can be expensive, but they don't have to be. Many career counselors and job search coaches set their fees on a sliding scale. Find the right one the same way you'd find a new dentist or doctor: Talk to people and get referrals.

INTERNET

www.rileyguide.com

This popular job-hunting web site with sharp advice and guidelines from search strategist Margaret F. Dikel offers a host of resources on many facets of a job search.

Also, don't overlook universities and community colleges. They typically provide career-related services to alumni, and some make these services available to the general public.

Many people in career transition value the benefits of a team approach to search. It's a good idea to mingle regularly with other individuals who are in the same boat as you, dealing with the same anxieties and ambiguities. No matter where you are in your career, you'd be surprised by how much you can gain by tapping into the ideas and perspectives of other job hunters. You may also uncover valuable prospects and referrals.

There are a variety of teams, clubs and organizations designed for people in transition and actively pursuing a search. Check your local Department of Labor office, community civic group and your local church or synagogue, which may sponsor a support group for job hunters and people in career transition. National organizations with a network of local chapters, like Forty Plus, Exec-U-Net and the Five O'Clock Club, require paid membership at some level, and provide strategic job-search counseling services as well as collegiality and support.

Be careful to distinguish these helpful job-search organizations from unscrupulous "career strategy" firms that offer to make you "marketable" and "give you the edge" in the job search process–for an astronomical fee.

Never pay a fee to any career-focused organization without a thorough understanding of the services it provides — and their proven benefits to other participants.

DEFINITION

The **hidden job market** *is a sector of the employment market that is only tapped through informal channels and by word of mouth. These jobs are never advertised to the general public.*

4. The hidden job market is more fertile than the public one

At least three out of every four jobs filled are never made known to the public. They are filled without ever emerging from the vast *hidden job market*. The overwhelming majority of job openings are filled by people who understand what the hidden job market is and how to navigate it successfully.

Another way to think about search is in terms of formal and informal channels to the job marketplace. Formal channels include:

- Classified ads
- Web site job boards
- In-house job postings
- Employment agencies
- Executive search firms (headhunters)
- Employment fairs

What do these channels have in common? Job applicants. Large numbers of them. Such large numbers, in fact, that one applicant's odds for ultimate success are very, very long because the competition is very,

■ **Applying for** *an in-house posting saves you from making secretive phone calls to prospective employers during office hours.*

very stiff. The most astounding fact about formal channels to the job marketplace is this: Combined, they account for no more than 25 percent of all jobs that are filled. Many career management insiders believe even that figure is high.

Informal channels to the job marketplace include:

- Networking
- Direct-approach strategies
- Creating opportunities where none exist

What do these channels have in common? Only the self-reliance of job hunters who use them. In other words, if you choose to pursue workplace opportunities by using some combination of informal channels, you're not in competition with an overwhelming number of people who are responding to the more formal, public job marketplace.

■ **Employers tend** *to be impressed by direct action, so get on that phone.*

Informal, hidden channels lead to at least 75 percent of all jobs that are filled.

The most effective search campaign involves active, ongoing navigation of informal and formal channels to the job marketplace. However, you may wish to use the 75-25 success ratio as a rough guideline for allocating your time to various job search activities.

5. A job search is a numbers game

In so many ways, a job search involves big numbers and long odds. Let's look at just a few of the ways a job search is a numbers game:

1 Competing with hundreds of people who respond the same classified ads in print or on line

2 Building your network of contacts and securing two new referrals from each of them

3 Trading numerous voicemail and e-mail messages to arrange meetings and interviews (it can take as many as seven phone calls just to connect live with a person you're trying to reach by using work or business numbers)

4 Moving through the interview process and meeting at least six people who want to know all about you

5 Encountering five rejections or dead-ends for every one search-related conversation or meeting that takes place

■ **Be prepared** *for the interview: You may be required to give a presentation for your interviewers.*

6 Competing with a short list of one, two, three, or four finalists for the job you've pursued aggressively

What's the point of thinking about job search as a numbers game? Simply this: The setbacks and disappointments you will probably encounter along the way are likely to far outnumber the thrills and triumphs. It will be easy to personalize the downturns and allow them to sap your energy and motivation. But understanding that the search is a numbers game will provide you with a way to separate your emotions from the process. You can distance yourself from a sense of personal rejection or failure by keeping sight of the number of influential factors that are beyond your control. And the greater the number of players on the field, the more of those factors there are.

The key idea to keep in mind about the job-search numbers game is that it always boils down to the most important numeral of all: one. Because it takes just a single job offer to make all the difference in the world to your career.

6. You can't predict how long your search will take

You'd like your search to be over and done with as quickly as possible. Depending on your profession and your industry, it may be. But it's more likely your search will stretch out for a significant period of time. If you launch your search with the idea that it's open-ended, you'll be doing yourself a favor.

VIP

Some job searches begin, advance, and conclude in a matter of weeks, even days. Others meander on for months, sometimes years. Rather than concentrating on a time frame, concentrate on time efficiency – and on doing everything you can to move your search ahead. The chronology will take care of itself.

7. The more time you put into your search, the sooner it will end

We've already seen that a job search is like a numbers game. As you move through it, keep sight of the law of averages: The more activities you engage in, the greater the likelihood of fruitful return. If you're employed, you have a very limited number of hours available to you during the week to devote to a search. Use each of those hours as efficiently as possible, and supplement them with weekend time.

■ **Don't let it** *get you down – the harder you search the less time it will take to secure a job.*

If you're not employed, you have time to make your search the focus of your days. Most people find that 35 or 40 hours of intensive job-search activity per week is not realistic, since it is emotionally draining and generally exhausting. But remember, an effective search requires quiet time for preparation, research, and planning, as well as "on" time for networking, interviewing, and follow-up communication. Also, expect to occasionally have days when you need to put your search on pause to clear your head. When you do, give yourself permission to take a break and go to a movie or take a long walk.

INTERNET

www.jobs.com

Jobs.com promotes itself as "the Internet's fastest-growing web site." It offers a job search resource center, an employer list, a résumé bank and other useful tools. Especially helpful for students making the transition into the workforce.

Spend as much time as you can on your search, but be careful to monitor the time you spend. The quality of the time you spend is far more important than quantity of hours you log.

8. Your attitude about the search process will influence its outcome

You can't conduct a job search without getting in front of people. You will need to present yourself to the work world and make a case for yourself. How well you do that will be determined to a great extent by what's going on in your head as you move through the search. Keep sight of the fact that just about everyone needs to look for work at one point or another. Most people go through the process several times throughout the course of their career.

■ **Take every opportunity** *to be productive, even if it is your lunch break!*

If you permit yourself to feel lost and adrift as you navigate your career transition, you will not be forceful and persuasive with the people who can help you. If you are bitter, angry, or resentful about your career situation, you will alienate the people who may lead you to a different situation. If you are not purposeful and focused in your self presentation, your search will not culminate quickly or easily.

INTERNET

www.monster.com

Not called Monster.com for nothing, this comprehensive job search site includes some 175,000 jobs and more than 30,000 employers. It also offers job-hunting advice by expert columnists.

■ **Job-searching may seem** *daunting at first but hard work and dedication frequently pay off.*

Don't make the mistake of holding out for the perfect job; it doesn't exist.

Focus instead on finding your way to an ideal job – one that engages your interests, taps your skills and abilities, aligns with many of your career values, and suits your personal style.

Another point to remember: The next job you take will probably not be the last job you'll hold. Nothing is forever. Evaluate each opportunity in the context of your career plans as you envision them currently, and in the larger context of your life.

■ **Being well-informed** *will impress employers. However, being yourself counts as much as any knowledge.*

9. You are what matters most

In the job search process, what's most important to your ultimate success is you yourself. There will always be individuals who conduct a more strategic search, build an arsenal of more persuasive tools, have a wider network of contacts, and conduct themselves more forcefully than you may be able to. By the same token, there will always be individuals who fall far short of your abilities.

Don't waste time and emotional energy comparing yourself with either camp. Work with what you have and what you can get. Remember that you are in charge of your own search. No coach, counselor, mentor, or strategist can get you the job that you want or need. You must do that yourself. To make that process as simple as it's going to be, work on your people skills. Learn how to be with people and, as best as you can, to make them feel comfortable. How you put yourself out into the work world – the ways you impress people and make yourself memorable – will determine how successfully you'll navigate its terrain.

Make sure you like yourself and approve of yourself, because if you don't, no one else will.

10. Your job search is just one part of managing your career

Chances are that you're going to be working for a long time. Your career will very likely take twists and turns that you can't even imagine right now. Managing your career effectively involves thoughtful work all along the way, not just during the job search.

A job search is a career episode.

Just as an apprenticeship, an assignment, a training course, a transfer, and a promotion are events that become milestones in your career, a job search is a process that has a beginning, a middle, and an end. It will become a reference point in your career. But a job search does not make or break a career. Its outcome gets you to the point where you can continue managing your career in a broader way.

As we've seen elsewhere in this book, managing your career effectively means taking the long view. Conducting a successful job search is a necessary, unavoidable part of managing your career that you will likely need to undertake more than once. To make sure it's as effective as it can be, keep your job search activities focused on the here and now.

■ **Sit down** *and take the time to find out about jobs that are suitable for you.*

A simple summary

✓ For most people, a job search is daunting. You may conduct your search more effectively if you think of it as a process, not an event.

✓ Six basic career situations prompt people to launch a job search. Whether you're employed or not, each of these career situations has a mix of benefits and drawbacks to an effective job search campaign.

✓ Your job search will not be effective unless you consider it a top priority. If you are not employed at the time of your search, make searching your full-time job.

✓ Your ability to describe what you can do for an employer is paramount to your success in job search. You can develop this ability through the foundational work of self-assessment, and by reviewing past accomplishments.

✓ Ten key concepts about the job search will enable you to develop and maintain a positive, productive view of the process of looking for work.

Chapter 15

Gearing Up for Your Job Search

N OW THAT YOU'VE GOT THE BIG PICTURE of job search in focus, you can
start on the process. I'll outline the fundamentals, such as looking at
your financial picture, before providing a list of essential job-search tools.
You'll find guidelines for using radar and spotting targets in your search
by gathering information. Finally, I'll look at the importance of a strategic
marketing plan, and how you can use it to move your search ahead.

In this chapter...

✓ Getting organized ✓ Your financial picture

✓ Command Central for your job search

✓ Essential job search tools

✓ Taking stock of what you have to offer

✓ Gathering and using information

✓ Where to look

✓ Developing your marketing plan

Getting organized

IF YOU'RE SERIOUS about landing a new job, you'll want to do everything you can to make the process efficient and ultimately successful. While you can't control all of the circumstances, events and outcomes that lie

ahead of you on the job search pathway, you can set yourself up to navigate them effectively.

■ **If you want** *to race ahead with your job search, plan well in advance.*

INTERNET

www.americas employers.com

America's Employers.com is sponsored by the Career Relocation Corporation of America (CRC). The site features information on job search essentials, recruiters, electronic networking and more, along with a resume bank, job listings and a company database.

It's a series of steps

A job search is not a process that's best left to chance.

■ **If you follow** *these steps, it won't be long until your dressed up for your first interview.*

A full-fledged search campaign involves a systematic series of initiatives and responses on your part that will eventually get you from where you are now to your first day in a new job.

The more organized and methodical you are with these steps, the more likely it is that your search will progress effectively and productively.

Your financial picture

REMEMBER THAT YOUR JOB *search may take longer than you anticipate. If you have a budget, review it and revise it in light of your career transition and the uncertainty that comes with it. If you've never looked at your financial picture seriously and set realistic guidelines for spending and saving money, do it now. Add up your monthly expenses to get a workable idea of how far your resources will carry you during your transition. Obviously, you'll need to save as much money as possible.*

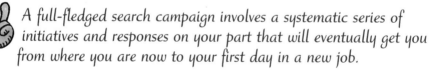

Cut the fat

Look for ways to trim expenses. Divide your expenses into two categories: essential and non-essential. Set very strict guidelines for yourself regarding what you must spend money on and what you like to spend money on. The first category consists of rent or mortgage payments, food, transportation, car and tuition payments, credit card payments, and other non-negotiable expenses. The second category consists of entertainment, dining out, hobbies and leisure interests, and many lifestyle services that you might forego – at least temporarily.

■ **Crack open** *the champagne when you have secured your new job. Until then, stick to your budget.*

INTERNET

www.employment spot.com

The Employment Spot features a compendium of must-see career and employment sites, an archive of feature articles on search, and capabilities for finding a job or posting a job.

Balance your budget

After you've developed an accurate tally of your monthly expenses, look at it in light of your financial resources. Work up a realistic monthly budget, and stick to it. Review your budget as your search progresses, and revise it as necessary. Remember that it's always a good idea to pad your budget slightly to allow for unforeseen circumstances or emergency situations.

Don't allow yourself to dip into your reserve if you're not required to use it. You never know when you will be.

Build into your budget the resources necessary to cover essential job search tools. You will almost certainly need access to a computer and a good printer. If you already have them, great! If not, you may wish to invest in them now, if your budget permits. The alternative is to rent computer time and services, usually on an hourly basis, from local services like Kinko's.

In addition to a computer, you'll need a variety of other essential resources that will facilitate your search. Be sure to allocate enough money to cover these purchases at the beginning of your search.

■ **In the long term,** *buying a computer could be a good investment.*

SAMPLE CHART OF MONTHLY EXPENSES

Essential Expenditures		Nonessential Expenditures	
Mortgage or rent payment		Dining out	
Food		Entertainment	
Credit card payments		Health club membership	
Car payment		Housecleaning service	
Tuition/student loan payment		Sports	
Transportation expenses		New leisure clothes	
Dry cleaning			
Job search expenses			

Command Central for your job search

TO CARRY OUT your job search efficiently, you must have an efficient workspace. If you're employed, you may have access to phones, faxes, the Internet, and other channels that connect you to the outside world. But you may not be able to use them freely to look for a job. If you're not employed, you'll need to be in contact with the world from home.

You can make your campaign much more effective if you do everything possible to separate your search from your personal life. Being at home presents a host of distractions that can eat up your time, drain your energy and destroy your focus. You will need to be ruthless in establishing boundaries and guidelines that will enable you to carry out your search in a businesslike way.

■ **Try not to get** *distracted while job-searching. Set yourself boundaries and guidelines to ensure success.*

Set aside a space

Set up an area of your home and devote it exclusively to your job search activities. Think of it as a home office – Command Central for your job search. Try to keep the activities and tools of your search completely separated from those of your home life, so that you preserve the comfort of your personal space.

If you find that your living situation cannot provide you with the privacy and tools you need, or is just not conducive to job search activities for any other reason, consider conducting your search from other locations. You might ask friends or business contacts if they can make workspace available to you for limited amounts of time. Be sure to cover any expenses you incur. Also, check out your local library for reading rooms and for Internet access. You can do a great deal of information gathering without ever moving away from the computer screen, wherever it may be located.

INTERNET

www.jobtrak.com

A helpful employment site that features information and resources for students, alumni, and college staffs. Also provides access to a variety of valuable services.

You'll need a phone

Don't expect to conduct an effective job search without an efficient telephone system. You will need a touch-tone phone with at least one line. You'll also need an answering machine. Consider these crucial parts of your workspace.

Cellular phones are fine for checking messages, but don't rely on them exclusively to communicate with people as you conduct your job search.

Wireless phones are not conducive to the conversations you will need to have with networking contacts and prospective employers. Those conversations sometimes turn into interviews. You simply cannot be effective as an interviewee when you're in motion, or when your connection is fading.

Trivia...

If you spend or plan to spend a lot of time on the Internet, consider installing a second phone line to your job-search workspace. Remember, being online means tying up your telephone line. Incoming callers will receive a busy signal, and may grow weary of trying to track you down.

■ **Allocate a space** *as your official job-searching area, so that you have everything you need at hand.*

Essential job search tools

CONDUCTING AN *effective job search requires a number of basic tools that facilitate the process. Acquire these and begin to use them before you attempt to move forward in your search. Here's a checklist of essentials:*

Telephone and answering machine

Digital, single-unit systems are preferable, since callers do not have to wait while recording tape rewinds.

Tips:

1. Record a brief, straightforward outgoing message. Remember, contacts and prospective employers will hear your greeting and form impressions of you based on it.
2. Do not limit the recording time of incoming messages. Some messages will contain critical information that you will want to hear in its entirety.
3. Consider using services like call waiting, call forwarding, and other features that make it easy for callers to communicate with you.

Calendars and appointment listings

Whether you use the old-fashioned appointment book, the Day Runner system, a Filofax, a software program, or one of the trendy Palm Pilots, you will need an efficient, reliable way to keep track of your appointments.

Tips:

1. Use a system you're comfortable with. If you're technologically-minded, go with computerized appointment listings. Consider a software package such as Microsoft Outlook or Stay Organized, Quick & Easy (from Individual Software, Inc.). If you're more of a low-tech type, stick with the pencil-and-book format. Don't use the event of your job search to convert to a new system.

   ■ **Be sure** *to keep a note of every appointment you make.*

2. In addition to a daily appointment listing, use weekly and monthly spread sheets. These facilitate the planning process and keep you organized. They're also a ready reminder of the volume of job-search activities you've got going on.
3. Maintain a portable calendar so you can check your schedule and arrange meetings when you're away from home (at an interview, for instance, or when you're returning phone calls on the road). Be sure your portable calendar includes phone numbers, since not every caller leaving a message has the presence of mind to leave a number with it.

Address file

You will need to keep careful track of all the people you speak to throughout your job search. That means all of your contacts, all of the people they refer you to, and all of the people you interview with, whatever the outcome. It's essential to keep a log so that you can follow up effectively and loop back to key contacts as your search progresses.

Tips:

1. Keep an address file in the medium that suits you best. Use a traditional address book, a specialized software program, or the address-book feature of your e-mail program

2. Regularly update and maintain your names and numbers address file. You never know when you'll need someone's contact details.

3. Use your address file to keep track of your job search relationships. You will need to remember who referred you to whom. It's important to track and sort your connections to people.

Stationery

No matter how much you may rely on e-mail, you will have to use snail mail during your job search. Invest in good-quality stationery for your cover letters and follow-up notes. You'll also need top-grade paper for the printed version of your résumé.

Tips:

1. Engraved or embossed stationery is always impressive, and you can consider it a worthwhile investment. However, using your software program to print your name, address, and numbers on your letters is perfectly acceptable.

2. Most people find white or buff stationery preferable. Gray almost always looks dingy, and blue somehow just doesn't work well. Stay far away from other colors, no matter what your profession or temperament.

3. Don't forget to have an adequate supply of matching envelopes.

4. Make sure your stationery and your résumé paper are compatible. (They don't have to match, but they should be complementary in terms of tone and texture of the paper quality.) You will frequently need to enclose your printed résumé with the cover letters you write. The letter, résumé, and envelope should look like a well-planned package.

■ **Remove any old contacts** *from your address file if they are no longer relevant to your job search.*

Business cards

If your job search calls for a good deal of networking (and most do), get yourself business cards and hand them out liberally. Remember, it's not always appropriate to hand out a résumé. But it's almost never inappropriate to give someone a card.

Tips:

1. In addition to your name, your card should provide some indication of your profession, area of expertise, or industry. People need a way to remember what work that you do, or want to do. You can be very specific (job title or areas of expertise) or fairly general (industry or functional area), but you should provide some reference to your career. Otherwise, your card will appear to be a social calling card.

2. Include on your card any and all numbers where you can be reached: telephone, fax, and e-mail.

3. Be sure the layout and type are reader-friendly, not confusing.

■ **If your profession** *is cleaning, make it clear on your business card, and distribute as many as you can.*

Filing system

Part of conducting an effective job search is maintaining records efficiently. It doesn't matter if you use accordion files to hold your paper documents or a computerized system of storing your communications. Just be consistent.

Tips:

1. You won't be able to store everything related to your job search in your computer. Keep a separate storage file for periodicals, newspaper clippings, annual reports, and all paper research documents that you accumulate during your search.

2. Keep a copy of every communication you send: letters, memos, e-mails, thank-you notes, and follow-up letters. Maintain them chronologically, by contact or by job search event (such as your pursuit of a particular position).

3. For maximum efficiency and accessibility, store all of your correspondence in the same place.

■ **Organization is everything:** *Keeping copies of all communication you make will benefit you in the long term.*

Taking stock of what you have to offer

IN VERY MANY ways, a job search is just like salesmanship.

When you're conducting a job search campaign, you will need to engage in many of the same activities that characterize an effective sales campaign.

Let's take a look at some of the ways job search and salesmanship are alike. Each involves:

- Learning about customers' needs
- Developing a thorough knowledge of the product or service
- Positioning its unique benefits to customers or clients
- Building sophisticated knowledge of the market for the product or service
- Gathering intelligence about competitors
- Communicating with prospective customers
- Demonstrating the benefits of the product or service
- Gauging the response of customers
- Following up with customers and addressing their concerns
- Requesting a decision to commit to the product or service
- Negotiating the terms of commitment
- Putting the commitment into effect
- Following up on the commitment to deepen the business relationship

■ **Write down what you** *have to offer and the ways in which can sell yourself to companies of your choice.*

The product is you

In a job search, of course, the product or service you're selling is you. Your challenge throughout the process is to be as thorough, convincing, and persuasive about yourself as the most effective salesperson could ever be. To meet that challenge, you'll need to be clear and convincing about how well you are equipped to fill the needs of your prospective employer and provide lasting benefits. In other words, you'll have to be able to describe and demonstrate what you will bring to the table.

■ **Think about yourself,** *then consider the best way to sell "you" to your employer.*

Assessing your skills

That points to the kind of awareness that can only be developed through the self-assessment process. As we saw in Part Two, career-related self-assessment is a way of stepping back and taking inventory of your personal and professional qualities, in order to identify the kind of work that will be most satisfying and fulfilling. Remember, the assessment process involves looking carefully at four key areas:

1. Interests

2. Skills

3. Values

4. Personality and style traits

As you're gearing up for your job search, be sure to invest time in a fresh inventory of your personal and professional attributes (and areas that need development).

Look especially at your skills; they rank highest among your marketable qualities.

■ **Give your skills** *a thorough inspection before thinking about selling them to someone else.*

Your résumé, your written and verbal communications, your networking conversations, and your interview techniques must showcase your skills clearly and convincingly. If you haven't analyzed your marketable skills recently, or if you've never taken stock of them, do it before you begin your job search in earnest. Refer to the exercises in Chapter 6, or work with a career consultant who can help you take an objective look at your attributes.

Gathering and using information

YOU CANNOT conduct an effective job search campaign without information. And you cannot gather the kind of information you'll need without doing research.

Most people are put off by the prospect of doing research. Somehow it seems to conjure up memories of slogging through endless term papers in high school or college. Typically, research seems like a boring activity that's more of a chore than a challenge. And that's why most people in a job search tend to be lackadaisical about gathering and using information.

Why you can't do without research

But research can make all the difference in the world to the success of a job search – or the lack of it.

Think of doing research as an ongoing process of gathering and using information to your advantage.

You simply cannot move a job search forward without engaging in that process. Remember, information brings knowledge, and knowledge is power.

■ **Knowledge of the company** *and the job you are applying for is vital, so make sure you do your research.*

Let's look at some of the ways you can use information in your job search. Research can enable you to:

■ Develop an understanding of different professions
■ Recognize and analyze industry trends
■ Identify specific organizations to target
■ Identify employment agencies and search firms
■ Locate sources of classified employment ads
■ Identify professional associations that meet locally
■ Locate support groups and organizations for people in career transition
■ Identify and locate key contacts
■ Prepare for interviews by learning about specific companies
■ Understand what salary range is an appropriate goal
■ Learn how to negotiate your salary and benefits

■ **Check the employment** *pages in the newspapers but don't rely on them exclusively.*

For those reasons and many others, research is an essential ingredient in your job search. If you do it well, it will pay off.

Research in small bites

To rid yourself of some of the dread of doing research, think of doing it in relatively small bites of time throughout your search, rather than in huge chunks of time up front. Let's face it, putting in an hour of research a day for a week seems far less daunting than putting in five hours all at once. And you'll be more productive, because you'll be able to retain your concentration and focus. Here's a model of how research can help you gain knowledge throughout your job search.

1. Finding and gathering facts

This is the stage that is the most confusing, because it's the most chaotic. The facts and tidbits of information that you're collecting are not yet connected in a systematic way, and do not form a picture that's understandable. In this stage, information is like pieces of a complex jigsaw puzzle that have been dumped onto the floor.

2. Gaining knowledge

■ **If you do** *your research you will get results.*

As you collect facts and review and analyze their meaning, you begin to recognize patterns and relationships that provide you with basic knowledge. Information comes together in more of a systematic way, and enables you to form a bigger picture. This stage is like recognizing and completing a key section of the jigsaw puzzle, which will allow you to move on to an even larger area.

3. Developing understanding

As you talk with contacts and add their ideas and perspectives to the information you've already gathered, you round out your knowledge with color and texture. Synthesizing objective information and subjective insight enables you to develop real understanding about a topic or situation, not just one-dimensional book knowledge. In this stage, the jigsaw puzzle is completed.

Don't think of research as an onerous chore that you can do just once and be done with. Think of it instead as unfinished business or a work in progress. It's a process you'll need to revisit and refresh periodically throughout your search. If you can turn it into detective work, instead of thinking of it as homework, you may even come to enjoy the process. And you'll probably be amazed at how much useful information you learn.

■ **If you have** *made any contacts in your desired field, listen to their ideas – you may gain invaluable information about your chosen career.*

RESEARCH RESOURCES

There are many excellent resources that can help you understand the importance and uses of job-search research, and provide you with an abundance of insights on how to conduct it effectively. Among the best are:

Researching Your Way to a Good Job, by Karmen N.T. Crowther
(John Wiley & Sons, 1993).
Using the Internet and the World Wide Web in Your Job Search,
by Fred E. Jandt and Mary B. Nemnich (JIST, 1997).
Targeting the Job You Want, by Kate Wendleton (Five O'Clock Books, 1997).
See the career and job-search bibliography, compiled and annotated by
Wendy Alfus Rothman.
The Business Information Desk Reference: Where to Find Answers to Business Questions, by
Melvyn N. Freed and Virgil P. Diodato (Macmillan, 1991).

These directories will also help you track down some of the information you need:
*City and State Directories in Print, Directories in Print, Encyclopedia of Associations, Encyclopedia of Business Information Sources, Professional Careers Sourcebook
The Job Hunter's Sourcebook*

Where to look

THERE ARE *three basic ways to do research:*

- Investigating print and electronic resources at libraries
- Accessing information on the Internet
- Networking with contacts for subjective information and perspectives

You'll need to engage in all three activities. It's best if you pursue them simultaneously, because different sources of information complement and enhance others, and will enable you to form more reliable conclusions.

The library

Find the largest library you can and use it. Big cities and major metropolitan areas have the libraries with the largest collections of resources. University libraries typically have excellent, extensive collections. Get acquainted with the library that will serve you best, and become familiar with its career and job-search resources. You'll find a wealth of information that's available in print, on CD-ROM databases, and online. It's usually helpful to take a guided tour of the library, if one is available.

There's never a need to do your job-search research in isolation. Collaborate with the librarians or information specialists on staff. It's their job to know what's available at the library, and to help you access information efficiently.

When searching, make it easy for your information specialists to help you by asking them specific, pointed questions, not general ones.

For example, do not ask the information specialist to "give me everything you've got on the pharmaceuticals industry." Instead, ask for "recent profiles of the top ten pharmaceuticals companies on the East Coast," or whatever it is that you need specific information about.

The Internet

If you're comfortable using the Internet, by all means take advantage of its ease and convenience. But be wary of spending an overabundance of time surfing the web. The Internet is far less scientific than a collection of library resources in the way it

- **The Internet** *can be an invaluable tool for research.*

organizes and presents information. Once you're on the web, it's easy to be lured from one site to another just to see what turns up. In many ways it's like trying to find a needle in a haystack. Be very careful to monitor the time you spend online.

Use the Internet as one component of the research process. It's very easy to access information online and collect enough of it to believe that you don't have to dig any deeper or look any farther. Don't be lulled into that false sense of security. While it's true that the Internet can yield virtually unlimited information, the quality of the information is extremely variable. Company websites, for example, will provide you only with the information they want you to have – not the more comprehensive, objective information you're likely to obtain through other sources.

INTERNET

www.hotjobs.com

Enables visitors to do a job search by keyword, by location, and by company. Also references jobs by industry sector. You can also access a feature that offers sharp, advice-filled articles by expert career counselors.

INTERNET

biz.yahoo.com/industry

Track down useful industry information at Yahoo's special industry site. It includes links to resources that will also enable you to research specific companies.

Tapping the various *search engines* is probably the best way to put the Internet to work for you throughout your job search. Use search engines to access information directories and indexes. In addition to specific company websites, online job search resources include helpful career sites, job listings, and electronic classified ads. Also, be aware that the Internet is transforming the way search firms recruit candidates for job assignments. Its impact on the search industry is likely to be at least as great as its impact on the travel industry.

■ **Reading books** *is the traditional method of research, but using the Internet to learn can be much more fun!*

SELECTED RESOURCES FOR INDUSTRY RESEARCH

1. *American Salaries and Wages Survey*
2. *Dun's Business Rankings*
3. *Encyclopedia of Associations*
4. *Standard & Poor's Industry Surveys*
5. *U.S. Industrial Outlook*
6. *U.S. Industry Profiles*

DEFINITION

Internet programs that seek and locate online information about a specific topic requested by the user are called search engines.

Researching industries

If you need industry information, use resources that provide top-line information and overviews. Don't delve too deeply at first. Begin modestly and tap a variety of print and electronic resources, including directories, industry surveys, trade journals, and general business periodicals, along with business sites on the Internet. Pull together as many different facts and perspectives as possible. Use the following guidelines the same way you'd use a compass in a dense forest.

When researching industries, look for:

- Industry trends of the recent past and present, along with trends that are taking shape
- Products and services developed and marketed by the industry
- Relationships with other industries
- Geographic location or concentration of the industry
- Professional associations that represent the industry
- Names and profiles of industry leaders and influential people

■ **To discover more** *about your chosen profession, study industry surveys and trade journals for relevant information.*

Researching companies

Once you've researched your target industry, you can begin to develop a list of target companies within that industry. You can identify these companies by several different criteria: geographic location, company size, revenue, and others. Accessing company information on CD-ROM is generally less tedious and more time-efficient than using print materials. As always during the research process, put together information from a variety of sources to gain the deepest, most well-rounded knowledge of a particular company.

Always check whether or not the company you're researching has an annual report and a web site. Although both of these resources will typically offer only selective, biased information about the company, they will enable you to see how the company wants to be perceived. You can get a feel for the public image the company wants to convey. You can also learn top-line information that will enable you to interview at the company more intelligently.

When researching companies, look for:

- Primary and secondary products or services marketed by the company
- History of the company
- Size of the company, by employees and by revenue
- Sales and earnings reports over time
- Key competitors
- Names and profiles of top management

SELECTED PRINT AND ELECTRONIC RESOURCES FOR COMPANY RESEARCH

✓ *Dun & Bradstreet's Million Dollar Directory* (on CD-ROM as Dun's Million Dollar Disc)
✓ Hoover's Handbooks (*American Business, World Business, Emerging Companies,* et al.)
✓ Moody's Manuals
✓ *Standard & Poor's Corporations* (also on CD-ROM)
✓ *Thomas Register* (also on CD-ROM)
✓ *Ward's Business Directory of Private and Public Companies* (also online)

Selected online resources for company research:

✓ Companies Online: www.companiesonline.com
✓ Company Sleuth: www.companysleuth.com
✓ Corporate Information: www.corporateinformation.com
✓ Hoover's Online: www.hoovers.com

The human factor

No matter how much factual information you gather, and regardless of where it comes from, you'll need to synthesize it and enrich it with the insights and perspectives only people can provide. That's why networking and its offshoot, informational interviewing, are so invaluable to the research process. Without the color and texture of human insight, information is one-dimensional.

The most effective, beneficial research consists of the synthesis of information gathered from traditional media and online resources, and the wisdom and impressions of experienced people.

If you're considering a significant change of career direction, the conversations you have with people will be perhaps the strongest influence on your choice. You will learn, by talking with people who are established in the profession or industry you're considering, about the benefits, drawbacks and potential opportunities you're facing. You will also gain knowledge of the profession, industry or company that is based in firsthand experience, not impersonal factual information.

Information interviewing can help you develop a tremendous amount of insight about organizations, industries, and professions. It will also help you build of network of professional contacts. For an in-depth guide to techniques and tips in this key area, check out *Information Interviewing* by Martha Stoodley (Ferguson, 1997).

■ **There's no substitute** *for the wisdom and insights of experienced people.*

> **DEFINITION**
>
> Information interviewing *means setting up interviews with people simply to seek their insight. No job is on the line, so you can both be more relaxed. The alumni association of your university can be a good way to find people you might want to meet this way.*

Developing your marketing plan

ONCE YOU'VE completed the first and largest segment of your job-search research, you'll be in a position to write your marketing plan.

It's essential that you develop a sound marketing plan, because it will serve as the blueprint for your job search.

Another way to look at your marketing plan is as the equivalent of a business plan for a startup enterprise. It will help you steer your campaign.

Five key areas

What goes into an effective marketing plan? Basically, the conclusions you draw from the earliest stages of your research. Your marketing plan reflects your ideal choices in five key areas:

- Geographic location
- Industry
- Companies
- Functional area
- Job titles

You will need to prioritize these five key areas. Be clear about your most important consideration in identifying and pursuing targets. For example, if you decide that you do not wish to commute more than 25 miles to work under any circumstances, your marketing plan will consist of only target companies within that radius.

Consider your options

You will also need to develop options within the five key areas. Try to identify three principal industries you might target. Within each, identify 15 companies you could approach. If possible, identify an alternative functional area to pursue (although your choice of functional area is often a result of your profession – accountant, for instance, or editor).

Then, identify several possible roles, or job titles, that you might want to pursue. In the functional area of Human Resources Management, for example, you may wish to investigate roles in staff development, training, recruitment, and compensation, based on your experience and areas of expertise.

What are you offering?

Your marketing plan must also include an outline of the conditions you're seeking in a job, and an outline of what you have to offer. Remember, a job search is like the sales process: both involve demonstrating benefits persuasively. You must be able to communicate how you will contribute and add value to your target companies.

Be very clear about the skills and abilities you want to hold out as your most marketable qualities.

Don't make the mistake of highlighting expertise that you don't want to use in your next job (or the job after that).

So if you're the world's best typist, but you don't want to type anymore, don't even mention that skill. Refer back to your self-assessment exercises to review your conclusions about what you will bring to the table.

What else is in your plan?

Other sections of your marketing plan can include:

1. Key contacts

2. Essential information sources (directories, publications, web sites)

3. Required reading (trade publications, business periodicals)

4. Appropriate search firms or agencies

5. Planned approaches (networking, direct mail, Internet)

6. Schedule of activities (first steps, follow-up initiatives, next steps)

■ **If you really** *want that job, you need to develop your persuasive skills – why not try them out on a colleague or friend?*

Your marketing plan will evolve as your job search advances. Don't expect to write it once and then lay it aside. Like so many other parts of managing your career effectively, your job search marketing plan is a work in progress. Try to remember that as you write your plan for the first time, and don't be reluctant to revise and recast it as your search unfolds. You will be more focused, and your search will be more effective.

■ **Networking is a fantastic way** *of making contacts, so phone that person you have never dared to until now!*

A simple summary

✓ To manage your job search effectively, you'll need to implement a series of systematic initiatives and follow-up activities that will eventually lead you from where you are now to your first day in a new job.

✓ An efficient workspace is critical to an efficient job search campaign. Essential campaign tools include a telephone and answering machine, calendars and appointment listings, an address file, stationery, business cards, and a filing system.

✓ An effective job search campaign is like an effective sales campaign. It's up to you to know and convincingly describe the qualities and benefits of the product and service you're selling – yourself.

✓ Gathering and using information effectively will give you a tremendous advantage throughout your job search campaign. Plan to tap into a variety of resources in print, on line, and through information interviews.

✓ A marketing plan is the blueprint for your job search. It summarizes the conclusions and decisions you reach through your research, and serves as a rudder for the progress of your job search campaign.

Chapter 16

Presenting Yourself in Print

I F YOU'RE LIKE MOST PEOPLE, writing your résumé is not at the top of your list of favorite things to do. But there's no escaping the fact that your résumé is an essential career management tool. It's in your best interest to have an up-to-date version no matter where you are in your career. If you're planning a job search, you need one fast!

In this chapter...

✓ Your résumé: an essential career management tool

✓ What your résumé does for you

✓ Paper vs. electronic ✓ Résumé formats

✓ What goes into a résumé?

✓ Résumé no-no's ✓ Writing your résumé

✓ Tips for developing an electronic résumé

✓ About cover letters

YOU DON'T NEED TO BE A PILOT TO BE A HIGHFLIER, WITH AN IMPRESSIVE RÉSUMÉ YOU'RE ON YOUR WAY!

Your résumé: an essential career management tool

IF YOU'RE GOING to launch a job search campaign, you must have a résumé. You will use it in several different ways, and with many different types of contacts. You may revise your résumé once or twice as you move forward, or you may tailor it to each search initiative you undertake.

Love it, hate it

You will probably develop a love-hate relationship with your résumé. You may trust in it one day, and lose all confidence in it the next. If you're like most career-minded people, you will have a lot of yourself and your identity bound up in your résumé.

All of this is understandable when you stop to think about why people use résumés – to get jobs. Finding a job is hard work. It demands lots of time, energy, and emotion. It can be very stressful, because it's a high-stakes activity: either you win big, or you lose out. And because the résumé is such an essential job search tool, planning and writing it typically trigger unhealthy doses of anxiety and stress.

■ **Don't be afraid** *of your résumé: If you put in the effort you will benefit from the results.*

Just do it

Those feelings can lead to procrastination about getting your résumé done. Chances are, you have neither the time nor the inclination to procrastinate (well, at least not the time). If you've committed to a job search, you want to get it moving and get yourself out in the marketplace as soon as possible.

Don't allow your résumé, or your lack of one, to get in your way. Get it done, and get on with your search.

Most people tend to feel that their résumé has to be the ultimate document – powerful, persuasive, unassailable, thoroughly enticing, and completely convincing. With standards like those, who wouldn't feel put off by the prospect of writing one? The truth is, your résumé will take on all of those characteristics if you give it the thought and effort it deserves – no more, and no less. In a job search, it's natural to want to demonstrate that you're the best candidate your interviewers have seen.

If you approach the task of writing your résumé with the idea that it has to be the best résumé the world has ever seen, you'll never get it finished.

What your résumé does for you

HERE ARE SOME *key ideas to keep in mind as you develop your résumé and put it out there in the job marketplace. These will enable you to shape and keep a realistic, useful perspective about the role of the résumé in finding a job and managing your career.*

Your résumé is simply a tool

Even though you will use it to pursue existing job opportunities, your résumé is not going to get you a job.

Only you can attract a job offer. Your résumé will serve as a bridge to conversations and interviews that may eventually lead to a job, but no one will offer you work based on a document alone.

Your résumé should open doors. If it stimulates enough interest on the part of whoever's reading it to want to meet you in person, your résumé is working as hard as it can. Think of it as an ad for you. If the ad prompts a prospective buyer to check out more about the product (you), it's done its job.

Your résumé is a conversation starter

Many people feel that a résumé has to provide, in a compelling and persuasive way, all the details about everything they've ever done. It doesn't. Your résumé has to provide only enough information to make contacts and interviewers want to know more about you. The details, subtleties, and nuances of your career should come out in personal conversations, not your résumé. Think of the difference between watching coming attractions and watching the movie itself: Good highlights make the larger product seem irresistible.

■ **Study your résumé:** *Interviewers will be sure to ask you questions based on the information you provided.*

During a personal conversation or interview, your résumé can serve as a roadmap. Typically, hiring managers or human resources professionals will keep your résumé in front of them as they conduct the interview (sometimes reading it as you speak). When that's the case, the information contained in it will provide a context for the conversation. If it contains highlights, you'll be able to describe details and finer points in a colorful, animated way.

■ **If asked questions** *about your résumé, be enthusiastic yet informative when answering.*

There are many ways to develop a résumé that works

One of the ideas about résumé writing that provokes great anxiety is that there are very strict rules and guidelines to follow, and that if you inadvertently break one, you won't get a job. That's nonsense.

The truth of the matter is that there's no single formula for representing yourself in a résumé.

There are some components of information that belong in every résumé, and there are some résumé formats that are customary and even expected. But there are innumerable ways to package the information that your résumé will present. Basically, your résumé is a document that showcases you and your career achievements. It should also capture and reflect some hints about your personality.

Make it your goal to be remembered

To be most effective, your résumé has to create quick and lasting impressions.

It has to work fast, like a seductive music video. That doesn't mean it should misrepresent you, distort any information or misstate facts. It means you need to be careful about what you want your résumé to emphasize, what you want it to imply, and how you want the reader to remember you.

If you want to heighten your chances of attracting interest and getting interviews, your résumé should portray you in a

Trivia...

You're going to be shocked when you learn how much time the average reader devotes to a first look at a résumé. It's less than ten seconds. If a reader is not captured by an impression or a bit of information during that span, the résumé will likely be trashed. If your résumé hooks and reels in the reader immediately, you can expect that he or she will spend slightly more time reading your document more carefully – about a minute. By then, the résumé has either succeeded or failed at generating interest in meeting you.

memorable way. Whether it's through your choice of language, the length or brevity of the document, its design and layout, or the way in which it organizes and presents information about you, your résumé should work to set you apart from the crowd – without reflecting poorly on your reputation or your qualifications for the job.

Be original

Often, the best way to be memorable is to be original. A bold résumé that takes chances and defies convention will not be convincing to everyone who sees it. But it's a good bet that a bold résumé will be remembered by many more people than it turns off.

One way to develop a résumé that's both memorable and persuasive is to look at many different samples, and then come up with something you haven't seen.

There are innumerable résumé resources for you to access, both in print and electronically. Find a book or software package that contains many different résumé samples. Be sure a number of the samples reflect your career level – that is, roughly the equivalent number of years in the workforce and roughly the equivalent educational background. (It's not necessary to locate a résumé sample that describes the same career background or objectives as yours.)

■ **If you were** *the employer and you received a résumé like yours, would you be impressed?*

NOTABLE RESOURCES ON RÉSUMÉS:

■ *Building a Great Résumé,* by Kate Wendleton (Five O'Clock Books, 1997)
■ *101 Quick Tips for a Dynamite Résumé*, by Richard Fein (Impact, 1999)
■ *Résumés! Résumés! Résumés!* Third Edition (Career Press, 1997).

Several software packages offer helpful guidance on résumé development, and typically include dozens of examples. Some of the most recent include:

■ RésuméMaker (Individual Software)
■ Résumés that Work (Macmillan)
■ WinWay Résumé (WinWay)

Review the résumés to get a sense of what's being accomplished, and how. Compare and contrast the different approaches to expressing career experience, and decide which elements you like and which you don't like. Try putting yourself in the shoes of a Human Resources executive or a hiring manager looking to identify prospective candidates for an open position. Ask yourself which resumes impress you in 10 seconds or in one minute, and which ones leave you flat.

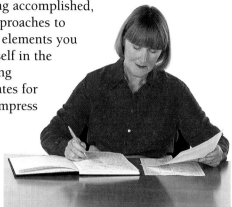

After you've reviewed a good number of samples and seen a variety of approaches, put the books aside and begin to develop your first draft. Use your own thoughts, ideas and words. Never copy from a sample or try to fit your background into someone else's format.

■ **It's wise** *to produce two different résumés, one that you can print onto paper and one you can send electronically.*

Paper vs. electronic

The Internet has transformed the way many people look for jobs, and how employers and recruiters find them. Résumés are routinely posted on job-search sites, and are passed among sites routinely. In fact, the Internet has given rise to a new phenomenon in the employment marketplace: the passive job search. People post their résumés online and wait to see what, if anything, will happen. Of course, this phenomenon greatly increases the volume of résumés received by employers and recruiters, escalates the competition among job hunters, and lengthens the odds of standing out. It's like upgrading a tropical storm into a full-blown hurricane.

How valuable is an Internet résumé?

There's no question that electronic résumés are an unavoidable part of the playing field in today's job-search marketplace. However, it's important to bear in mind that electronic résumés play only to the public job market – the sector that is accessible to everyone. They are used to respond to classified ads in print and online; to post with employment agencies and recruiters; and to register with job banks and other databases online.

As I discussed in Chapter 14, the public job market accounts for only one of every four jobs that are actually filled. When all is said and done, navigating the Internet for job opportunities is just one more way of participating in the free-for-all of looking for work in the same places where most other people look for it.

There's no escaping paper

If you're going to conduct an intensive job search, sooner or later you'll be asked to post your résumé online. You will probably want to do this, if only to cover all of your job-search bases. However, bear in mind that electronic résumés require a different composition and different features from the traditional paper résumé. (A little later in this chapter I'll give you some tips for developing an electronic résumé.) Even if you're just conducting a passive job search, sooner or later you'll need a traditional paper résumé that you can present in interviews.

The bottom line is this: To conduct an effective job search, you're going to need a traditional paper résumé.

It's going to serve you in many more job-search situations than an electronic résumé. And a traditional paper résumé provides you with a better opportunity to be distinctive and memorable. It's in your best interest to develop and write your paper résumé before you start thinking about an electronic version.

Résumé formats

ONE OF THE FIRST *decisions you'll have to make when developing your paper résumé is how you want to organize the career information you're presenting. You have three basic format options: chronological, functional, and combination. Each has distinct advantages and disadvantages. Let's take a quick look at all three.*

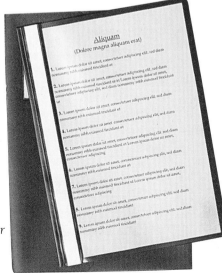

■ **The way you present** *your career information in your résumé is extremely important – the chronological résumé is the most common choice.*

The chronological résumé

The *chronological résumé* is by far the most widely used format. It's the easiest to develop, it's the safe choice in the job marketplace, and it's the format required by agencies and recruiters.

DEFINITION

A résumé that organizes career and educational history in reverse chronological order, beginning with the most recent and working back, is called a chronological résumé.

Advantages
- steady, progressive employment and achievements
- Familiar to interviewers from all backgrounds
- Serves as a compass for career discussion during interviews

Disadvantages
- Implies that your next job will be a progressive outgrowth of your most recent one (a disadvantage if you're looking for a change)
- May reveal gaps in your employment history
- Ineffective at highlighting skills and accomplishments of various career points

Consider this format if
- Your goal is a job in your present or most recent industry, or a related one
- You're looking to advance along a vertical career path – that is, to take on more of what you've been doing up to this point
- You have a steady employment history without a record of job-hopping every few months

The functional résumé

The *functional résumé* is the format of choice for individuals who are planning and seeking a major career change. It places emphasis on transferable abilities and plays down specific employers, job titles, and dates.

DEFINITION

A résumé that organizes career and educational history by functional areas, drawn from the entire span of one's work experiences, is called a functional résumé.

Advantages
- Highlights skills and competencies that can apply across industries and organizations
- Portrays your strengths as a sum total at present, not confined to particular jobs or career situations
- Downplays or hides gaps in employment history – and your age

- **When writing your résumé,** *emphasize your accomplishments.*

Disadvantages
- Suggests to some interviewers that there's something about your background you want to hide
- Less effective for points of reference in interview situations
- Agencies and recruiters will usually not accept it

Consider this format if
- Your current career goals do not match your work history or you have little actual experience in the area you're pursuing
- You have gaps or inconsistencies in your employment history
- You're re-entering the workforce after a long absence, or you'd like to steer clear of any clues about your age

DEFINITION

A résumé that organizes career and educational history by emphasizing functional experience within a reverse chronological order is called a combination résumé.

The combination résumé

As you might expect, the *combination résumé* synthesizes elements of the chronological and functional formats. It carries the impact of the functional résumé, yet typically does not put off interviewers who are accustomed to the chronological format.

The combination résumé is the most flexible format of all, because there are many ways to synthesize your career and educational information. One way is to lead with your most recent employer and create functional areas of achievement under that umbrella (for example, under the employment heading of Acme Corporation you would list your accomplishments within functional areas like Project Management, Market Research, and Customer Service). Another way is to lead with a list of credentials and accomplishments, and follow this with a chronological listing of employment, volunteer work, and education.

Advantages
- Showcases competencies and skills within a particular employment context
- May demonstrate growth and development within a particular organization or industry
- Can play up your abilities as well as your credentials, such as job titles and the organizations you've worked for

Disadvantages
- The most difficult format to develop and execute convincingly
- Typically lacks consistency in sections
- May imply you're going to extraordinary lengths to conceal some information about your background

- **Even austronauts must** *submit résumés when being considered as candidates for space expeditions.*

Consider this format if:
- You've had a long tenure with a single employer
- You're planning to leverage your experience in one industry to find a job in another
- You wish to draw attention to the places you've worked as well as what you accomplished there

Just out of school

If you're a student making the transition from academic life to Planet Work, there's no need to pretend on your résumé that you're more experienced than you really are. Your résumé should begin with a section on your educational background, then detail any experience you've gained within that context: associations, clubs, school newspaper, student theater group, and so on. If you've held part-time, temporary or seasonal jobs,

they should also be included on your résumé. That information will give prospective employers clues about the kinds of work you know, and some of the skills you may have already developed.

- **If you have** *just graduated, don't be tempted to exaggerate about your work experience in your résumé.*

> ### Trivia...
> *Performing artists and entertainment-industry professionals require a special kind of packaging for their career information. They compile lists of credentials, which serve as the sum of their career achievements. Actors, for instance, will list their parts in theater, film, and television, often on the back of professional portraits. Directors, too, will compile a list of credentials in the media where they've worked.*

What goes into a résumé?

THERE ARE CERTAIN *elements that you can consider required in any résumé, no matter what format you choose. There's also a wealth of optional elements that may appear in your résumé. Make your decisions about these according to your job objective, your career history, and the amount of space you have available.*

Résumé essentials

All résumés, no matter what format or medium you select, must contain at least three principal areas of information. These are the key sections of your résumé, and they are non-negotiable.

Contact information

You must say who you are and how you can be contacted. Do not label or categorize this information, just put it right at the top of your résumé. It must include:

- Name
- Mailing address
- Telephone numbers: work, residence, wireless and/or service, as applicable
- Fax number, if applicable
- E-mail address, if you have one (if you don't, get one)

Work history

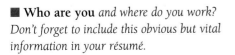

This is the body of your résumé – the part that takes up the most space and sells you the hardest.

Prospective employers pay the most attention to the work history section.

Depending on your choice of formats, you will organize this section according to the chronology of your work history, the functional areas of your expertise, or a combination of the two. If your résumé should not take on one of the three traditional formats, your work history might consist of lists of credentials: productions you've been involved in, acting jobs you've done, clients you've served, projects you've worked on, and so on.

Label this part of your résumé to cue readers and interviewers. Some suggested labels for the body of your résumé, depending on your career situation, are:

- Summary of Experience
- Professional Background
- Career History
- Summary of Accomplishments
- Employment History
- Career Highlights
- Selected Accomplishments

- **Who are you** *and where do you work? Don't forget to include this obvious but vital information in your résumé.*

Education and training

This section follows the body, and often concludes the résumé. It provides information about your formal education and/or professional training. The farther in time away from your educational credentials you are, the less emphasis they should receive. Here are 11 tips on listing information about your educational background:

1. List your highest level of education first, and work backward.

2. If you have specialized or professional training that relates directly to your job objective, list it first.

3. If you've gone to graduate school, also include your undergraduate credentials.

4. If you have a college degree (bachelor's or associate's), do not list your high school credentials.

5. If you did not acquire a college degree, consider listing the curriculum of any courses you pursued.

6. If your formal education did not extend beyond your high school degree, list that credential first.

7. If you did not complete high school, list the curriculum of any courses you took.

8. List your GPA only if it's less than three years since you've been in school.

9. Include any honors and awards you may want the world to know about.

10. Do not list fraternities or sororities. Not everyone looks favorably on them.

11. If you're a student making the transition to the work force for the first time, your educational credentials belong at the top of your résumé.

■ **If you attended** *any courses provided by your work, be sure to describe them in your résumé.*

Optional sections of a résumé

There are many kinds of information that may be included in your résumé. Choose to include them or not based on these criteria:

■ How you want to be remembered in the workplace
■ How far along in your career you are
■ How people in the field you're pursuing like to perceive serious, career-minded individuals like yourself
■ How much space you have after completing the three key sections

Optional sections of your résumé include:

Objective

Recommended only if you are pursuing a very specific, focused job, or if you have limited or no experience in the workplace. Otherwise, an objective might pigeonhole you and cause résumé readers to exclude you from consideration for any other positions.

Summary

The summary is probably the most powerful component of any résumé.

An Objective describes where you like to be headed in your career, but a Summary describes where you've been and what your experience amounts to. It's a profile. It does the work of a headline on a newspaper.

A good summary statement provides an overview of the information that follows in the body of your résumé. It's a positioning statement that grabs the reader's attention, piques his or her interest and paves the way to more detailed information about you.

If you choose to include a summary statement on your résumé, you can label it in several ways:

■ Summary
■ Summary of Qualifications
■ Professional Profile
■ Career Profile
■ Overview

■ **Don't automatically include** *an objective on your résumé. It is only necessary if you are applying for a very specific position.*

Or, you can include you summary statement without labeling it at all. You can simply hang it at the top of the page, just beneath your personal information, and let it speak for itself. You may wish to consider offsetting the summary statement with rules or italicized type.

Special skills

Especially appropriate if your career centers on very specialized expertise. You may wish to list, for example, computer hardware or software knowledge, or language proficiencies.

Certificates and special training

List these if they relate directly to your career objective. If they enhance your stature or position in the job marketplace, include them.

Associations and affiliations

Include current (not past) membership or active involvement in any professional or civic associations that relate to your career focus or job objective. Be very selective about which associations you list. Avoid any that might be controversial or antagonistic to any readers of your résumé.

Awards and recognition

List any career-related awards you've garnered, but don't go overboard. It's nice to be singled out for recognition, but you don't want to put yourself across as superhuman. Also, consider making a reference to your awards in your summary statement and providing fuller details in this section.

Military history

If you've served in the military, you may wish to include your credentials in your résumé. Briefly outline your tour of duty and include accomplishments, awards, and citations.

■ **Make sure that your** *résumé gives details of everything you believe to be relevant to the position that you are appluing for.*

INTERNET

www.provenresumes.com

This site has very possibly more information about résumé writing than you could ever use. It includes listings of workshops and resources, and booklets that you can download immediately.

INTERNET

www.4resumes.com

At this specialized site from the 4Anything Network, click to access résumé writing tips, guidelines, postings, coaches and more.

Professional development

List any courses, seminars, workshops, or training experiences that relate to your career focus, or recent positions held. If you include this section in your résumé, it should immediately precede or follow the Education section.

■ **If you have attended** *any training schemes or workshops, be sure to include them in your résumé.*

Résumé no-no's

AS YOU'VE SEEN, you have lots of choices and options in developing an effective and distinctive résumé. There are few hard-and-fast rules. However, there's still some of that old conventional wisdom about résumé writing that's hanging around like humidity after a thunderstorm. It's time to blow it away forever.

Here are some suggestions on what to leave out of your résumé if you want it to work for you:

1. Don't label your résumé with the word résumé. Your reader will know what it is.

2. Don't include salary history or information. Save that for personal conversations and interviews.

3. Don't include personal statistics other than the contact information you need at the top. Leave out your age, height, weight, health, marital status, and parenthood status. It is illegal for prospective employers to ask for that information, so there's certainly no need to volunteer it.

4. Don't include references, or write that they are available on request. That's obvious. When an employer wants to contact your references, he or she will ask you for them.

5. Don't include testimonials or tributes from other people. They will make you seem like you're either selling too hard or in need of an extra push.

6. Don't include your photograph unless you're an actor or a model. It's illegal to make hiring decisions based on looks alone, so don't invite an employer to break the law.

7. Don't include hobbies or interests unless they support your job objective. Save these for networking and interviews, and use them to enrich your conversations.

Writing your résumé

NOW THAT WE'VE *covered the formats and options that are available to you in developing your résumé, you might want to take a crack at the writing. Here's a list of key points to consider as you do.*

Fifteen tips for developing an effective résumé

1. Describe accomplishments, not responsibilities. What you have done in the past gives employers clues and expectations about what you can do for them now and in the future.

2. Quantify your accomplishments wherever possible. Use numbers, dollar figures, and percentages to dramatize your accomplishments and convey their significance. Describe revenues, profits, savings of costs or time, number of projects, number of subordinates or team members, and so on.

3. Give your résumé the length that's appropriate for your career situation and for the industry you're in. It's not true that all résumés must fit onto one page, and especially not if you have to use a tiny type size to squeeze it in. It's generally not a good idea to exceed two pages (except if it's the electronic version of your résumé), unless subsequent pages are lists or addenda.

4. Limit the scope of your résumé to the past 10 to 15 years, unless there's something extraordinary about you or your background that happened before that. In general, people want to know where you are and what your career focus is right now, along with the some of the accomplishments that got you there.

5. You can refer to early career episodes and experience with a general statement that wraps up the body of your résumé, such as "Previous experience included increasingly responsible positions in sales and marketing," or "Prior career experiences included teaching elementary school and publishing a successful desktop newsletter."

6. Don't use "I" or any other pronouns in writing your résumé. Write your accomplishments using powerful action verbs.

■ **Mention relevant previous jobs**, *but ideally concentrate on what you are doing now to pursue your career!*

7. Don't write complete sentences. Look for ways to economize on words. Use short, bulleted statements that pack some punch and can be easily absorbed by the reader.

8. Draft your résumé first, then revise it several times. All good writing happens in the rewriting. You won't get it perfect the first time.

9. Make sure the writing in your final version is perfect. There's no excuse for typographical errors, misspellings or faulty grammar. These are deadly when they appear in a résumé, because they reflect poorly on you. Don't rely exclusively on the spell-check feature of your computer. If spelling and grammar are not your strong suits, get someone else to bring a fresh proofreading eye to your résumé.

■ **Never write** *the final draft of your résumé by hand – it will look much more professional if you use a word processor.*

10. Produce your résumé on a computer or word processor, and print it using a laser, ink-jet or letter-quality printer. Résumés produced on a typewriter are no longer acceptable. Don't even think about writing it by hand.

11. In designing your résumé, use lots of white space. It makes the document simpler to read and navigate. A one-page résumé that has crowded, dense blocks of type is less pleasing (and less effective) than a two-page résumé with a breezier feel.

12. Don't mix typefaces unless you're a trained graphic designer. Most people prefer consistency in type choices, which usually makes for a résumé that easier to read.

13. Use boldface and italics sparingly in your résumé. Be consistent in using display techniques to offset information. Words that appear in all capital letters or underlined (except for résumé section headings) tend to be distracting eyesores.

14. Print your résumé on a high-quality paper, preferably a 20-pound bond or greater. Most résumés should be printed on white, off-white, or beige paper. Stay away from gray. Use other colors only if they're appropriate to your industry, never just to stand out from the competition.

15. Remember that your résumé is a work in progress. Don't hesitate to revise your résumé to fit your objectives if they shift or change as you move forward in your job search.

Tips for developing an electronic résumé

AS WE'VE SEEN *earlier in this chapter, electronic résumés are becoming increasingly common. The Internet has had a huge impact on the employment marketplace, and on job search strategies. It will continue to exert influence on how people look for jobs – and how employers seek candidates to fill positions.*

■ **Technological** *knowledge is vital these days, so impress potential employers with your electronic résumé.*

Unless you are relying strictly on networking to uncover your next job, you will eventually have to forward your résumé by e-mail or post it on an online job site, or both. When you come to that bridge, don't cross it with your traditional paper résumé; save that for presentation purposes in snail-mailings and especially in interviews. Instead, adapt your résumé into a second version that you'll use exclusively online.

For optimal effectiveness, electronic résumés require you to follow special guidelines about length, format, writing, and design.

Length

Most traditional paper résumés are one- or two-page documents. Those lengths provide a comfortable framework for most people who will read your résumé, and refer to it during interviews. But electronic résumés generally take the human factor out of the equation. They are scanned by information-seeking computers that do not have short attention spans. That means your document can be as long as you like.

Writing style

Résumé-tracking computers scan for information about your skills, expertise and credentials, rather than the action-oriented accomplishments that are the core of your traditional résumé.

So for your electronic version, you should use language in a different way. Focus on nouns – not action verbs, as in the traditional résumé. Instead of writing "audited," reframe your information to include the word "auditor." Rather than writing "managed," use "management." Stay away from "trained," but definitely include "training." You get the picture.

VIP

List credentials liberally, along with the software packages you know well or moderately well. Remember, the more information you include in your electronic résumé, the greater the likelihood of scoring a hit with employers' tracking software.

Design considerations

Your electronic résumé requires special attention to design – or the lack of it. Your online résumé will sometimes be seen by people as well as computers, so you need to make sure it will look good on a computer screen. Many professionals recommend using a *sans-serif* typeface (such as Arial, Helvetica, or Tahoma) to facilitate scanning and eliminate distractions. You can use upper and lower cases freely, but don't use bold face type or bullets in your electronic résumé. These can produce garbled text on some computers. Italicized text is less risky, but use it sparingly.

DEFINITION

The little "feet" that appear on the top and bottom of printed characters such as the T and E are called serifs. When none of the letters in a typeface have those feet, it's called a sans-serif ("sans" means without) typeface.

All text on your electronic résumé should appear flush left, not centered.

Also, do not justify the text. Think of your electronic résumé as the stripped-down version (except for its length). It should contain only text, unadorned and unencumbered. You'll have to work carefully to provide the simplicity that electronic résumés demand.

About the only design element called for by traditional and electronic résumés alike is space. Your résumé requires plenty of it to facilitate scanning. So remember to give your electronic version plenty of room – at least as much as your paper presentation version.

ONLINE GUIDELINES

For additional information and guidelines on developing and posting your online résumé, check out *Cyberspace Résumé Kit* by Mary B. Nemnich and Fred E. Jandt (JIST Works, 1999). It outlines many ways to tap into Internet job-search techniques, and provides colorful details on a host of cyber-résumé topics. In addition, it features listings and ratings of more than 80 Internet résumé sites.

About cover letters

NO DISCUSSION *of résumés would be complete without at least a few words about cover letters. Normally, the two documents go hand in hand.*

When you're sending a résumé by traditional snail mail, you must enclose a cover letter – that's non-negotiable.

When you're faxing a résumé, it's advisable to send a top sheet or, preferably, a top sheet and a cover letter. If you're sending your résumé electronically, it's sometimes recommended that you attach a note, although many résumé sites ask for just the electronic résumé.

What a good cover letter does

Cover letters are more challenging than they seem. A good, effective cover letter is not merely a simple announcement that a résumé is enclosed. Instead, it is an enticement to read the résumé. Cover letters offer you an opportunity to grab the reader's attention right away, and draw him or her to the career information detailed in your résumé. What's more, a cover letter provides you with a chance to make an impression by talking to the reader in conversational language, rather than in the clipped, action-packed verbs of the accompanying résumé.

Most important of all, a cover letter is an opportunity to present yourself as you wish to be remembered.

In other words, it's a chance for you to show something of your personality. Your language and your use of words can be informal or elegant, serious or lighthearted, incisive or questioning, direct or roundabout. It gives the reader clues about who you are, and a context for the information that's detailed on the accompanying résumé.

■ **In the cover letter** *you must persuade the employer in a concise manner that you are the right person for the job.*

Goals met

What work does the cover letter really do?
A good one can accomplish several goals:

- Target your résumé to a strategic contact
- Pique reader interest in your résumé
- Describe your interest in and enthusiasm for a particular job or an organization
- Demonstrate your savvy about an employer's needs
- Highlight some of your special qualifications or career accomplishments
- Dramatize the fit between your background and an employment situation
- Set the stage for ongoing communication

Art and science

Effective cover letters require a canny blend of art and science. Capturing your personality, developing reader interest in your background, and enticing him or her to review your résumé is the artful part. Following accepted letter-writing format, and using language and grammar correctly, is the science part. Most résumé-writing guidebooks and resources contain sections on cover letters, too. Check them out the same way you investigate the résumés themselves: See what each one accomplishes, get a feel for how you would make it your own, and then move on. Never copy sample letters or adapt template letters to your own needs. Look to them only for guidance.

■ **Don't be afraid to** *go it alone. You should not need guidance for every single step.*

■ **A good cover letter** *will favorably predispose the reader to look at your résumé and consider you for an interview!*

Your writing skills

Of course, effective letter writing requires effective writing skills. Not everyone has them. If you're not comfortable putting words together to express ideas, it's not likely that you'll develop a knack for good writing overnight. (However, writing is like a muscle: The more you exercise it, the more well developed it becomes.) You may wish to enlist the help of someone who's more comfortable with the printed word. Take a stab at putting your thoughts down in rough-draft form, then turn to a friend or colleague for input and editing.

Simple writing guidelines

Whether you're composing a cover letter, a fax cover sheet, or an e-mail cover file, follow a few simple guidelines about communicating in print:

1. Write for the ear, not the eye. In other words, write as you would speak. Read your writing aloud, and if it sounds unnatural begin again. You may wish to speak your thoughts, even mentally, before you attempt to capture them in print.

2. Be concise. The best writing has a snappy, breezy pace that's easy on a reader's attention span.

3. Structure your writing. Think of a letter or a memo as a story with a beginning, middle, and end. The progression from one section to another should be fluid and natural.

4. Draw from your résumé. It's okay to borrow some of the language from your résumé, to dramatize selected points about yourself or your background.

5. Remember cover letters are vehicles for communication. They offer you opportunities to form positive impressions, and to be persuasive about your qualities and qualifications.

Ryman
SUSPENSION
FILE F.CAP

■ **It's so important** *to be organized – it's essential you keep a copy of every letter you send so you can refer back to it.*

6. Always proofread your writing. Do not rely exclusively on the spell- and grammar-check features of your software program. Although these features are useful for picking up misspellings and some grammatical errors, they cannot track all typographical errors or misused words. That requires a human touch.

7. Keep a copy of every letter you write, either on paper or in a computer file. It will refresh your memory about your exchange with a contact, and document the substance and history of your communication. You may also be able to borrow phrases from one letter to suit another.

Remember: always revise your letter or memo. Remember, all good writing happens in the rewriting.

A simple summary

✔ Your résumé is an essential career management tool. Think of it as a tool to facilitate your search, not the ultimate document about your life and times.

✔ The most memorable résumés are often the ones that break with convention and make a distinctive presentation of career information.

✔ Certain categories of core information belong in every resume, but you have many choices about what other information to present for added personality.

✔ The three traditional résumé formats chronological, functional, and combination – are workable options for most job hunters.

✔ Even if you eventually decide you need an electronic version of your résumé, you will always need a traditional paper résumé.

✔ A cover letter or memo should always accompany your résumé. Cover letters provide you with an opportunity to form lasting impressions and draw attention to the more detailed career information in your résumé.

Chapter 17

Presenting Yourself in Person

A BIG PART OF MANAGING YOUR CAREER is hunting down a series of suitable work situations. That means looking for a job is an activity you'll likely engage in not just once, but many times during your career. Does that idea excite you, or exhaust you?

In this chapter...

✓ Why job interviews make you nervous

✓ Thinking constructively about interviews

✓ Strategies for effective interviewing

✓ Different kinds of job interviews

✓ Preparing for interviews

✓ Your career commercial

✓ Your OARs: showcasing key skills

✓ Basic guidelines for effective interviewing

Why job interviews make you nervous

WHAT IS A JOB INTERVIEW, *anyway, and how is it different from a social conversation, a networking occasion and an information-gathering meeting? All of them focus on an exchange of ideas and information, usually between two individuals. All involve verbal communication. Some of these exchanges are less formal and more relaxed than others. But by nature, the interview has one major characteristic that sets it apart from other kinds of career conversations: There's a job at stake.*

They have what you want

In typical interview situations, it's normal to feel like you're at a disadvantage. After all, your interviewer has something that you want – a job. Most people experience the interview as an all-or-nothing contest: If you're successful, you land the job, and if not you go away empty-handed. There's no middle ground. So even before the event begins, you're likely to feel pressure to be persuasive and convincing enough to win what you've come for.

But the stress of interviews goes beyond that, and hooks into another common fear that most people find extremely unpleasant – fear of rejection.

By design, interviews are judgmental. You're being scrutinized not only for your experience and job qualifications, but for your manner, conviviality, wit, appearance, confidence, modesty, and a host of other qualities that are never addressed but are inevitably noticed. You may have impeccable career credentials, yet fail miserably in an interview because you didn't "click" with the other person in the room. Not only do you walk away without the prize, but you may feel like you were not qualified for it. No wonder interviews are stressful!

■ **Remember the interview** *is a two-way process – wanting the job is as important as the employer wanting you!*

Thinking constructively about interviews

LET'S FACE IT, *a job interview will never be relaxing. But you can choose to think about an interview in constructive terms that may reduce your anxiety and enable you to manage the event effectively. That means making the interview work on your terms as well as your interviewer's. Let's take a look at just what that means.*

■ **Be honest with yourself –** *does the job fulfill your expectations?*

You can check them out

Of course, employers use the interview situation to check you out, but most people lose sight of the fact that the interview is also an occasion for you to check out the employer. You can (and shoulbe checking the requirements of the position, along with the organization, its culture, its personalities, and the prospect of blending in with all of these.

Use the interview situation to form a vision of what your working life might look and feel like for a long time to come. Then ask yourself if that vision feels right for you.

Did they impress you?

An interview or series or interviews will provide you with information and provoke impressions that will lead you to one of these conclusions:

■ You and your qualifications match up with the position that's open
■ You and your qualifications do not match with the position that's open
■ You feel compatible with the organization, but not in the position you're interviewing for
■ You do not feel compatible with the organization or the people who work there

If you're not sure how you feel about a job opportunity after the first interview, you need to continue the process and seek more information that will enable you to draw a solid conclusion. Remember that managing your career effectively requires you to make thoughtful, considered decisions about the work situations you choose to become involved in. Don't yield all the power to the people on the other side of the desk. Interview situations are judgmental, but keep the judgments moving in both directions.

309

Strategies for effective interviewing

JOB INTERVIEWS *call for the very best self-presentation you can muster. If you haven't interviewed for a long time, or if you're about to embark on the interviewing phase of your first job search, chances are you're somewhat anxious. Most people fear being confronted with tough, even brutal questions from their interviewers. Other interviewing phobias include going blank, losing focus, appearing tentative rather than forceful, and giving "wrong" answers to questions about skills, qualifications, or accomplishments.*

■ **It doesn't matter** *whether you are applying for a job as a waiter or as a brain surgeon, you should always be well-prepared for the interview.*

Was it memorable?

The truth is that relatively few interviews turn out as badly as job candidates envision they will. A far likelier outcome is that the interview will not be at all terrible, yet not really memorable in any way.

As a job candidate, your best goal for successful interviewing is not to avoid a disastrous event, but to ensure an extraordinary one.

Five key strategies

How do you accomplish that? With five key interviewing strategies:

1. Know yourself and your professional attributes, and be able to describe how you can make contributions and add value.

2. Understand the interpersonal dynamics of interviewing.

3. Prepare carefully for each and every interview.

4. Be meticulous about follow-up activities, such as letters and phone calls.

5. Maintain an affirmative, constructive point of view during interviews – and their aftermath.

Different kinds of job interviews

■ **Be prepared:** *There are various types of interviews and interviewing techniques!*

DON'T EXPECT your job search to begin and end with a single interview. Keep in mind that job search itself is a process, and the interviewing stage is a process within the process. You won't have all of your interviews at once. What's more, it's likely that your pursuit of any job opportunity will involve several interviews, with people from a variety of areas and at different levels. And, in the larger context of your job search campaign, it's likely that you'll encounter several different kinds of interviews. It's helpful to sort out some of their similarities and differences, so let's take a brief look at each of them.

Interviews with human resources managers

Human Resources (HR) professionals are often (but not always) the first interviewers you'll meet. It's important to understand that they are *gatekeepers*. When organizations are hiring, HR departments typically manage the process. It's their job to control the influx of candidates and narrow it to a more manageable pool. Also, HR managers are often the first point of contact when job hunters make unsolicited approaches to an organization.

> ### DEFINITION
> *It's the HR department's job to control the influx of job candidates and narrow it to a more manageable pool. It's their responsibility to open or (more typically) close the gates on your candidacy, so they are often referred to as gatekeepers.*

■ **Impress the company's** *human resource's person and you'll be one step closer to getting an interview with your potential next boss.*

A general focus

Because HR managers are required to manage the hiring process in many or all areas within an organization, their technical knowledge and expertise is usually limited.

HR managers should know a little about a lot of areas, not a lot about any particular area. What all this means for you as a job candidate is that interviews with them tend to be very general.

Typically, they will focus on your employment history, your career thinking, your personal attributes, and some general knowledge of the functional area you are pursuing.

That is not to say that interviewing with an HR manager will be a cakewalk. Keep in mind that HR managers are, in a very real sense, professional interviewers. They conduct dozens or hundreds of interviews each year. To move the interviewing process forward and take your candidacy to the next level, you will need to make favorable impressions about your professional qualifications and your personal qualities.

What your goals should be

In interviews with them, your goals are to present your background as substantive and accomplished, and to present yourself as a potential asset to the organization. Be careful to describe your background and accomplishments without using jargon or too much technical detail. Concentrate on conveying your professional profile, your personal attributes and your knowledge of the organization you're interviewing with.

Interviews with hiring managers

If you get past the HR department (and remember, not all interview processes begin there), the next step is to meet with the functional manager or supervisor to whom you would report. When you interview with a manager, you're interviewing with the person who could be your next boss. This kind of job interview is the most pivotal in the relationship-building process between a job hunter and a prospective employer.

■ **Be aware** *that your interviewer is potentially your next boss – striking-up a rapport .is vital!*

VIP

In effect, when you interview with a hiring manager, you're already on the job — because it's then that the relationship between you and your next boss begins (and sometimes ends). It's at this stage that most employment deals are made or broken.

Let's get technical

Unlike HR professionals, hiring managers are likely to focus on your technical expertise and proficiencies. Of course your prospective next boss is interested to know who you are and what your personal style is like. But he or she is also keenly interested in what you can do. For that reason, your goal in interviewing with hiring managers is to describe your career accomplishments in a compelling way that underscores the value you will bring to your interviewer's organization.

■ **Getting the job** *depends upon who you are and what you can do for the company.*

Focus on your accomplishments

Hiring managers want to know if you've got what it takes to provide solutions and fill existing or potential needs. To convince them that you can, focus on how you've made a difference at work in the past. Remember to demonstrate what you will bring to the table. You can do this by describing your accomplishments in concise, convincing short stories. Think of them as the equivalent of verbal snapshots. To be most effective with a hiring manager, think of yourself as a storyteller. Describe the ways you've made an impact in previous work situations. By inference, you'll be describing some of the ways you'll enrich your interviewer's organization now and in the future.

And finally

1. Other points to remember about interviewing with hiring managers include:

2. Learn as much as possible about existing needs and goals, so that you can present yourself as a problem solver.

Work to keep the interview conversational. Don't let it become an interrogation. Listen carefully to the interviewer's questions and ideas, respond persuasively, and ask probing questions throughout the interview.

■ **Be confident** – *the interviewer needs to know that you can make a difference.*

3 You are building a relationship. Be attentive to every personal and professional nuance in the process, especially the follow-up.

4 Find out as much as you can about next steps. Be specific, so that you're not left wondering when the next communication will take place. As your interview closes, take the initiative. Ask, "When can we continue our conversation about the position?"

Assume that your interviewer wants you to succeed. Typically, the organization has needs to be met and problems to be solved. Your interviewer is anxious to accomplish those goals as soon as possible.

Interviews with senior managers and executives

A formal meeting with your prospective boss's manager may be part of the interviewing process. Typically, this kind of interview occurs after one or more interviews with the functional manager to whom you would report. The good news is this: If the functional manager recommends that you interview with one or more higher-ranking executives, the chances are good that you are well on your way to an offer.

A courtesy interview

An interview with a senior executive is often a courtesy interview. If it does go well, you may be out of there in a hurry. But the senior executive is typically expecting that it will go well, since he or she has a vote of confidence about you and your qualifications from the functional manager. Often, an interview with a senior manager or executive is a formality – a sign-off. Don't minimize its importance, but keep sight of the probability that you're close to your goal: a job offer.

■ **If the senior executive** *interviews you, you're nearly there!*

Interviews with peers

Sometimes a functional manager will want you to interview – formally or, more typically, informally – with other members of the department, division, or group. These are usually the people with whom you'd be working closely every day – your coworkers. It's an opportunity for you to present yourself in a less stressful environment than an interview with a hiring manager, and to see who you might be working with.

As in an interview with a senior executive, chances are that favorable impressions about you have been conveyed in advance. In other words, the hiring manager has talked to your prospective peers about you, and asked them to meet you and share their impressions. This kind of interview is often unstructured and more sociable, but one rule always applies:

Whatever you say and however you behave will get back to the hiring manager.

Follow their lead

Your goal in interviewing with peers is to keep things on a favorable course. Interview with peers on their terms. Follow their lead in gauging the level of formality, use of humor, disclosure, and opinion. Go where they take you. Most often, peers simply want to know what it will be like to work with you day in and day out. They can't know if you don't show them. Give them a good look at your personality – not just your job-search "game face." And take advantage of the occasion to get a better idea of how things really work in the department and in the organization.

■ **Interviews with peers** *may seem casual, but be careful what you say – you want to make the right impression!*

Interviews with a panel

Panel interviews are rare, although they are sometimes conducted in the public service and not-for-profit sectors. If you are scheduled for a panel interview, expect to meet with a mix of managers and prospective peers.

This can be tricky, because at the same time you're trying to impress each of them, they're trying to impress each other.

Expect the inquisition

A panel interview may feel like an inquisition. Your goal is the same as in any interview: to present yourself as an asset. But you must do so with skill and diplomacy, because a panel interview is a group experience. Part of what participants are looking for in this situation is a demonstration of your cooperative spirit and interpersonal skills. Answer questions thoughtfully, and direct your responses primarily to each questioner. But acknowledge the presence of the other listeners, and include them in your responses.

■ **Interviewing in numbers** *might seem threatening, but a panel interview isn't intended to be like an official interrogation.*

INTERNET

www.askthehead hunter.com

This "insider's edge on job search and hiring" is presented by Nick Corcodilos, real-life recruiter and author of Ask the Headhunter (Plume, 1997).

Interviews with search firms and agencies

Interviews with recruiters for search firms – typically called headhunters – can resemble those with Human Resources managers in that they typically focus on general information about you and your accomplishments. However, if a recruiter has extensive knowledge of your industry or business (and there are many specialists who do), the interview can resemble one with a hiring manager in that it will specific and technically focused.

Form an alliance

In interviewing with a search firm, set yourself the goals of building a relationship and forming an alliance. Remember, search firms and agencies, like human resources departments, are gatekeepers. If you interview successfully with them, they will advocate for you.

Keep your perspective

Interviewing successfully with search firms and agencies calls for some special guidelines and perspectives:

1. Be open-minded. Reputable recruiters do have assignments to fill, and there's every reason to believe, if you're talking to the right recruiter, that one or more of them could be for you.

2. Be wary. Because recruiters do have assignments to fill, you may find yourself learning about opportunities that don't feel quite right for you. Don't be bullied into pursuing them. Find out as much as you can from the recruiters about any opportunity proposed to you, and evaluate each one carefully. Pursue the opportunity only if it seems to be one you'd pursue on your own.

3. Assume that the recruiter wants you to succeed. The search firm he or she represents typically has a large commission at stake. You may be the successful candidate that will help them earn it.

■ **Don't be persuaded** *by skilled recruitment agents to take a job that doesn't feel right.*

4 Be candid about your salary requirements. Search firms need to know your compensation level in order to match you with an appropriate position. Questions about salary level cannot easily be deflected.

5 Remember that you are developing a relationship. Work to build and nurture an alliance. If a recruiter holds you and your qualifications in high regard, you can be sure they will propose your candidacy for any appropriate assignments they attract. Be attentive to every nuance in the interviewing process, especially follow-up.

SEARCH FIRM RESOURCES

For additional information and guidance on working with search firms, consult these helpful resources:

■ *The Directory of Executive Recruiters*, a reference guide published annually by Kennedy Publications
■ *Job Seeker's Guide to Executive Recruiters*, by Christopher W. Hunt & Scott A. Scanlon (John Wiley & Sons, 1997)
■ *Kennedy's Pocket Guide to Working with Executive Recruiters* (Kennedy Publications, 1996)

Preparing for interviews

GOOD PREPARATION *is at the heart of every successful interview. It's not a good strategy to simply show up. If you want to be persuasive and convincing in an interview, you must be able to demonstrate how you can contribute to the organization and add value. To accomplish that, you must be able to talk about yourself and your career accomplishments effectively.*

■ **Proper preparation**
shows — don't put it off, just do it!

You also need to present the image that's appropriate to the position you're interviewing for. You'll need to field tricky, sometimes difficult interview questions. And you will need to do engage your interviewer in a dialogue that will enable you to learn everything possible about the position that's open – and communicate why you're the right one to fill it.

Gathering information

Interview preparation has two basic components: gathering information about yourself, and gathering information about the organization you're interviewing with. If you've completed your career assessment exercises (see Chapters 5 through 8) and the career review that leads to the résumé, you've got a rich variety of information about yourself. Now you can turn your attention to learning about the organization. See Chapter 15 for more on how you learn about an industry and the organizations in it.

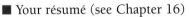

The base of knowledge you acquire will provide you with a significant strategic advantage in the interview.

You will be better prepared to ask pointed questions about the position that's open, and you will impress your interviewer with your thoroughness and your planning skills. And that's not a bad impression to make!

Your interview arsenal

Good interview preparation requires you to be thoughtful and attentive in a number of key areas. Your interview arsenal must include:

- Your résumé (see Chapter 16)
- Your career commercial (I'll get to that later in this chapter)
- Knowledge of your marketable skills and competencies (see Chapter 6)
- Awareness of your personal attributes and areas for development (see Chapter 7)
- Verbal summaries of your key accomplishments (more on this in a moment)

In addition, you must devote time and attention to personal factors that will influence the outcome of the interview:

- Grooming
- Clothing
- Manner
- Body language
- Attitude and demeanor

■ **Don't underestimate** *the power of a charming smile.*

AN IMAGE GUIDE

If you think you'd benefit from an in-depth guidance in creating the right interview and workplace image, check out *VGM's Complete Guide to Career Etiquette: From Job Search Through Career Advancement*, by Mark Satterfield (VGM Career Horizons, 1995).

You'll also find a wealth of books on interviewing strategies in the careers sections of bookstores and libraries. Among the most popular is *Knock 'em Dead: The Ultimate Job Seeker's Handbook* by Martin Yate (Adams, 1998. You can check out the website at www.knockemdead.com.

Your career commercial

A SUCCINCT, colorful career commercial is perhaps the most powerful tool you can use as a job hunter. It's critical to have one, and to be ready to use it in any interview situation. If you've been through the interview process at all, whether recently or in the past, you'll recall the moment after the introductions and the small talk when the business conversation really kicks in. You know when that moment arrives because your interviewer says, "So, tell me about yourself,"or "What's your background," or "Tell me what you do."

Your response to that all-important conversation starter will shape the image of how your interviewer remembers you.

It's important to keep in mind that, to a very large extent, people will remember you the way you tell them to remember you.

That's why it's so important to "script" your career commercial and put it to use, with some refinements and adjustments, in every interview situation.

■ **A career commercial** *can be useful without having to seem artificial and insincere.*

What is a career commercial and how does it work?

1. It's a concise overview of your career background, skills, and personal attributes. It is highly selective in conveying information.

2. It is not a narrative of your résumé. It is a big-picture, colorful synopsis of the career information your résumé details.

3. It portrays your background the way coming attractions portray a movie: by providing a glimpse of the best parts.

4. It sets the tone for the rest of the interview and a context for the discussion that's about to take place. What you talk about in your commercial gives interviewers information and impressions to shape the questions they will ask throughout the rest of the exchange. This means that you have an opportunity to manage, to a degree, the direction the interview takes and how it flows.

5. Unlike a résumé, your career commercial is three-dimensional. It is a powerful message that is delivered in person – by you. It shows animation, expression, and dimension that will reach the person who hears it and influence his or her perception of the information presented.

6. It helps interviewers quickly understand where you see yourself going and what you'd like to have happen in your career.

7. It is your most influential, most powerful, and most critical job-search tool.

■ **If you make** *your speech concise, interesting, and varied, you will have the whole table hanging on your every word.*

Using your career commercial

Now that you know what a career commercial is and how it works, here are ten tips on developing and using it.

1. Keep it short. Shoot for 60 to 75 seconds. Do not exceed 90 seconds, or you will lose your interviewer's attention.

2. Look back at the summary statement, or profile, on your résumé (see Chapter 16). Your career commercial should reflect and build on that overview of your background. Both are tools that summarize your career focus, skills, and strengths.

3. Construct your career commercial by drawing from these possible areas of focus (you will not be able to include them all):

■ **Keep your** *career commercial short – don't get carried away by the sound of your own voice*

A SAMPLE CAREER COMMERCIAL

Kathy is the owner of a successful events-planning business. She keeps an open mind about her career path and stays on the lookout for promising opportunities. A client referred her to a contact at a midsize firm in the public relations field, who was considering contracting for events management work. Naturally, Kathy was interested in winning the contract. When she interviewed with the contact, she was focusing on selling the services of her firm exactly as if she were on a job interview.

Here's Kathy's career commercial:

"I'm an events planner. I like to say that I help professional people do good business and keep good memories. I plan and stage various kinds of promotional events, and make sure they're in keeping with the public image of my clients.

"I've been planning and managing successful events for more than ten years. During the past three years I've done a lot of work in the entertainment industry, staging press parties and program-launch events for clients like The Attitude Channel and Movietime. I've also planned major sales conferences in the media industry, for Pace Magazine and others. Before that, I specialized in shareholder meetings for large corporations.

"I broke into this field by planning weddings. I've always had a good ability to clarify people's ideas and hopes about an event, and then make them a reality. Planning dozens of weddings sharpened my skills in coordinating teams, paying attention to details, playing up images, and bringing everything together in festive, memorable events.

"I have a reputation for being imaginative, thorough and dependable. About 70 percent of my business now is repeat business. What I'm planning to do next is bring my background and expertise to the public relations area. I'd like to contribute to the public events efforts of midsize firms like this one. I have a wide variety of experience to bring to bear, and I could make an immediate impact.

"That's the short version of my story! I know I've covered a lot of ground. What part of my background can I tell you more about?"

- Identifier – how you refer to yourself
- Profession or industry background
- Specific companies or clients you've been associated with
- A career accomplishment that you're proud of
- Skills and strengths for which you want to be remembered
- Educational background and/or specialized training
- Awards or recognition you may have received
- Personal attributes you wish to emphasize
- Where you're going in your career, or what you'd like to have happen as a result of this interview
- An open-ended question to draw the interviewer to one or more of the key areas you have mentioned

INTERNET

www.careerbuilder.com

Career Builder links with more than two dozen other career sites, and provides information and advice on many areas of job search, including interviewing.

4 Develop your career commercial by writing it, then revising it and revising it again. Don't expect your first draft to be the final outcome.

5 Write for the ear, not the eye. Remember, you will be speaking your commercial. As you rewrite, change any words that do not sound conversational when you read the commercial aloud.

6 After you've written, revised, and read your commercial aloud to check for length, select four or five key phrases that will help you remember the flow of your commercial from beginning to end.

7 Do not memorize your commercial – you'll sound like a robot when you deliver it in interviews. Instead, memorize the four or five key phases, and let them link you to the ideas that will enable you to tell the story.

8 Remember that your career commercial is not a walk through your résumé. It's an attention-grabbing blurb to stimulate more detailed conversation.

9 Practice delivering your commercial as often as you can, to anyone who will listen. Practice in front of a mirror, too, and check your facial expressions as you speak.

10 Refine and tweak it to fit specific interview situations and objectives. Use a more informal version of it in networking meetings.

- **Rehearse your commercial**, *but don't deliver your "script" parrot-fashion*

Your OARs: showcasing key skills

DESCRIBING HOW YOU *have made contributions and added value in your previous work situations is pivotal to your success in any interview. Interviewers want to know what you've done in the past so they can get a clear idea of what they can expect you to do for them. It's critical for you to express your past accomplishments in a way that showcases your skills with impact.*

Naturally, the accomplishments that you describe in an interviews should include many of those you've included in your résumé, since your interviewer is likely to refer to them. But you may wish to describe other accomplishments, or alternatives to the highlights that are included in your résumé. As your interviewer poses questions, he or she is expecting to hear meaningful, substantial responses that demonstrate your skills, your personal qualities, and the ways you have made a difference in previous career situations.

Showcasing your skills

You can beef up your interview arsenal by preparing a number of short, demonstrative stories that describe your key accomplishments and showcase important skills. Use these stories to respond to questions throughout the interview. First identify the skills you wish to emphasize in a particular interview situation, then craft the short stories that demonstrate those skills in the context of your key accomplishments. Use the acronym OAR as a framework for your accomplishment stories.

■ **If you've previously** *ran your own business, don't be afraid to talk of your achievements.*

1. Overview: Begin your accomplishment story with a simple reference to what it's about. Identify a workplace problem or situation that you responded to.
2. Actions: This is the heart of your accomplishment story, where you describe all of the actions you took in response to the problem or situation. Be clear that the actions demonstrate your workplace skills.
3. Results: Conclude your accomplishment story with a quick reference to the results your actions produced. Quantify those results as concretely as you can.

SAMPLE OAR

Here's an example of an OAR at work in an interview situation. Bob is interviewing for an Assistant Creative Director's position at a midsize advertising agency. He has a background in the magazine industry. His interviewer is a Senior Vice President on the creative side of the agency. He wants to learn about Bob's approach to the creative process, and poses a fairly open-ended question in the interview: "Bob, which of your campaigns did you like the best?"

Bob had a number of OARs worked up, and responded with this one:

Overview: "I'm proud of all of my campaigns, but one was successful very quickly. I lead the creative team when we were asked to redefine the image of Seek magazine in the advertising marketplace. Advertisers didn't think our readers were very loyal."

Actions: "I developed a strategy to identify some of our high-profile readers and have them talk about the magazine and how much they liked it. I managed a research team, conducted the interviews, and worked up a creative concept that positioned us as slightly irreverent. I wrote the slogan "How to find out"and the copy that we used in print ads. I also directed the storyboard development for the TV spots."

Results: "We ran the print and the TV spots alternately for six weeks. After that I conducted focus groups to gauge the response, and they were tremendously positive. The salespeople brought the message to advertisers, and for the next half of the year our page count jumped by 40 percent."

Notice how Bob's accomplishment story has a beginning, middle, and end. It progresses according to the OAR framework. Also, notice how the story is peppered with action words that capture and describe Bob's skills.

Downstream with your OARs

Here are eight tips on developing and using your OARs:

1. Keep them very brief – 60 seconds or less.

2. Be clear about the message of each accomplishment story.

3. Refer to the skills and competencies you demonstrated in reaching each accomplishment.

4. Quantify results wherever possible.

5. Develop at least a dozen OARs to describe the skills you want to emphasize in interviews.

6. Write and revise each OAR. Edit each one as tightly as possible.

7. Don't memorize your OARs word for word; just memorize the framework for each.

8. Practice verbalizing them before your interviews.

INTERNET

www.careerpath.com

CareerPath provides a compilation of job listings from major newspapers and employers across the country. You can search companies by industry, geographic location or keyword.

Basic guidelines for effective interviewing

AS YOU MOVE *through the interview process, keep in mind that in each situation, your immediate objective is to get the next interview. Of course, your ultimate goal as a candidate is to receive a job offer. But don't expect to receive an offer after just one interview – very few hiring deals are closed so quickly.*

■ **Practice makes perfect:** *Don't worry if you didn't get the job after your first interview.*

Your best strategy is to jump the interview hurdles one at a time. Keep the process moving forward by getting the green light to proceed to the next stage.

No matter how many interviews you sit through, each one is different. You start with a clean slate each time. However, every interview situation calls for behaviors and conduct that are not only appropriate, but also essential for success. Here are some general guidelines to follow in all interview situations.

Managing time

1. Be on time all the time. Allow for the possibility of transportation- or weather-related delays. It's better to be slightly early than slightly late. If you are unavoidably detained, call to say so.
2. Always get an idea of your interviewer's time constraints. Ask, "About how much time do we have today?"

Carrying baggage

1. Show up for interviews carrying as little as possible. Do not bring shopping bags or any tote bags that contain things you don't need for the interview. Limit your baggage (other than handbags) to a single briefcase, and be sure it contains only essential materials.
2. Carry an umbrella if the weather calls for it. Try to leave it in a coat closet or receptacle outside your interviewer's office.

Taking notes

1. You may wish to write some things down during the interview. Be sure your interviewer won't find it intrusive. Ask, "Do you mind if I jot down a few notes as we speak?"
2. If you choose to take notes, be careful to keep your attention on the conversation.
3. Never try to write lengthy phrases or sentences; they will distract you from the rhythm of the conversation. Write trigger words only, and flesh out the ideas later. Do not allow note taking to prevent you from keeping good eye contact with your interviewer.

■ **If you have** *to travel to your interview, give yourself time to leave your luggage in your hotel room.*

Minding the dynamics

1. First impressions are lasting impressions. Take the initiative during the first moments of the meeting to make your interviewer feel comfortable. To break the ice, make thoughtful small talk – no matter how trivial it may seem. Your interviewer will appreciate the gesture, and you will loosen up too.

2. Head off a one-sided interview. If your interviewer insists on doing all the talking, try to break in and interject with observations or questions. If your interviewer expects you to do all the talking, take the initiative to ask questions and draw out conversational responses.

■ **If your interviewer** *does all the talking, they will have learned nothing about you – even worse they might just forget you.*

3. If your interviewer seems distracted, bored or inattentive, you may wish to test his or her interest. Ask leading questions like, "How does my experience in this area match up with your needs at this time?"

4. Remember that an interview is not merely an exchange of information. It is also the beginning of a relationship with great potential. Invest in building the relationship from the earliest moments of the interview. This means revealing not only your professional qualities, but your best personal attributes as well.

Using body language

1. Begin your meeting with a firm, but not aggressive, handshake.

2. Take your cue from the interviewer on where to sit, if it's not already obvious. Avoid deep sofas or plush chairs if at all possible.

3. Keep a straight posture in your chair. Lean forward slightly toward your interviewer to convey your interest. Keep your feet flat on the floor. As the interview progresses, you may wish to lean back in your chair and cross your legs if your interviewer does.

■ **Remember, everyone** *hates a weak handshake.*

1. Don't fold your arms across your body – that's a defensive, "closed" position that will make you appear remote and inaccessible. Keep your hands in your lap. It's acceptable to use your hands to be expressive, but not to excess.

2. Keep strong eye contact. It's important to look directly at your interviewer when he or she is speaking, and as you speak. But be careful to avoid staring. Pull your gaze away from time to time to provide a break and maintain ease and a mutual comfort level.

3. Vary the tone and modulation of your voice. Avoid droning. You can accomplish this most effectively through practice. As you prepare for interviews, listen to yourself speak. Try tape-recording some of your responses to interview questions you can anticipate. Remember that you need to keep your interviewer engaged.

4. Smile – as frequently and as genuinely as possible.

Talking about money

Don't be the first to bring up the topic of money.

Of course you want to know about salary and other compensation. But your best strategy in the interview process is to resist the urge to ask until you get to the later stages. Early on, concentrate on learning about the needs of the employer. Ask about existing problems and reasons for the job opportunity. Keeping your focus there will give the employer the welcome signal that your pay package is not your first priority.

1. If your interviewer asks you about compensation, try to deflect the question. Say, "At this point I'd like to focus on your needs and the opportunity for me to contribute. I'm sure the question of compensation will work itself out."

2. If it becomes clear that your interviewer wants specific information about your current or most recent salary, or the salary level you're seeking, gauge your response carefully. You may be able to deflect the issue one more time, but be careful not to annoy your interviewer. Say, "As I've said, at this point it's finding the right situation that's most important to me. If the match is right, I'm sure the salary details will fall into place."

■ **The golden rule** *when negotiating your salary is never to name a figure first. If you do, you will probably lose the negotiation.*

3. If you feel like your back is against the wall, defuse the question and preserve the comfort level in the room by quoting a fairly wide salary range. Say, "I think my background and accomplishments place me in the 45 to 50 range" (meaning thousands of dollars, of course). You may wish to be slightly more specific. If so, say, "My earnings now are in the high 40s." Or, "My current salary level is in the mid-50s."

4. Never quote an exact figure. Do not say: "I'm looking to make 55 thousand." For all you know, $65,000 may be in the budget and available to you. But you'll never get it if you set your sights too low.

5. If you must quote a salary range, find out if it's in your interviewer's ballpark by following your quote with a leading question. Ask, "How does that line up with the compensation for this position?"

■ **At the end** *of the interview be bold – why not ask the interviewer if they are going to offer you the job?*

Following up

1. Never end an interview without asking about next steps. This information will provide you with a context for your follow-up efforts.

2. Write a follow-up letter within 48 hours after each interview. Use it as an occasion not only to thank your interviewer for meeting with you, but also to describe again why you are right for the position. You can also mention afterthoughts or points that you were unable to express in the interview.

3. Honor the agreements you make with your interviewer. If you say in your letter that you'll call in two weeks to find out where things stand, make sure you do.

Other perspectives

In interview situations, think as a problem solver. Articulate ways you have provided solutions and added value to organizations in the past.

1. Show enthusiasm. A positive attitude is compelling and convincing.

2. Always try to move the interviewing process ahead. Remember your goal at all times is to get the green light to the next interview.

3. Never evaluate a position definitively until you've secured an offer. Until then, you're working with incomplete information and your own highly subjective impressions. Don't judge an opportunity before you're clear about all of its dimensions.

■ **Success often lies** *in not "being" the best, but appearing to be the best!*

Remember that the candidate who receives the offer is not necessarily the one with the strongest qualifications. Often, the successful candidate is the one who interviews best.

A simple summary

✓ Job interviews are stressful events. The stakes are high, and it's typically winner take all. One perspective to keep in mind is that interviews are occasions for a process of two-way investigation, not one-way interrogation.

✓ Your job search is not likely to end with a single interview. Typically, as you pursue each opportunity you identify, you will move through a process that includes several different kinds of interviews. Some will be more specialized and specific than others.

✓ Key interviewing strategies, including your ability to describe how you can make contributions and add value, will help you deliver an effective, memorable interview – and avoid an ordinary one.

✓ Your interview arsenal includes your résumé and several key tools. Chief among these is your career commercial, a short verbal overview of what your have to offer. It affords you an opportunity to manage the lasting impressions your interviewer forms about you.

✓ Every interview situation represents a clean slate. You must manage each one as a unique, stand-alone event. Following general strategic guidelines will enable you to present yourself effectively and move the interviewing process forward – your goal every time.

PART FIVE

MANAGING YOUR CAREER FROM HERE

THIS FINAL PART FOCUSES on managing your career while you're working – in effect, moving ahead while in place. You'll start by gaining some new perspectives on settling into a new job and *launching* the professional reputation that will stay with you there.

You'll find these helpful for making *headway* in any new work situation. You'll learn about behaviors to adopt and blunders to avoid at work. After taking an in-depth look at career reputation and strategies, you'll see why skills and abilities are probably not enough to get you as far as you can go in your career, and you'll discover what else you need to get there. Finally, you'll learn about networking which is the most *important* career management activity you can pursue. Also, you'll learn the Ten Commandments of networking for career vitality.

Chapter 18

Your New-Job Honeymoon: 100 Days of Harmony (or Less)

CONGRATULATIONS! YOUR SEARCH IS OVER and you've accepted an offer of employment. Now you can relax for a while, take a low profile, coast through the first few weeks on the new job, and see how things take shape, right? Wrong. During your earliest period of time in a new job – about a hundred days, or even less – you formulate the image and reputation that will, for the most part, stay with you as long as you stay with the organization. It's not a time to rest on your laurels. In fact, it's a time to do careful and conscientious work on several fronts – and not all related to your job responsibilities. In this chapter, you'll learn how to manage your contributions and workplace presence during your first hundred days. And you'll see how important it is to develop relationships with your coworkers, learn the ropes within your organization, and tackle your work productively.

Ready to start the clock?

In this chapter...

✓ Make-or-break time

✓ Your action plan for being new

DON'T RELAX JUST YET – YOU NOW HAVE TO IMPRESS YOUR EMPLOYERS IN THE WORKPLACE!

Make-or-break time

YOU'VE ACCEPTED *an offer of employment. You've agreed on a start date. Maybe you've been able to take some time for yourself before you start the new job. As Day One approaches, you're probably struggling with a strange blend of emotions: pride, exhilaration, anticipation, apprehension. All of those feelings are unavoidable when you're heading into a new job, and all of them are healthy.*

If your job search has taken longer than you expected it would, you're probably relieved that it's over at last, but you can't rest on your laurels just yet, or you may be back out on the job search battlefield before you know it.

Your first hundred days (roughly three months) on the job set the stage for all the days that follow. All that you do during that time span – the impressions you make, the behaviors you show, the initiatives you take, the alliances you form – will add up to a generalized, lasting judgment about you: thumbs up or thumbs down.

In other words, your professional image and reputation are set during your first hundred days on the job.

And because this is true, you owe it to yourself to manage that phase of your career as carefully as any other.

Special status

During your first hundred days, you're going to be scrutinized up one side and down the other. Your work will be evaluated more carefully than it may ever be again. What's more, all of your coworkers are going to be checking you out. Your peers will be circling you to see if you can be trusted. Your managers will be looking at you very closely, not only to determine how quickly you'll contribute, but also to make sure they made the right decision by hiring you. Your subordinates, if you have any, will be watching your every move, both to see how you land and to find out where they stand.

■ **First impressions count:** *In the early days you must try to prove how capable you really are.*

The good news is that, throughout all of that, you have some rope. You can make a couple of mistakes that will be forgiven, as long as they're not utterly disastrous, because you're new and the organization is still in love with you. In fact, they're likely to be so enchanted by your presence that you'll be unable to do any wrong at all – for a time. What all of that means is that, figuratively speaking, you're on a *honeymoon*.

DEFINITION

In the workplace, an employee's earliest days and weeks with an organization are typically known as the honeymoon *period. It is a time of adjustment, evaluation, and relationship building, typically colored by an exchange of admiration and idealism.*

Should you be literal about counting down a hundred days? Probably not. Honeymoon periods vary by organization. Larger, established companies are likely to cut more slack for new employees than smaller ones. In fact, many large organizations have a formal trial period of one to three months before the employment agreement becomes permanent. Benefit plans may not be active during that time, and a new hire is not considered "official" until he or she successfully completes the trial period. It's a little like probation.

Other organizations, especially smaller companies, entrepreneurial businesses, and high-tech operations, move much more quickly. You're likely to feel pressure to get acclimated and to contribute almost instantly – or be replaced.

Regardless of whether your honeymoon period is a hundred days, a month, three months, or three weeks, this time is crucial to your ultimate success there – and satisfaction, and so you should plan carefully and use the time wisely.

■ **If you work** *for a small company there is a greater chance that you'll be thrown in at the deep end. Your aim is to prove that you are a swimmer!*

Investing in yourself

Fairly or unfairly, first impressions are lasting impressions. That's why you're careful to look your best in interviews, say the right things when asked to describe yourself, and smile when you're meeting someone new.

During your honeymoon period, the people around you will form impressions about you that will endure. When things settle down and business relationships gel, your coworkers and managers want to feel comfortable with you. If you care anything at all about interpersonal dynamics (and you should), you'll want them to feel comfortable with you, too. But what's even more important to the ultimate outcome is feeling comfortable with yourself.

In other words, when the honeymoon period is over and you settle into the everyday rhythm of work, you should be "fully present," which means participating with all of your strengths, personality traits, and even your weaknesses. You should feel free to be, for the most part, who you really are – not a specially edited version of yourself that you have to present in the workplace. To gain that freedom, it's essential for you to manage your honeymoon period carefully, with the right blend of modesty, self-assurance, flexibility, and accessibility. It's a fine line to walk, but it's the way to success.

Being new and broadcasting it

One of the best things you can do for yourself before you begin your job is to assess your tolerance for being new to a situation. If you're like many people, you find a certain comfort in knowing how things work:

What's most familiar is what's most comfortable. But in a new job, nothing is familiar. How well will you wear those clothes? Will you feel a need to take charge of everything and bring things under your personal control? Or can you tolerate a period of uncertainty, in which you're essentially "out of the know" until you learn the lay of the land and stake your ground in it?

Try to remember that your coworkers and managers want you to feel new for a while. They want you to struggle just a bit, as they did, and own up to being the new kid on the block. After all, each of them was new to that work environment at one point or another. And now that their honeymoons are over and they've established themselves, they have a veteran status that you haven't yet earned. They will appreciate a certain measure of deference on your part, tempered by another measure of your own self-confidence.

Another thing to remember is that being new and being out of the know means that, at least for a time, you're vulnerable. It's in your best interest to acknowledge that and to ride with it in the beginning. Show your coworkers and managers that you're an open book. Don't pretend that you're not vulnerable – to others or to yourself. That can work against you by making you seem inaccessible and remote. To a greater or lesser degree, everyone is tender in a new situation. When you're starting a new job, it's just your turn.

■ **You're the new kid** *on the block, so be prepared to listen and learn from your colleagues.*

Telling the outside world

It's a good time to contact everyone who has helped you during the course of your search. You will want to keep your contacts informed of your whereabouts. Assume that they will want to know how your search has turned out, and where you've landed. Most importantly, communicating with your contacts as you gear up for your new job is another opportunity to express your thanks for their role in contributing to your campaign. Don't make the mistake of thinking that some contacts have not been helpful. Everyone who networks with you, gives you an idea or an opinion, refers you to another contact, or simply enables you to draw a conclusion plays a role in your search, however large or small. Be thankful for what you've been able to learn from your contacts, and let them know that you are.

Your action plan for being new

BECAUSE YOUR HONEYMOON *with a new company is so important, you should have an action plan for navigating this phase of your career. Concentrate your energy and effort on establishing yourself well in the new situation, and keep a perspective of its place within the larger context of your career.*

Your first priority is to learn the ropes in your organization. That means finding out how things work, who the players are, what's valued the most, and who's best at delivering it. Think of yourself as a sponge: Observe and absorb as much as you possibly can. But you can't do that alone – you will need help from the people around you. Getting it can be tricky, since your coworkers don't yet know you. You'll need to earn their trust over time.

■ **Try to learn** *as much as you can from your colleagues in the early days.*

Getting to know your colleagues

One good way to learn how navigate in your new organization is to seek guidance from people at your level or higher, but not from the highest-ranking members of the management team.

Get acquainted first with many of your coworkers, but don't get too chummy with anyone just yet. Have lots of one-to-one conversations with your coworkers in the office, but try to go out to lunch or coffee with several at a time.

■ **Don't take** *your coffee breaks with just one group of your coworkers – take the time to talk to all of your colleagues.*

Don't pair off for the more social conversations, because you may send signals that you're developing partnerships. And since you don't yet know people well, you're not in a position to know how those partnerships might be perceived.

INTERNET

www.careerresource.com

Whether you're new in your job or a veteran, you'll find valuable career-management information and insights here. Designed to help you enhance your career and improve your performance, this site presents learning strategies, tips for managers and executives, solutions to workplace problems, and a host of other resources.

Keep yourself accessible to as many of your coworkers as you can. Get a sense of their personalities. After you've become acquainted with a number of them, choose one or two at your level or higher and ask for their opinions on things within the organization. You might want to ask each for their take on what it is that you, as a new employee, really need to know about how things work. That conversation can be tremendously helpful both ways: You'll gain invaluable perspectives, and the coworkers you ask will sense that you're placing your trust in them – and will probably respond with candor and sincerity.

Develop relationships with peers as well as subordinates, if you have any. Remember that the tone you set now is the tone that will stay with you throughout your association with the organization. If you come across as remote and aloof, people will not warm up to you – and may even be reluctant to work with you on team projects. If you come across as too personal and intimate with people, you may be perceived as a talker and a gossip. People may not trust you. It's important to strike a balance between the two extremes.

■ **Fitting in is easier** *if you show a friendly, helpful manner.*

Assimilating the culture

One of your major challenges during your honeymoon will be fitting in. Watch your coworkers, and see how they behave. What do they talk about? How do they dress? How do they relate to each other? What's the general tone of their conversations? Assess what you need to do to gain their acceptance. You may find it necessary to adapt some of your behaviors to gain their trust and confidence. It's important to establish rapport and respect early on because, as time passes, it becomes harder to do. Keep your radar up, and watch for signs of approval (or disapproval) from your coworkers. Think of them as members of an exclusive club that you want to join. Ask yourself, what will it take to get them to open the door for me? In short, what will it take to fit in?

Every organization has a distinctive approach to business and its own ways of getting things done. These customs, policies, and procedures form its *culture*, you should make it one of your top priorities to learn your organization's culture inside and out. What's more, every organization has an external, public, image as well as an internal one. Your mission is to figure out the internal one and assimilate it as quickly as possible. (There'll be time enough to be concerned about your organization's external image later on, after you've established yourself within the inner sanctum.)

Interpreting the fine points

As you're assessing the culture of your new organization and attempting to fit yourself into it, keep in mind that small quirks and details harbor big concepts and beliefs. Observe the habits and rituals within the organization, and ask yourself their meaning. For example, do people close their doors when they're working or leave them open? What about during meetings? Do they close doors for large meetings and not smaller ones? What do the patterns suggest about the work ethics, levels of trust and suspicion, and the nature of communication among the coworkers? What do the patterns suggest about the behaviors you want to show?

Pay attention to how managers communicate with their subordinates, and vice versa. How are ideas, initiatives, and assignments communicated – in person, in writing (memos or e-mail), or by voice mail? Even though all three forms may be used, it's likely that one predominates. You'll need to get comfortable with that form, pronto, as well as figure out what it suggests about your work environment. Lots of voice mail might signal a bustling, lightning-fast workplace pace. Lots of e-mail might signal not only rapid-fire pacing, but a preponderance of reticent managers or coworkers who may not be as accessible as you'd like them to be.

■ **How do your** *colleagues behave in meetings? If you watch closely you will learn a lot about the way the organization operates.*

Notice, too, what happens when people gather, both formally and informally. Is anyone ever late for staff meetings and, if so, how is their lateness perceived? What about missing meetings altogether? Is lateness or absence construed as rudeness or poor time management, or a dedication to more urgent things? Does it signal business or boredom? And what's the impact of the lateness or absence on that person's reputation? Don't forget to watch the patterns at more informal gatherings, too, such as birthday celebrations, baby showers, going-away parties, and other festivities. Is participation by everyone expected or simply requested? Who attends, and who stays away? What do those patterns suggest to you about your own participation?

Connecting with colleagues

As you make your choices about who you'll reach out to for guidance, be careful not to alienate others. You'll run the risk of being seen as one who excludes, rather than includes, your coworkers. During your first hundred days, you'll need to work hard at developing workplace relationships. That means seeking people out, not hiding at your own workstation. No matter how anxious you are to make a mark and succeed at the work you do, resist the urge to keep your nose to the grindstone. Let people know you're thinking about them, wondering how their work is going, and how they might advise you on some of yours.

Try to visit with coworkers regularly, if only for a few minutes. Keep up your interest in them, and keep them interested in you. It's important to establish just the right balance of openness and caution in communicating with them.

■ **There's no need** *to be overly friendly with people you don't know very well yet, but you must make an effort not to alienate yourself from your colleagues.*

One useful guideline to follow at your new job is to assume at first that everything you say will find its way to someone else. People talk. And when you're new, they're talking about you. In time you'll learn who can be trusted and who can't, but for now consider yourself on the campaign trail.

That doesn't mean being phony or inauthentic. While it's true that you may have to temper some elements of your real-world personality, don't make the mistake of adopting a workplace role every day. It's not only exhausting, but most people can ultimately tell the difference between someone who's acting and someone who's being genuine, and they'll usually prefer the latter. Your mission is to show yourself and your true colors whenever appropriate, but never carelessly.

Playing the political game

As far as the political game goes, the rules are different everywhere. You'll have to learn the game board at your new organization and how intense the political scene really is. In most organizations, maintaining success requires a certain gamesmanship that's more about making your presence known than defeating others. Some organizations have unbelievably diabolical, cutthroat political scenarios permeating their culture. In those places, winners are few and losers are many. One guideline that will serve you well, no matter what the political landscape, is to avoid manipulation. Put yourself out in front, so to speak, but don't take a win-at-all-costs attitude.

■ **One way to avoid** *being manipulated by coworkers and peers is to demonstrate how capable you are early on.*

Another aspect of astute politicking is to understand the impact of the company you keep. Keep in mind two unwritten rules about the relationships you develop: gilt by association and guilt by association. In other words, you'll be seen as golden, or tarnished, according to the reputations of the coworkers you surround yourself with. Get to know who gets things done and try to associate with them, both to develop relationships and to get their perspectives. Also, get to know which of your coworkers are "dead wood," and steer clear of them.

Obviously, you'll want to tap into the grapevine. This can be tricky, because you don't want to be perceived as a gossip or a rumormonger. Again, it's a matter of choosing the right coworkers to trust. Remember that trust develops over time, so don't think you'll be able to open yourself completely all of a sudden and have your gesture reciprocated. Instead, gain the confidence of your coworkers by turning to them for information about how they things get done. Try not to focus your inquiries on people. For example, don't ask, "How well does Bill get along with Tom?" Instead, ask, "How well does the sales division blend with marketing services?" Taking individuals out of the conversation keeps it objective and businesslike.

■ **Seeking advice** *is a great method of learning, but be careful not to become too close to your colleagues too quickly. Avoid personal conversations until a level of trust is built by both parties.*

Doing your work

As you're working to fit in and validate the hiring decision about you, you'll need to be especially attentive to the volume and caliber of your work. Some organizations start their employees off with a relatively light workload, simply to afford them a chance to settle in and learn the ropes. More typically, organizations have a backlog of projects to complete in a hurry – many, no doubt, that piled up while the search for their new hire (that's you) was going on.

In today's fast-paced, technology-driven work environment, you'll be expected to get up to speed very quickly while at the same time being watched very carefully. The good news is that your honeymoon allows you just a little bit of wiggle room to make a mistake or two. Your first couple of blunders will be written off to your inexperience in the new environment. When your honeymoon is over, though, all bets are off.

Here are a few guidelines for managing your work output during the first hundred days:

1. **Don't do anything radical.** Of course you want to get off to a flying start and justify your organization's decision to hire you. But you can do that without setting the place on fire. Don't set out to accomplish sweeping changes right away, because you may be setting yourself up for early failure.

2. **Add value from Day One.** Contribute to the collective effort of your unit, division, or, if you work for a very small firm, the entire team. Become a part of the picture, not the entire picture. Think of yourself as adding a hue to the palette of the workplace: You bring something unique, and you add to the mix of colors already in place. Make an impact by being productive.

3. **Establish your work-style parameters.** Be careful to work at or just slightly above the pace and intensity you'll settle into after your honeymoon is over. Don't spend your first hundred days working 12- or 14-hour days if you don't plan to keep up that pace later – you'll set precedents that you won't be able to break without looking like you're slacking off.

■ **Don't overload** *yourself: If you take on too much in the beginning you'll be expected to maintain the same work levels in the future.*

4 Think quality. Make sure that the work you do is excellent, not just passable. There's a huge difference between excellence and perfection, and your goal is the former. Achieving excellence in your work output is something you can usually do with the right blend of skill and application. Achieving perfection is something you can rarely do. And because the attempt to reach perfection consumes so much valuable time, it's almost always counterproductive. Be insightful enough to recognize the difference between being perfect and being excellent, and apply it to your work habits.

5 Keep your focus on your career. Think of your first hundred days as an investment not only in the job you've just accepted, but in your entire career, so it's vitally important to stay focused. Live your life in a way that will enable you to contribute at maximum output during that critical time. Be sure you get the rest you need to be highly productive, and avoid filling your personal life with too many activities or concerns that will distract you from your work and have a negative impact on it. Your honeymoon period will be over more quickly than you think, so play it for all it's worth while you've got it going on.

6 Keep a balanced perspective. Success in your new job is not only about completing tasks and projects. It's also about developing and building relationships. Getting to know your coworkers, subordinates, and managers is part of the work you need to do. Proceed thoughtfully and steadily. Remind yourself every day that the impressions you make during this period will shape your reputation for a long time to come. Be sure they're the impressions that you want your coworkers to have.

Getting along with your boss

The relationship you develop with your boss is the key to your success in the organization. If your boss enjoys your presence, trusts you, values your work, and appreciates your contributions to the organization, you're set. If your boss doesn't like you, no matter how good your work is or how well your coworkers get along with you, your career will go nowhere. Developing the right relationship with your boss takes work followed by lots of maintenance. It's a process to initiate during your first hundred days and to continue open-endedly after your honeymoon period is over.

■ **Be sure to communicate** *with management on a regular basis – that way they'll know how well you are doing.*

It's your job to help your boss get his or her job done. Think of your working relationship as a collaboration. Here are a few guidelines to follow in managing that relationship:

(a) Communicate. As often and as thoroughly as possible, it's absolutely crucial to keep your boss informed about whatever you achieve, large or small. By doing so, you enable your boss to talk to his or her managers about things that are getting done or need to get done.

■ **Don't be afraid** *to express your opinions to your boss. He hired you because he thought you would be an asset to the company – so speak up!*

(b) Provide solutions. Think of yourself as a troubleshooter, and work to solve problems that fall under your boss's areas of responsibility. Your accomplishments will also be seen as your boss's accomplishments. You may not think that's entirely fair, but it's a fact of life in organizations. Your boss will value your ability to make him or her shine.

(c) Express your opinions. Chances are that your boss does not want you to keep your opinions to yourself. A robot can do that. Your boss wants to know what you think, even if it's not in agreement with what he or she is thinking. If you have any disagreements with your boss, express them privately. It's important to stand behind your ideas – and equally important to be flexible. Don't dig in your heels. There's a big difference between conveying an opinion and waging a standoff.

(d) Acknowledge your boss's authority. Your boss is not your boss for nothing. Chances are that he or she has racked up a number of significant contributions along the way. Even if you don't know what they are, presume that they are valued within the organization. Your boss gets to have the final say on how things go. When it's your chance to be the boss (if you ever want to be), you will too.

(e) Be accountable for your actions. When you succeed, take credit. When you fall short, take the blame. Don't wear a suit of Teflon armor in the workplace – no one appreciates a finger-pointer.

(f) Be open to constructive criticism. As a newcomer, you are, after all, in a learning mode. If your boss critiques your performance, your style, or your workplace approach, take it with

■ **The boss is often** *seen as the bad guy, but if you want to follow in his footsteps, learn from his knowledge and experience.*

the idea that he or she genuinely wants you to succeed. Be sure you understand the point of the criticism, and ask for specific examples that will place it in context. Value your working relationship with your boss. Remember that you don't have to be great friends to work well together. You just need to work well together.

A simple summary

✓ During your first hundred days in a new job (or, more precisely, your first significant block of time), you will form a lasting image and mold your reputation. Your behaviors, your initiatives, the alliances you develop, and the impressions you make will set the stage for your tenure with the organization.

✓ Being new to a work situation is not easy. One of the best things you can do during your earliest time in a new job is to develop a tolerance for being the new kid on the block. It's only a temporary label, but wearing it gracefully will help you learn more and develop better relationships with your coworkers.

✓ Your major challenge during the first hundred days is fitting in. It's crucial that you get acquainted with your coworkers, learn the parameters of the organization and how things get done, and understand and absorb the culture of the organization.

✓ Developing workplace relationships is a big part of the work you need to do during your first hundred days. It's important to make yourself accessible to as many of your coworkers as possible and to seek guidance and insight from a select few.

✓ It goes without saying that your work will be evaluated very closely during your first hundred days. You'll need to manage your contributions carefully. You'll also need to get along with your boss, because he or she holds the key to your next hundred days, and maybe beyond.

Chapter 19

Attitudes to Adopt, Blunders to Avoid

WHEREVER YOU ARE ON YOUR CAREER PATH at this point – entering the workforce for the first time, in your first hundred days on a new job, or in midcareer and midjob and wanting to overhaul your workplace image – this chapter can help you form an action plan for behaving in the workplace. First, I'll give you pointers on how to behave at work and how not to. You'll learn about ten key mindsets that are vital to your success and satisfaction on the job.

In this chapter...

✔ Managing your image and attitude at work

✔ Ten mindsets for mastery

✔ Habits to have and hold

✔ Dealing with politics

✔ 15 action steps for getting along and getting ahead

SILVER SERVICE TREATMENT ISN'T REQUIRED IN THE OFFICE, BUT A GOOD ATTITUDE WILL TAKE YOU FAR

Managing your image and attitude at work

NO MATTER WHERE you are in your career, it's important to be thoughtful about your conduct and presence in the workplace. You can't cultivate a positive, professional image by chance. Nor can you develop and maintain a solid reputation just by relying on fortune. Although it's true that your basic professional image and reputation are set during your first hundred days on the job, there is always room for refinement and improvement.

■ **Make sure** *you are always dressed to impress*

Like a marriage or any relationship that's built for the long haul, your workplace image and identity can be shaped and perfected over time, and you should always be prepared for periodic maintenance.

Most people never receive any formal training in how to behave in the workplace. There's never a shortage of adult-education courses or conference seminars on handling office politics or negotiating a rich compensation package, but more wide-ranging programs on workplace conduct are few and far between. In fact, the subject of personal conduct and behavior in the workplace is so panoramic that no single training course or formal education program could ever do it justice.

People typically learn about workplace conduct as they move forward in their careers. Most people just show up for work, experience the daily challenges, routines, crises and crashes, and eventually settle into a framework of responsive behaviors that feel comfortable enough to them and appear right enough to others. Occasionally, some people tap into resources that can influence their workplace conduct in a positive way, such as personal development books, courses, lectures, and the guidance of mentors. But for most people, knowing how to act and react in the world of work involves a whole lot of trial and error – and lessons learned the hard way.

INTERNET
www.smartbiz.com

Although the Smart Business Supersite positions itself as a "how-to resource for small business," serious career-minded people in many different workplace situations will find useful resources "to help you run your business or department smarter."

INTERNET
www.dbm.com

This site is sponsored by Drake Beam Morin, a large firm that specializes in business-to-business career consulting and transition services. You can access information categories on online learning resources; news, tips, and trends; and managing your career.

While no single source or resource can provide you with all the "how-to" guidelines you'll ever need to succeed in the workplace, there are strategies you can adopt right away to make your work situation satisfying and rewarding – now and in the future. These are broad, smart strategies that will travel well with you to any career situation, beginning with the one you're in right now. They involve your image and professional identity, your attitude toward work, and your approach to your coworkers and your job. These strategies are important not only for enhancing the position you're in now, but also for managing your career over the long haul.

■ **Learning how to** *conduct yourself in the office takes time and develops with experience.*

Ten mindsets for mastery

PROBABLY THE MOST VALUABLE *strategy you can adopt to enhance your presence and success in your workplace is to crystallize several key mindsets about your work and your contributions to your place of work. No one will do this for you. In fact, no one can. This is an ongoing effort you need to make by yourself, because it's about yourself – and how you go about your work. Let's look at ten important mindsets to adopt and some reasons why each is so vital to your success and satisfaction.*

1. Expect the unexpected

One of the best things you can do for yourself to increase your productivity (and enhance your well-being) is to learn how to deal with uncertainty in the workplace. It's just not possible to wake up each workday and be able to anticipate everything that the day will bring. Part of working life is responding skillfully and gracefully to unanticipated challenges. No matter how dull, routine, or boring your job may seem at times, there are always crises, emergencies, fires to be put out, and communications to make. You'll be in a better position to respond to unexpected events if you leave room for them in the mental toolbox you bring to work.

■ **Crises happen often** *in the workplace, so don't panic – the important issue is how you intend to respond to each situation.*

Many people are not comfortable responding to things they cannot anticipate. They can feel blind-sided by surprises or unexpected turns of events and may need time to comprehend what is happening and decide how to respond. If that sounds like you, it's probably true that you like lots of structure and predictability in your work life (and maybe in your personal life, too). Try to develop a higher tolerance for the unknown, the uncertain, and the mysterious. You'll be better equipped to roll with the punches of the workday, rather than just responding to the safe and familiar challenges you can foresee.

2. View the glass as half full, not half empty

You may think that choosing between these options is like choosing between beige and ecru. In fact, it's more like choosing between positive and negative, because those are the moods and attitudes that correspond to each of those options.

■ **Think positively and** *you'll increase your likelihood of success.*

Most people do not like to be around negative thinkers. They are like toxins. Negative thinking can sour any situation and rob people of pleasure. People who have a natural tendency to protest, challenge, sulk, whine, and complain will test the patience of their coworkers and peers and eventually alienate most of them.

Be on the lookout for opportunity and possibility in workplace assignments and situations. Leave negativity where you find it.

You'll form better relationships with coworkers, subordinates, and managers – and they'll form more rewarding relationships with you.

3. Make it known that you want to keep learning

One of the best ways to enhance your value in the workplace is to continually develop new skills and competencies. That's a good strategy not only for managing your current situation, but also for managing your career. It's in your own best interest to push to expand your horizons. Develop technical skills as well as broader, more managerial abilities. If you're clueless about where to begin or which skills to develop, ask trusted coworkers for recommendations.

■ **Never be afraid** *to ask – most people are more than glad to help.*

Although you should make it know that you want to keep learning, no one appreciates a know-it-all. Part of the mindset of continual learning is coming across to your coworkers as not having all the answers. If you did have them, there'd be nothing left for you to learn. Show people that you're a sponge, not a sage. Learn from what others have to show you. Be open and receptive to their input and ideas.

Finally, when you encounter a workplace project or situation that baffles you, don't try to figure it out by yourself. If there's something you don't know or don't understand, ask someone. No one will think you are weak. In fact, people are likely to appreciate you more, because you'll be revealing that you're just like they are: at times, in need of a little help.

4. Be accountable for your actions

Give credit where credit is due, and take credit when it belongs to you. By the same token, accept responsibility for your mistakes, oversights, errors of judgment, and lapses. Don't engage in finger pointing. Don't automatically bounce blame toward others. But don't accept blame when it's not yours to own.

One of the keys to developing a strong workplace presence is being accountable for your actions, responsibilities, obligations, and commitments.

Be sure to do what you say you're going to do. If you fail, for whatever reason, acknowledge that you were not able to follow through. If possible, try again. As you become increasingly comfortable, take risks – calculated, not reckless, risks. Managers and supervisors would rather see you reach for goals and ambitions that are slightly on the high side than constantly meet goals and ambitions that are easy marks. Sometimes, the effort that you make in stretching past your own boundaries is more valuable, and more rewarding, than reaching a goal that's safe and easy to attain.

5. Break the bonds of perfectionism

Even if you take tremendous pride in your work and in the way you do it, remember that there is such a thing as overdoing it. Of course you invest yourself and your professional identity in the work that you do. It's natural to want it to reflect your drive for excellence. But "hyper-excellence" benefits no one and can actually detract from your productivity. Sometimes, the most excellent work you can do is to let go of a project and move on to the next one.

■ **Doing extra work** *often seems the only way to complete a never-ending project, but if you do too much your work will suffer and so will your health!*

Perfection in the workplace is rarely attainable. And when it is, it typically requires efforts that are not only extraordinary but beyond reasonable expectations. When you're caught in the grip of workplace perfectionism, it can be helpful to draw an important distinction: the difference between a perfect solution and an ideal one. It's likely that the latter is not only more attainable, but more appropriate to your situation.

Perfectionism can enslave you. It can eat away at your time, alienate you from coworkers, fill you with anxiety, and, worst of all, set you up to experience profound disappointments. You're unlikely to ever achieve the perfection that you seek. And even if you do, what price must you pay and, in the end, who will appreciate it as much as you? Channel your workplace energies into a caliber of work output that will be appreciated and valued by as many people as possible.

> ### Trivia...
> *Your boss wants you to do good work. Your boss also wants you to do a lot of work. If you're a perfectionist, ask yourself what would please him or her more — one project completed to an exquisite culmination, or five projects completed well and on time? If you're still not sure, ask.*

6. Keep quality a top priority

Wherever you are in your career, produce work that is of high quality. That's not a contradiction with the caution against perfectionism. Instead, it's a reference to standards of work that are high and exemplary. It's in your best interests to become known for doing work that is consistently good and sometimes great. To attain that, you'll need to walk the fine line that separates high-caliber output from hyper-excellent output.

Learn to pace yourself. Set your goals, and determine how much time and effort you'll need to achieve them. If you find you can't do a quality job in the time allotted, ask for an extension or adjust your goals. And don't be afraid to consult others (especially your boss) if you suddenly realize your goals are not attainable by the time promised.

Becoming known for doing high-quality work often means acquiring a reputation as the one who does the work the way it ought to be done, and an example for others to follow. Whether or not that's a role you'd like to take on, it's important to remember that you owe it to yourself and your place of work to do your job well. Remember, too, that compromising on quality really means compromising your integrity and your talents.

■ **You can demonstrate** *your talent without having to attain perfect results.*

7. Make your presence known in meetings and gatherings

Managing your career well means making yourself visible to managers, supervisors, coworkers, and subordinates alike. No matter what your work situation, you bring unique qualities, competencies, and ideas to the workplace. The people you work with want to see them, and they want to show you theirs.

If you're invited to a meeting, assume that others want to hear your thoughts and opinions, and volunteer them as often as you can. Thoughtful, more introverted personality types sometimes have difficulty breaking through the quick, snappy pace of meetings dominated by think-out-loud extroverted types (see chapter 9). If that's you, push yourself harder to enter the fray. Chances are that when you finally do get a chance to speak, people will listen attentively.

No matter what your personality type, it's important to make your presence felt at meetings. Remember that you are being paid a salary to make contributions and add value to a collective effort. People expect you to add your thoughts to the mix, unless you demonstrate to them over time that you're reticent or reluctant to do so. And if you do, you can expect to attend fewer and fewer meetings – and perhaps fade from the scene completely.

When you attend informal workplace gatherings, be sure that you're seen there. Participate in the spirit of the event at least for a time, even if you're tired or your heart's not really in it. You don't have to be the life of the office party or a goodwill ambassador spreading sparkles in the hallways. But it's in your best interest to show your coworkers and managers that you regard them highly enough to socialize with them – even if it is part of the job.

8. Be assertive – but be careful not to be overly aggressive

Formal meetings and informal gatherings are not the only occasions for you to make your presence known. In fact, it's a good goal to be assertive as often as you can and in as many situations as possible. This kind of behavior may come naturally to you; if so, fine. But if you're the kind of person who typically needs a push to stand up and be heard, train yourself to provide the push.

■ **Try comparing your work** *to cycling: If you are assertive you'll race ahead, but if you are aggressive it can be dangerous!*

Many people are reticent about asserting their opinions and expressing their ideas because they fear rejection or ridicule. Often, a hesitancy to be assertive goes hand in hand with a quest for perfectionism. Self-doubt is the real enemy of individuals who are uncomfortable with assertive behavior.

It's important to remember that your managers and coworkers want to know what you think. If you don't share it with them, they will eventually turn to others – and away from you. Also, not being assertive makes you an easy target for ambitious people to prey on. They will walk all over you. Remind yourself every day that you have talents, skills, abilities, ideas, opinions, and beliefs that are unique and valuable. These are the tools you bring to the workplace. If you never open your toolbox, no one will know what's inside.

Remember, too, that there's a difference between being assertive and being aggressive.

One is generally an asset, the other is generally a liability. Most people appreciate an aggressive approach to competitive activities such as sports, but it's not universally well regarded in workplace situations. It's a good bet that your managers and coworkers will admire you for an aggressive approach to your work. But keep your aggressions channeled toward work activities – and away from your coworkers.

9. Teach yourself to think on your feet

Whether you're aware of it or not, being at work requires you to make quick decisions and responses. It's important to stay in the moment. You will be required to show original thinking, sometimes under pressure. You will not always have the opportunity to think things through as carefully as you might like. When that happens, you'll need to feel confident about expressing your thoughts extemporaneously.

Many people feel exposed and vulnerable when they're pressed to express ideas or opinions on an impromptu basis. They may feel hesitant to share thoughts that don't seem fully shaped or conclusions that don't seem fully formed. Even if you haven't had a chance to reach your ultimate conclusion about a question or issue (your "final answer"), it's important to express your thoughts and inclinations as they exist in the moment. People want to know where you stand. Show them.

■ **If you can think** *on your feet in awkward situations you'll do well.*

Learning to think on your feet is like developing a muscle group. The more you exercise it, the suppler it becomes. Train your thought processes to remain flexible and resilient. You'll be stronger at responding to on-the-spot pressure, and your managers and coworkers will gain a richer sense of how you think and what you're made of.

10. Never believe you're indispensable

Regardless of where you are in your career, it's a mistake to think that your organization cannot get along without you. No one is irreplaceable. Many people who have spent long years with a single organization begin to feel that the relationship will go on forever – or at least as long as they want it to.

Don't be lulled into a false sense of security.

No matter how talented you are, how well you do your job, who you know, or who knows you, you are not untouchable or indispensable. No work situation lasts forever.

One of today's workplace mandates is to do more with less. As organizations continue to look for ways to trim costs and reduce overhead, older workers are routinely replaced by lower-salaried younger workers. Mergers take place. Downsizings occur. Industries fluctuate, and jobs that were once vital become extraneous. If you're holding one of those jobs, you many find yourself staring at the prospect of unemployment.

A strategy that will enhance your career and your marketability is to think of your current work situation as finite. Even if you're committed to it open-endedly, there's a very good chance that the job you hold now will not be the job you hold ten years from now, or even five. You may choose to move on or end the association for another reason. Or, it may be ended for you unexpectedly. Thinking of your current situation as finite practically compels you to think about and prepare for the next phase of your career. And that's a big part of managing your career effectively.

■ **A confident demeanor** *will get you a long way.*

Habits to have and hold

IN ADDITION TO DEVELOPING mindsets and following big-picture strategies for career success, you can develop habits that will strengthen your presence in the workplace, enhance your ability to make contributions, and make your experience of work more satisfying. Think of these as tactical maneuvers for on-the-job success. No matter where you are in your career, practicing these habits will yield immediate payoffs. You will notice a difference in your productivity, in the quality of your interactions with others, and in your general disposition about your work situation.

■ **Whether it is** *right or wrong, appearance counts!*

Invest in your appearance

Your workplace appearance – your hair, your clothes, your shoes, your fingernails – the way you look – sends out signals to others that can be positive or negative. If you think your appearance doesn't matter to others, think again. It does. Give it the consideration it deserves, and be thoughtful about how you look when you show up for work.

Investing in your appearance means attending to to two important areas – dress and grooming. You do not have to spend lots of money to enhance your appearance at work, but don't hesitate to spend the money you need to spend. Here some basic guidelines.

Dress

Keep your work wardrobe in line with that of your coworkers. Observe what they wear, what clothing styles seem appropriate and inappropriate, and then dress to fit in. You don't have to look like everybody else, but you do have to look right for the situation. Take cues from what you see around you, such as the formality or informality of others' clothing, and use them to inform your own style.

■ **If your appearance** *is sloppy, colleagues may assume that your work is sloppy too.*

What you wear to work reveals a lot about your attitude. You can impress others as serious or frivolous, approachable or remote, quiet or flamboyant, respectful or nonchalant. Be clear about the signals you want to send to coworkers, and choose the workplace wardrobe that will help send the messages you want to convey.

If you need specific guidance about workplace dress or building a wardrobe that's right for you, consult some of the many resources that address image and style. Among the most notable are:

a. *Chic Simple Men's Wardrobe* by Kim Johnson Gross, Jeff Stone and Woody Hochswender
b. *Chic Simple Women's Wardrobe* by Kim Johnson Gross, Jeff Stone and Rachel Urquhart
c. *How to Gain the Professional Edge – Achieve the Personal and Professional Image You Want* by Susan Morem

Grooming

Grooming has to do with personal hygiene and the appearance of your body. There's very little margin for error here. Everyone has a responsibility to attend to personal cleanliness.

Women need to pay particular attention to hairstyle, makeup, and nails. Men need to be attentive to facial hair (including ear and nose hair), as well as the hair on their head. Men also need to keep their fingernails clipped and clean. People of both genders should be careful with fragrances – heavy perfumes or colognes are generally not appropriate (or welcome) in the workplace. And everyone who speaks needs to be attentive to their teeth and breath, for obvious reasons.

■ **Keep yourself well-groomed:** *Nothing smartens your appearance more than well-manicured hands.*

Communicate effectively and efficiently

Make efficient and effective use of the telephone and voicemail; computers, software programs, and e-mail; and internal memos. How you use these tools (and what you manage to get done with them) conveys a great deal about your approach to your work and your coworkers. You have complete control over how well or how poorly you put communications tools to use. Practice using each of them until you're completely comfortable and masterful.

Respond promptly to calls, messages, and requests

A typical workday is likely to be filled with requests for action from you. Respond to them as quickly as possible – not only to fill the requests and meet the needs of the people who are asking, but also to get the tasks off your plate. Develop a reputation for returning calls and responding to voice mail and e-mail messages promptly. It's a sign of personal organization and effectiveness.

Attend to details

Even if you're a big-picture person, be attentive to the micro view of things. That doesn't mean change your ways, but it does mean that paying attention to details is sometimes the best quality control you can do. Whether you think so or not, people notice the small things. Subtleties are lost on some, revered by others. Don't make the mistake of believing that you can overlook the fine points.

■ **Always be prompt** *when returning phonecalls and e-mails – it will earn you a good reputation.*

Create patterns for your work – and stick to them

Everyone has a different workplace style and a different approach to the challenges of the workday. Find the ways that work best for you and establish patterns. For example, you may be able to respond to e-mails most effectively, and without interruption, at the end of the day. Set that pattern and stick to it. Think about the best time of the week to complete any administrative work you have, set a pattern to attack it then and stick to that time. Creating patterns means setting and working within a loose (and flexible) framework for completing work tasks: particular times of day, days of the week, and so on.

Set workday goals – and keep them reachable

Without goals, most people fall far short of their capabilities. Goals help you organize and concentrate your efforts. Set large and small goals often, and pursue them actively. If you fail to reach them at first, revise your goals and be sure they're attainable (see the SMART guidelines for setting goals in chapter 13). Goals ensure that your work is purposeful. Well-planned work is typically more effective, and more productive, than work that is not well organized.

Be approachable to your colleagues

If you are remote and inaccessible in the workplace, your career will go nowhere. Even if you are feverishly doing your work and pursuing your goals, find time to be available to your coworkers. If your workspace is an office with a door, be very selective about closing it. Keeping your coworkers shut out will give them the impression that you're aloof and unapproachable – not a good reputation to have. Much of succeeding at work has to do with making other people feel comfortable around you.

Get your hands dirty when you need to

Few workplace qualities are more off-putting to most workers than "task snobbery." In almost every job, there are substantive tasks to be done and there are menial tasks to be done. Don't give all the grunt work to your subordinates or other members of project teams. They dislike menial work as much as you do. Enhance the cooperative spirit by doing some of your own photocopying, faxing, typing, and other clerical or administrative work. You'll send positive messages to the people around you and, believe it or not, they are very likely to work harder at completing their share of the grunt work.

Don't pinpoint problems without providing solutions

Managers and supervisors don't want you to complicate their lives even further by identifying problems in the workplace. Instead, they want you to simplify their lives by developing and implementing solutions. In fact, they're paying you a salary to do so. Talking too frequently about what's wrong will put you in a bad light and eventually work against you. Coming up with the idea or solution to fix what's wrong makes you a "can do" person, not a whiner or a naysayer.

■ **There are jobs** *that we all hate doing, but sometimes it's best to get your own hands dirty rather than always designating the unpopular work to your subordinates.*

Steer clear of the gossip wheel

In any workplace environment, there's talk. Wherever there's talk, there's gossip. And wherever there's gossip, there are also bad feelings, questionable intentions, and negative thinking that's neither constructive nor productive. It will get in your way and drag you down. Stay away from the rumor mill – there's nothing you can do about rumors anyway. Gossip is not your friend. It's your archenemy, lurking in the hallways to sabotage your career.

Dealing with politics

Regardless of where you are in your career, your level, your profession, your organization or your job, it's inevitable that you will encounter workplace politics. You'll need to develop a strategy for confronting the political gambit, put it to use, and live by it. Some people choose to ignore politics altogether and elect to focus every ounce of their workplace energy on their work. That's a noble idea and a fine strategy for some people. For others, it's like choosing to ignore the weather.

The political game can be exhausting, and it can sap your productivity. Believe it or not, attending to politics can consume 80 percent of a typical workday or more. Most people agree that the effects of workplace politics are best described by some combination of five dramatic "D" words: distracting, draining, demoralizing, depressing, and debilitating.

■ **Don't listen to gossip** – *it is best to form your own opinions rather than pay attention to rumors.*

For many people, going with the political flow means going to extraordinary lengths to impress other people. Playing politics can also mean schmoozing, stroking egos, currying for favor, brown nosing, boot licking, and other vulgar activities. While some people are willing to engage in such activities to gain advantage, others reject the political gambit outright on principle. For them, playing politics means being phony – which is only slightly preferable to being dead.

No matter how energized or repelled you are by workplace politics, it's not your best career strategy to stick your head in the sand. It's important to realize that there's no such thing as a work environment that is free of politics. Where there are people, there is political maneuvering. While it's not within your control to change the existence of workplace politics, you can control how you respond to it. Basically, you can choose to ignore the political scene, participate in it energetically, or acknowledge and manage it to your benefit. Your choice is well worth careful consideration.

Having needs met

Every workplace brings together a mix of unique personalities. During each and every workday, they are required to carry out the tasks and responsibilities of their jobs – sometimes alone, sometimes in collaboration with others. In a perfect working environment, people would find ways to cooperate with one another. In anything less, they are left with the challenge of finding ways to merely co-exist. When a cross-section of people cross paths, conflict is inevitable.

■ **Sometimes conflict** *in the workplace is unavoidable. Try to resolve it as quickly as possible.*

Try as they might, people do not leave their human personalities at the doorstep when they show up for work. They arrive at the workplace with different baggage and different needs.

The political game is always about having needs met.

Of course you have needs, too, and part of figuring out how to respond to the political scene in your workplace is deciding how best to have your own needs met as you meet the needs of others.

Your best strategy for dealing with workplace politics is to try to figure out what people are really looking for and, without compromising yourself or your own needs, give it to them. You don't have to be phony about it, and you don't have to overdo it. Most of all, you don't have to sacrifice anything you don't want to sacrifice. By the same token, be sure that others meet your needs, too. In order to accomplish that, you need to help people understand what your workplace needs are. Be communicative about them, but don't be demanding about them.

Taking small steps to acknowledge and indulge people's workplace needs, without going overboard, will enable you to establish wider and wider circles of comfort – your own and others'. It's far better to go to work every day in an atmosphere that's reasonably comfortable than one that's not comfortable at all.

Being politically nimble

Outlining survival steps and strategies for dealing with politics at work is a little like planning one's wardrobe outfits for each day of the coming year. Every workplace has a different dynamic; every organization has a different culture. And every work situation will have its unique brand of politics. To manage it, you need to understand where it stems from (in other words, what's at the heart of most of the political maneuvering at your place of work). You need to make a decision about how to respond to it, and then stick to your decision.

No single resource – not even a combination of mentors, self-help books, and online support – can possibly prepare you for all of the political scenarios you'll encounter, or provide you with the tools you'll need to respond to them. If you must, refer to one that addresses the topic in an ambitious, imaginative way, such as *The Complete Idiot's Guide to Office Politics*, by Laurie Rozakis, Ph.D. and Bob Rozakis.

Rather than trying to master ground rules and guidelines for maneuvering political situations you may or may not encounter, you might wish to work on building some of the personal attributes that will enable you to respond to and navigate the political scene deftly and effectively. Sharpen your skill at dealing with politics by heightening your ability to be:

- Flexible
- Accommodating
- Observant
- Quick thinking
- Authentic
- Considerate
- Compassionate
- Inclusive
- Communicative
- Intellectually nimble
- Intuitive
- Confident
- Articulate
- Resilient
- Versatile

■ **Good communication** *and people skills are greatly valued in the workplace.*

15 action steps for getting along and getting ahead

MOVING FORWARD *effectively in your career is less about maneuvering for advantage and more about taking initiatives to grow, renew, and develop professionally and personally. It's about doing good work and working well with others. It's about understanding your strengths and weaknesses, capabilities and limitations, career values and goals, as well as working to the fullest extent possible within the personal framework they create.*

There are many initiatives you can take to ensure that you're approaching your work situation with all you can bring to it and to your career. Here are 15 action steps that are time-tested and sound. Let them inspire 15 more of your own.

About working with others:

1. Develop and nurture strong professional relationships within your organization and on the outside.

■ **Sharing information** *and resources will make you more popular at work.*

(2) Model the collaborative spirit.

(3) Share information and resources with others. Be inclusive in the work you do, not exclusive.

(4) Learn to appreciate and value different personal styles in the workplace.

(5) Adapt your behaviors and decisions to acknowledge and accommodate other people's preferences.

(6) Establish appropriate boundaries with colleagues and associates, and honor them.

■ **You don't have to** *compromise your identity to fit in with other people at work.*

(7) Without compromising your identity or your personality, work to fit in with others, not stand apart.

About your personal approach to work:

(8) Develop patience with the pace of your career. Do what you can to move it forward, but don't be defeated by not winning promotions or perquisites that are beyond your control.

(9) Always be clear about workplace expectations – your managers' and your coworkers'.

(10) If you find yourself in over your head on a project or assignment, do the best you can to complete it. Never give up on it.

(11) Turn workplace anger around, and use it to your benefit. Channel your aggressions toward work, not people.

(12) Develop your skills and your versatility. Seek new knowledge, new expertise, and new ways of providing workplace solutions.

(13) Learn how to say no when necessary – but pick your spots carefully.

■ **If you are finding** *a project extremely difficult, don't give up. Simply take a break and your head will be much clearer.*

14. Find ways to expand your job. Take on more and bigger responsibilities as time and scheduling allow.
15. Reach and maintain a careful, deliberate work-life balance.

■ **If you follow** *these 15 steps, it won't be long until your employers take notice of you!*

A simple summary

✓ Cultivating a positive, professional image doesn't happen by chance. Like so many other aspects of career management, it takes work and maintenance.

✓ You can enhance your career by adopting smart strategies that relate to your image and professional identity, your attitude toward work, and your approach to your coworkers and your job.

✓ Ten key mindsets – about you and how you go approach your work – are vital to your workplace success and satisfaction. Specific workplace habits will enhance your productivity, improve the quality of your interactions with others, and elevate your general career disposition.

✓ Workplace politics is an unavoidable reality of career management. How you respond to the political gambit at work will influence your success on the job – and in your career.

✓ On-the-job initiatives and action steps will enhance your workplace presence and performance, and heighten your career success.

Chapter 20

Managing Your Reputation

I F YOU'VE ACHIEVED A CERTAIN MEASURE OF STABILITY in your career right now, chances are you're not going to initiate a major change in the immediate future. That means the bulk of your career-management energy can be focused on steadier, ongoing career actions that will help move you forward even as you remain in your present situation. Among the most essential of those activities is managing your reputation.

In this chapter...

✓ What's in a reputation?

✓ The making of a reputation

✓ Gaining perspectives

✓ Guidelines for managing your reputation

✓ Feedback

✓ Reputation checklist

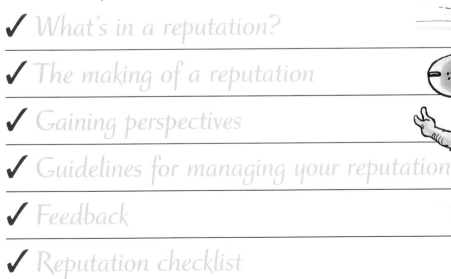

YOUR REPUTATION IS A BALANCE OF MANY ELEMENTS

What's in a reputation?

IN THE SIMPLEST TERMS, *your reputation is how people perceive you and what they say about you. Although reputations are are highly subjective and conditional, and everyone has a different caliber of subjectivity to offer, workplace reputations are vitally important because they can affect your career destiny.*

Perception vs. reality

The perceptions people have of you may be in line with what you already know to be true about yourself, or they may be completely out of alignment with your self-concept. In others words, there are always two levels of truth: reality and perception. But the funny thing about your reputation at work is that, often, perception is reality: How others are disposed toward you will affect your success, satisfaction, and career progress.

■ **The better you relate** *to your coworkers the more resilient your career is likely to be.*

As is the case with so many other career-related factors, reputations reach far beyond a person's skills and abilities.

Reputations are made of other people's perceptions, opinions that typically summarize one person's disposition toward another person.

Depending on the person, their opinion may focus on tangible skills and workplace abilities or on one aspect of a person's character, however accurate or distorted that assessment may be. Opinions can cover the gamut of perspectives and content:

■ "Jack's a real go-getter. He can get just about anything done."
■ "Liz gets hung up on details. She has trouble seeing the big picture."
■ "Lenny's tough to work with because you never know what he's thinking."
■ "Teresa doesn't take direction well."
■ "José's great in meetings. He keeps people laughing all the time."
■ "Wanda takes forever to get things done. Everybody else leaves her in the dust."

- "Bill is a real space cadet – really out there."
- "Janet will find a way to be the leader because she's good at it."
- "Eric doesn't know which end is up."
- "Trina will go after something until it's just the way she wants it."

Notice how few of these opinions do justice to a person's total character. And notice how few of them refer to skills and talents. No matter what their style or content, though, they are usually one-dimensional. Reputations, then, are basically collections of one-sided subjective ideas about a person that may have little in common other than the name of the person they describe.

INTERNET

www.careermag.com

Career Magazine's web site features valuable articles (by Caela Farren and other specialists) on managing and advancing your career, and on a host of topics that relate to employment and working life.

Obviously, your reputation is formed by the people you work with. There are ways that you can help form it, develop it, shape it, strengthen it, maintain it, and, if you need to, change it. When you choose to be thoughtful about influencing your reputation in any way, you are choosing to manage it. And that's a wise choice to make because, as career development sage Caela Farren has expressed so often, if you don't manage your own reputation, other people will. You decide which option you prefer.

By yourself or by consensus?

Managing your career well, for both success and satisfaction, is not something you can easily accomplish alone. If you try, you will eventually hit a wall that will block you from further growth and progress. Regardless of your profession, one way or another you work with other people – coworkers, managers, subordinates, customers. And the people you work with contribute enormously to how smooth and satisfying – or how rough and wretched – your career path is.

So, shape your workplace public image and handle your own "PR".

- **If you're** *really serious about your career, you can't afford to create a bad impression with those you work with.*

The making of a reputation

THINK OF MANAGING *your reputation as controlling the information that people use to describe you. The information includes facts, which are objective, and impressions, which are subjective.*

Facts and impressions can be divided into two categories:

■ What you know and don't know about yourself
■ What others know and don't know about you

These categories combine and interact in a variety of ways, mostly relating to workplace contexts such as style, leadership qualities, project participation, goal orientation, and time management. Whatever the workplace context, information about you exists in one of the following combinations:

■ What you know about yourself + what others don't know about you
■ What others know about you + what you don't know about yourself
■ What you know about yourself + what others know about you
■ What you don't know about yourself + what others don't know

Let's look at how a couple of these combinations play out in workplace scenarios. Given combination 1, suppose you hold a job as a marketing project manager. One day, in reviewing layouts for a promotional brochure, you use your natural proofreading skills to catch a critical copy error. Your coworkers are astonished that they missed it, but you caught it. The reason? You remembered your excellent proofreading skills and used them in reviewing the project. But since proofreading is not normally a major part of your job, your coworkers had no knowledge of your skill in that area. It took an unexpected demonstration on your part for them to find out.

Given combination 2, suppose you're that same marketing project manager from the first scenario. It may be your opinion that you juggle a number of simultaneous projects well and that you're effective in making sure that each one advances according to schedule. Other people have noticed, however, that when you need to give attention to more than two projects at once, your decision-making abilities slow down. They

■ **The way you show** *your style at work reveals more about yourself than you may relalize.*

have decided, unbeknownst to you, that as a manager you tend to "jam at the switch" when the project traffic gets heavy. However, unless they inform you about that tendency, you'll remain clueless about their conclusion. Here's the key question: Is it better to know or not to know what others think. If you chose the first option, you chose well.

The key to managing your reputation is working to maximize the information in category 3 and minimize the information in category 4.

The more that is publicly known about you — by your managers, peers, coworkers, and subordinates — the easier it will be to develop and maintain a solid, positive reputation.

Unnerving surprises will happen less often. People will know what they can typically expect from you and how you're likely to react in certain situations. That may lead eventually to new challenges and responsibilities that play especially toward specific characteristics of your reputation.

Looking at what others look at

Managing your reputation well includes influencing the ways other people think about you. Naturally, that process involves finding out how others see you and what they think about you. If you're like almost everyone else, that might sound a bit scary (or maybe very scary). The good news is that you probably have some sense already, even if it's just a hunch. Ask yourself, directly and with all sincerity, "What would my coworkers say about me?" If you're honest and candid with your answers, you may find that learning more about your reputation is not as excruciating as you thought.

It's helpful to be aware of some of the broad workplace themes that reputations generally revolve around. People will always have opinions about the character of others, but career reputations molded around several key themes and questions, including:

a Reliability: Do you deliver and come through? Do you actually do what you say you're going to do?

b Quality of work: Are your work contributions thoughtful and high in quality, or careless and transactional?

■ **The quality and standard** *of your work has a great bearing on your reputation.*

c Work style: Do you include others and tap into their talents as resources, or are you a Lone Ranger?

d Thoroughness: Are you typically prepared and deliberate in your approach to work, or do you tend to react to it as it comes?

e Motivation: Are you driven toward collective benefit, or are you mostly out for yourself?

f Time efficiency: Do you meet deadlines? Do you honor time boundaries or disregard them?

How reputations are created

How is a person's reputation formed? How does it solidify? How accurate or inaccurate must a reputation be? These may seem like trite questions, but the truth is that they have monumental significance to career development and management.

■ **To you,** *your working habits are an everyday feature of your life, but they have a substantial bearing on how others perceive you.*

To whatever degree they're aware, the people you work with are engaged in a continual process of making observations, evaluations, and conclusions about you.

The perceptions of others may be completely accurate, but it's more than likely that they are only somewhat accurate (and maybe even completely inaccurate) because they are subjective.

So at any time, it's probable that you are carrying out your career in two places: the world of truth as you know it, and the world of other people's impressions.

Let's take a closer look at what that means. Suppose you're an account manager, and you schedule two important client breakfasts during the same week. You inform your supervisor that you'll be in the office later than usual on Monday and Thursday so that you can meet with your clients over breakfast on both days. On Monday morning, you arrive at the office at 9.15 – 45 minutes past your typical arrival time – and a good half-hour after most of your coworkers

■ **Take note:** *People at work are always forming impressions and opinions about you.*

arrive. Some of them notice that you're later than usual. Then, on Thursday, you entertain a client over breakfast and arrive at the office at 9.40. Your coworkers notice again and begin to share their impressions and conclusions (mostly negative and resentful) about your lateness.

Here's how the perception process works – and how reputations are formed: A few people observed that you arrived at the office late. They evaluated your lateness as nonchalance and disregard for time. They concluded that you are an arrogant coworker who disdains rules and regulations. Unless you or your supervisor tells them, they may never know the real reasons for your lateness – the reality of the situation – that you were out meeting with important clients, perhaps winning new business for your firm.

If you continue to arrive at the office after everyone else and if your coworkers are not clued into the real reasons for your "lateness," your reputation as a disrespectful maverick may solidify. The only way it won't is through communication: Your coworkers must understand the real reasons for your arrival, and that means it's up to you to make sure that they learn – either by telling them yourself or by making sure your supervisor does it for you.

Here's another example. Suppose you have a complex, detailed financial projection to complete within a very short timeframe. To meet the challenge, you need as much concentration time as you can get for the next two weeks. You have an office with a door and, although most people work with their office doors open, you decide to close yours to avoid interruptions. While you're working on this complex project, the solitude enables you to focus and make terrific progress. But your coworkers, who can't see you, are wondering what you're up to – and why you're not including them.

In this situation, people observed that you were spending a great deal of time in your office with the door closed. They evaluated your need for concentration as a choice to exclude them from your work – perhaps because it is highly confidential. They concluded that you are aloof and remote in your approach to work and that you are not a team player. Unless they learn the reality of the situation – that you are working intently behind closed doors to complete a major project – they may continue to avoid you because they assume you don't wish to interact with them.

■ **Your way of working** *may not always be understood by your coworkers, so explain your motives if necessary.*

Gaining perspectives

MANAGING YOUR REPUTATION *effectively involves knowing where you stand with the people you work with. It's critical that you have an accurate sense of their perceptions of you, so that you can know which behaviors are working for you and which are working against you. The ultimate goal, obviously, is to define areas for improvement and development and then work on them. That's not to say that managing your career well means doing everything you can to please everyone around you (you'll never succeed in pleasing everyone). But it is to say that your coworkers at all levels hold great influence over what happens to you in your work situation and, by extension, in your career.*

INTERNET

www.asktheemployer.com

This site gives perspectives on many career-management topics, including managing your reputation and succeeding at work. It also provides e-mentoring insights for career enhancement.

VIP *Reputation management requires you to gain a perspective on yourself that's different from your own.*

Only other people can provide you with that. The impressions of your coworkers will provide you with a multifaceted view of yourself, one facet for each coworker, which you can compare with your own view. At all times, it's worth your while to know what your managers, peers, and subordinates have decided about you.

■ **In order to gain** *a balanced view of your reputation, don't be afraid to seek others' opinions.*

INTERNET

www.shrm.org

Sponsored by the Society for Human Resource Management, this site provides access to a wealth of work-related news, information, and resources. It also keeps you in touch with the hot workplace issues and trends that the HR community is thinking about.

Many people make the mistake of waiting for their formal performance appraisal to learn what others are thinking about them. The problem with that strategy is that formal appraisals typically occur only once or twice a year, at most. That's a very long time in which perceptions can solidify. And whether they're accurate or not, perceptions about you will solidify over time. But if you work to maintain a fresh awareness of others' perceptions, you preserve the opportunity to influence and improve your reputation as necessary.

Apart from formal performance reviews, how do you become aware of what others think about you? It's simple: You ask. You have to take the initiative to find out where you stand and then decide what you can do about it.

■ **Having someone** *to talk to on an informal basis can be invaluable, particularly in a highly structured organization.*

Guidelines for managing your reputation

BY FOLLOWING *a few simple guidelines, you can assess, repair, and improve your reputation whenever you need to. Of course, you should establish a periodic maintenance schedule and add it to your career action plan.*

Find and engage mentors

Perhaps the most beneficial way to gain perspectives about yourself and direction on managing your reputation is to develop associations with *mentors*. Serving as a mentor is sometimes a formal role instituted by an organization, especially for younger workers who have been identified as high-potential contributors. But for anyone, the best and most useful mentoring takes place informally.

Find individuals in whom you can place your trust and confidence. Ask if you can turn to them periodically for their perspectives and advice on career-related issues. You should cultivate more than one mentor. In fact, it's helpful to identify mentors both within your organization and on the outside. But remember: Relationships with mentors are special, so think quality, not quantity.

Successful mentoring relationships run deeper and are more confidential than typical relationships in your network of contacts. Develop and deepen your relationships with mentors over time.

Get feedback from your managers and colleagues

The best way to keep your ear to the ground to learn about your reputation is to ask periodically for feedback from the people you work directly with. Getting feedback on your workplace style and contributions is crucial for developing an awareness of how you're valued and how your reputation is shaped.

Gaining sincere and useful perspectives on yourself and your contributions to the workplace can be a delicate matter. You may learn things about yourself that are surprising, even shocking. You may have "soft spots" or "flat sides" that you were unaware of – and that may hurt you to find out about.

Your challenge is to accept opinions and impressions as valuable, useful, and constructive information. If you approach others genuinely wanting to see yourself as they see you so that you can develop and improve, people will usually respond genuinely. Remain open and receptive to what they think and say.

Adapt and develop your style and your presence

Managing your reputation well requires you to respond to the thoughts, impressions, and conclusions of your managers and your coworkers. In order to enhance, improve, or recast your reputation, you must demonstrate your responsiveness. This can take a considerable amount of time.

It's worth reiterating that managing your reputation does not mean capitulating to every single criticism or whiff of negative opinion that comes your way. In the long run, you will still want to be who you are in the workplace, not who others want you to be. But it's useful to develop an awareness of what behaviors you might do differently to achieve a wide, solid foundation of support.

Feedback

PERIODICALLY SOLICITING *the opinions of your managers and coworkers will help you give shape to and understand your real and perceived images in the workplace. The information that you receive will enable you to identify gaps between your self-concept and the perceptions of you by others, as well as to measure how large they might be. The process of seeking the ideas and opinions of others in the workplace is called getting* feedback.

Many people think that getting feedback always means hearing bad news. Not necessarily. Ideally, useful feedback achieves a balance of favorable opinions and constructive criticism. To manage your reputation effectively, you need to seek out and be able to hear to both positive and negative feedback. Whether or not you accept it or respond to it is a different matter entirely.

Asking for feedback

Getting feedback is a far less formal way of learning about others' perceptions of you than a performance review, which tends to provoke anxiety and involve other issues besides reputation. However, getting feedback that's useful and actionable requires some planning and preparation on your part so that you can be sure the event yields the kind of information you want it to. Basically, the planning and preparation involves implementing a framework for the process to ensure that it's not haphazard and random. After all, you're seeking information that will help you understand and manage your reputation. Take the event seriously, but don't anticipate it with unnecessary anxiety.

■ **Always ask for feedback** *on the work that you have done – you can learn a lot from other people's advice.*

The guidelines to follow in seeking feedback are analogous to the traditional structure for a well-written newspaper story: who, what, when, where, and how. By giving some attention and forethought to each of these areas, you'll be managing the process of getting feedback as well as it can be managed. Here are a few guidelines to spark your own thinking about how to proceed with the process.

Who

Decide whose information will be most valuable. Target people with whom you have direct contact and who are in a position to experience your workplace contributions and presence firsthand.

Identify coworkers from different levels to ensure that you receive a well-rounded perspective. Consider managers, peers, and subordinates. Tell them that their thoughts and impressions will be helpful to you on the job.

What

Be specific about the feedback you'd like to receive. "How'm I doin'?" captures the right spirit but is too vague. Instead, confine your request for feedback to specific projects, events, or situations. Say something like "I'd like your feedback on my presentation to the team yesterday."

■ **If there is someone** *whose opinion you value highly, try to arrange a meeting with him or her, whether formal or informal.*

During the actual feedback session, be prepared to help your coworker be specific. Ask him or her pointed questions that relate, for example, to your nonverbal communication during a presentation, your use of visual aids, or the humor of your anecdotes.

When

When you initially ask for feedback, avoid the tendency to let it happen on the spot. Say that you'd like to focus for just ten or 15 minutes on the project or event, and propose a mutually convenient time.

The ideal time to conduct a feedback session is at significant milestones during a project or shortly after a project concludes. The closer in time you are to a particular project, event, or situation, the fresher and more vivid your contributions will be in the minds of others – and the more valuable their feedback to you.

Where

Choose the location of your conversation carefully. Avoid places where interruptions may make it difficult to focus. Office areas, for example, tend to be flooded with phone calls, e-mails, and drop-ins that may be distracting. Cafeterias, restaurants, break rooms, and even transportation situations are typically more conducive to an informal, focused exchange.

Be sure to pick a location that provides a certain amount of privacy. Avoid hallways and restrooms.

How

During the feedback session, be clear about your intentions: You're asking for thoughts and impressions about your performance or contributions, just to know how you might improve and develop.

Keep the conversation informal. Remember, this is neither an interview nor a formal performance appraisal. This is an opportunity for you to obtain privileged information – the impressions and conclusions of another person – about you. Manage it well.

■ **A little preparation** *on your part prior to the meeting will help you obtain the information you want from the other person.*

Responding to feedback

The final part of your responsibility in seeking feedback is managing how you respond to it. With the right attitude and sufficient forethought, you will be able to absorb what you hear and integrate it into your workplace presence and approach. Begin with the assumption that you will hear some impressions that may not be easy for you to hear. Bear in mind, however, that it's easier to hear about them in an informal feedback session than in a more formal performance appraisal – or, worse, not at all. You may be pleasantly surprised by what you hear. Remember, feedback isn't necessarily bad news. If you do hear evaluations that are less than positive, take them for what they are intended to be: constructive criticisms. That is, after all, what you are seeking.

No matter what you hear, follow the unwritten code of honor in receiving feedback: Do not get defensive.

Nothing will alienate your coworker or manager more than hearing your irate justifications for the behaviors he or she is telling you about. Remember that you are receiving subjective impressions. They may or may not jibe with your own impressions, which may be, after all, equally valid.

Be sure to ask your coworker or manager about behaviors that you could be increasing – or eliminating. Ask something like "What could I be doing more of?" Or, "What am I doing that I ought to be doing less of?" Try to press for specific examples, and help your coworker avoid generalizations. Remind him or her that details make impressions vivid and memorable.

Finally, remember to express your thanks to your coworker or manager for his or her candor. It's not only business etiquette, but social grace. Your coworker or manager has, after all, done you a tremendous favor by sharing information that can help you manage your reputation and your career. Thanking him or her is the right thing to do, and the first step toward making your exchanges happen more regularly.

■ **The old-fashioned handshake** *is a good expression of common courtesy.*

Reputation checklist

YOUR WORKPLACE REPUTATION is built on three corners of a solid foundational triangle. Each corner plays a different role in the formation, development, and advancement of your reputation, and each takes on special emphasis at a particular point in your association with an organization.

The three corners of the reputation triangle are:

■ Skills and competencies
■ Personality traits
■ Workplace attributes

Your reputation focuses mainly on skills and competencies when you are new to an organization, before you've developed a history of performance there. Your skills and competencies (see chapter 6) are what you bring to the table.

As time passes and you become integrated into the workplace and culture of your organization, emphasis shifts to your personality traits (see chapter 8). These add shadings of color to your reputation that enhance or detract from it.

When you acquire a veteran status with an organization (the amount of time necessary to reach that status is different for each organization), your reputation revolves mainly on key workplace attributes. These attributes synthesize your skills, competencies, and personality traits and showcase them in the context of your particular workplace environment. In other words, your reputation will focus principally on what you have achieved and demonstrated in your current work situation.

■ **Although the way** *people regard you will change with the length of time you are in your job, you can't afford to become complacent in your attitudes to others or to your work.*

Here are key areas that workplace reputations center on:

How you think

■ Creativity (generating ideas)
■ Seeking alternative solutions (looking at flip sides, generating different perspectives)
■ Shaping and developing rough ideas
■ Critical thinking
■ Translating work understandably
■ Communicating clearly

■ **The way you communicate** *your ideas is as important as the ideas themselves.*

How you approach your work

■ Prioritizing work
■ Beginning projects with a sense of urgency and purpose
■ Leading a team and maximizing their efforts
■ Defining and describing boundaries, rules, procedures
■ Delineating roles
■ Motivating others

How you interact with others

■ Adding humor or levity to the workplace
■ Generating support from other contributors
■ Sounding out others' ideas and opinions
■ Delegating work and distributing it based on others' strengths
■ Modeling the collaborative spirit
■ Demonstrating compassion regarding others' needs

How you carry out your responsibilities

■ Delivering your work on time
■ Meeting budgetary guidelines
■ Delivering high-quality work
■ Following through on what you plan
■ Initiating new projects
■ Making productive use of down time

■ **A dash of humor** *can help in almost any situation, especially one that is slightly tense.*

How you expand your role

- Acting as liason between management and other workers
- Representing and communicating others' points of view
- Seeking and acquiring developmental resources
- Seeking and establishing alliances with other organizations
- Representing the organization to the outside world
- Volunteering for additional roles and responsibilities

- **Try to be open** *to others' suggestions, even if you do not necessarily agree with them.*

A simple summary

✓ Managing your reputation is not a career stage. It is a steadier, ongoing activity that is vital to effective career management.

✓ Your reputation is shaped by the stories people tell about you – managers, peers, subordinates, and associates. If you don't take the initiative to manage your reputation, others will do it for you.

✓ Reputations encompass not only factual, objective information about your skills and abilities, but also the subjective impressions of others about your personality traits and workplace attributes.

✓ Managing your reputation well requires you to acquire and maintain a perspective of yourself that is different from your own self-concept. Only other people can give you that.

✓ Effective reputation management involves four cardinal rules: establishing relationships with mentors, seeking feedback, remaining flexible, and adapting your workplace style and presence.

Chapter 21

Networking for Career Vitality

IN OUR FINAL CHAPTER, WE'LL LOOK AT A KEY STRATEGY for managing your career wisely and well – networking.

In this chapter...

✓ What networking is

✓ Career networking

✓ Why network?

✓ Putting yourself out to others

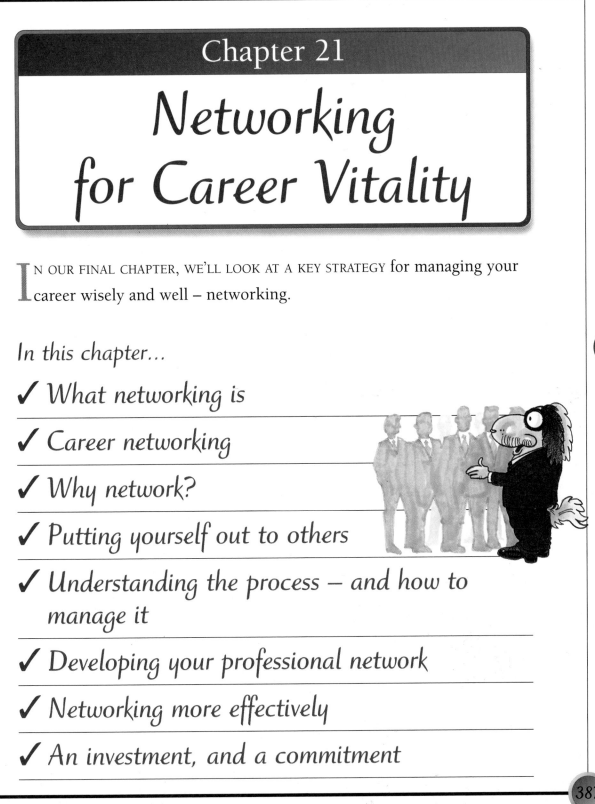

✓ Understanding the process – and how to manage it

✓ Developing your professional network

✓ Networking more effectively

✓ An investment, and a commitment

NETWORKING AS PART OF YOUR CAREER MANAGEMENT STRATEGY IS COMPLEX YET HIGHLY IMPORTANT

What networking is

IF YOU ASK PEOPLE *to describe their understanding of networking, you'll get a range of responses as varied as the people themselves. You'll quickly learn that the word means different things to different individuals. Most people will define networking as an activity characterized by one or more of these traits*

- You do it when you're looking for a job
- It requires contacting lots of people
- It involves asking for help
- There's a hushed, "undercover" feel to it

DEFINITION

The New Merriam-Webster Dictionary *defines* networking *as "the exchange of information or services among individuals, groups, or institutions."*

It's not the whole picture

In a certain way, each of those characterizations is accurate – slightly. Like a cartoon caricature, each of them focuses on a single trait about networking and distorts it. The truth is that none of those characterizations captures the full spirit and meaning of the term networking as it applies to effective career management. Alone and collectively, they portray an exaggerated picture of an activity that's crucial to your career vitality.

We do it every day

Let's look at networking both generically and specifically. It's a good bet that as you progress through your life you're networking all the time – probably without knowing it. Think about how you find a new dentist, or a new doctor. How do you make your choices about what movies to see, or CDs to buy? How do you decide which books to read, or TV shows to watch? How do you know which car to buy?

For all of these questions, the answer is the same: You talk to people. You get opinions, and work them into your thinking and decisions. Whether you're aware of it or not, that's a form of networking. Even if you don't actively solicit opinions, chances are you allow the thoughts and positions of others – people in the media, teachers, politicians, clergy, and others in high-profile positions – to influence your choices. That can be a form of networking, too, because it involves reaching beyond yourself, your thoughts, and your personal resources.

- **Networking can be as simple** *as keeping in touch regularly with a client or supplier.*

A skill and an art

Generally speaking, networking involves interactions and exchanges with people. It's an activity that's often carried out informally and intuitively. In certain contexts, though, networking can be highly purposeful and intentional – it can be used to achieve important goals. For many people, it's an ongoing activity that has limitless intrinsic value: the process itself yields rich rewards. For all those reasons, networking can be viewed as both a skill and an art.

Career networking

CAREER NETWORKING *has a specific focus. It involves relationships and interactions with career-minded people. Like everyday networking, which usually centers on exchanging referrals and recommendations, career networking involves relating informally to other people, although it can get a bit more formal.*

The focus of career networking is usually one of three areas:

■ Researching a career choice or change
■ Advancing a job search campaign
■ Actively managing your career while you're working

In short, networking is not an activity to do only when you're planning a major career change or conducting a job search campaign. It's an activity that will benefit, enrich, and advance your career at any stage. If you've just landed a new job, now's the time to begin your career management networking. If you're holding a job and you haven't been networking to manage your career actively, now's the time to begin.

■ **Keep abreast** *of issues in your company or industry by meeting informally with colleagues.*

Why network?

PEOPLE TAKE *to the idea of networking in a variety of ways – some of them pretty negative. Ask a couple of people how they feel about networking, and some of the responses are likely to be:*

- "I can't be phony like that."
- "I don't want to be so dependent on others."
- "Why would anyone want to talk to me?"
- "That's for people who have an agenda."
- "I could never manipulate anyone that way."
- "It's demeaning to ask people for their help."

In some circles, networking has a very bad reputation: Many people have been burned by job seekers who say they're looking for information, and ask instead if there are any positions open. Others describe being taken advantage of by career climbers who are out for nothing but personal gain. And too many people who think they're doing good networking wind up putting their contacts on the spot – which alienates everyone and is productive for no one.

■ **At first you may be** *reluctant to network, but once you see its benefits, you'll soon change your mind.*

Almost everyone has heard of networking, yet almost no one can agree on what it is or how to go about it. So let's get a few things straight about networking.

It is about interacting with people and building relationships. But it is not about just taking from people.

Networking is about allowing others to be helpful, but it is not about being dependent. It is about being positive with other people, but it is not about being inauthentic.

You can't do without it

Unless you're the keeper of a lighthouse that you built yourself, managing your career effectively is not an activity you can do in isolation. It's a process that involves ongoing relationships and interactions with others. Even if you turn out work that is

■ **A successful career** *is built upon solid relationships with others in your industry.*

consistently excellent, make all your deadlines and meet all your responsibilities, you won't have all the resources you need to manage your career to the level of success that's available to you. You'll need other people to facilitate and advance the process. You'll need visibility. And you'll need to work at putting those together.

One way to think about managing your career effectively is to think not about what you know or who you know, but about who knows you.

If you're cynical about the power of networking, consider these facts and their implications:

- A personal referral can generate as much as 80 percent more results than an unsolicited cold call.
- In business circles, more than seven of every ten new jobs are filled via a process of referral.
- Most individuals are in a position to identify 200 or more personal contacts.
- Receiving just two referrals from every contact can double and re-double the size of your network very quickly.

Networking for your goals

Networking can be a very efficient way to accomplish career goals. In fact, it's critical for managing your career effectively. Even if you're career-minded, you may be having difficulty thinking about what it's like to actually engage in networking activities. You may be visualizing yourself at a gathering, networking with others. If you are, you're also thinking about how comfortable the process feels. And chances are, you're either very comfortable or not comfortable at all.

■ **Keep your address**
or contacts book up-to-date
– you never know whose
phone number you may
require next.

Putting yourself out to others

LET'S BE CLEAR: *Career networking does involve interacting and building relationships with others. It means putting yourself out there to other people. If you're shy or reserved by nature – more of an introverted type (see Chapter 8) – it's going to be a little harder for you. You'll need to keep giving yourself a little push. But if you keep a constructive perspective on networking and a focused frame of mind, putting yourself out there will get less and less difficult as you continue to do it.*

Fears and barriers

Many reserved, reflective people write off the idea of networking because it seems inauthentic. Introverts tend to think of networking as making small talk. To them, there's very little that's less genuine than small talk because it seems to lack meaning and depth. If that describes you, it may be helpful to think of small talk as a tool or device to use just to break the ice and clear a path for more substantive conversation. You don't have to keep your verbal exchanges at a superficial level once you connect with another person, but you do have to connect.

Another reason many quiet types balk at networking is fear of rejection. They tend to think people will be disinterested or turned off by their ideas and observations. That results in distorted ideas of how conversations with new people will go – and a dread of them. Let's say the odds are 50–50 that approaching a stranger will go well. Introverts who are anticipating rejection are actually facing much steeper odds because they've already decided the encounter will not go well, which makes it even harder to initiate conversation and engage in it.

Believe it or not, the biggest networking challenge for introverts (and for cynics) is not the art of conversation, but the art of constructing and keeping the frame of mind that will get them to engage in the process. To meet the challenge and rise to it, let's look carefully at some deeper perspectives about networking.

■ **Don't be afraid** *of networking with new people: The more you do it, the easier it becomes.*

A constructive perspective

In their wonderful book *Power Networking: 55 Secrets to Personal & Professional Success* (MountainHarbour, 1992), Donna Fisher and Sandy Vilas describe networking as an attitude and a way of life. They're quick to qualify the book's title, as "power" networking refers to a power that comes from a spirit of giving and sharing – not the brand of power that is associated with authority, influence, and egoism. In that sense, networking can be seen as interacting with others in an ongoing process of collecting and sharing information for the mutual benefit of yourself and the people you network with. It's an activity that empowers you.

The most important part of that description is the piece that refers to mutual benefit. Don't be confused: networking is never one-way. By nature, it involves exchange and reciprocity.

Networking is about giving, as well as getting, information and ideas.

Some people think of networking as selling or influencing. Think of it as telling, not selling. Another common misperception about networking is that it involves a hidden agenda, and manipulating people in order to carry out that agenda. It does not. The best networking is the kind that enables people to be helpful to one another willingly. If you think networking is nothing but sucking up to others to gain their favor, think again. It's simply a process of sharing resources.

Finally, many people are reluctant to engage in networking because they think it means putting pressure on friends, contacts, and associates to influence others. It does not. It means acknowledging that other people are in your circle of experience, and demonstrating your connectionand commitment to them.

■ **Be positive** *in your attitude towards networking: It is part of a vital, healthy career.*

Understanding the process — and how to manage it

NETWORKING IS A TERM *that's used loosely to define a wide range of interactions with many different kinds of people. In* Successful Networking *(Barron's, 1997), Dena Michelli and Alison Straw identify several different types of networks. The distinctions are helpful in breaking down the broad concept of networking into manageable parts.*

Think of your large-scale network of contacts as consisting of three divisions that often overlap and intersect:

- ■ Your personal network
- ■ Your organizational network
- ■ Your professional network

Let's take a closer look at each of these networks, and identify the kind of contacts that belong in each.

Your personal network

The hub of your personal network is your family and friends, along with acquaintances from your community, church or synagogue, schools you attended, and clubs or associations you belong to. The people who belong in your personal network are basically people you would socialize with, spend your leisure time with, and invite into your home. Of course, those criteria could apply to some people you know from work, but the primary sources of your personal network are outside of work.

■ **Your personal life** *is based on a network of relationships. Networking in your career is a formalization of this structure.*

Your organizational network

Your organizational network consists of contacts developed primarily through your workplace. The larger the organization you work for, the wider your field of potential contacts. The hub of your organizational network is the people you work directly with – on project teams, committees, task forces, and interdepartmental efforts. However, your organizational network can extend beyond the walls of your workplace and include customers, vendors, consultants, and even competitors. Think of your organizational network as, quite simply, the people who in some way share a connection to the place where you work.

■ **The network** *in your place at work is similar to a spider's web – it connects all aspects of the organization.*

Your professional network

Your professional network is more far-reaching. It consists of individuals who cluster around common work and leisure interests. Think of your professional network as people who do the same or a related kind of work as you. Certainly these could include people from your organization, but the primary sources of your professional network are outside of your organization: colleagues, associates and even clients from other organizations.

Your professional network is the one that will be most valuable to you in managing your career. It's in your best interest to invest time and energy in developing and nurturing it.

How the three work together

There is a dynamic interaction among the three distinct networks. They intersect and link with each other in a variety of places to form a larger, more comprehensive system: your full network of contacts. Keeping your career vitality requires you to maintain your connections in each of them, and place increasing emphasis on building relationships with organizational and professional contacts. It's very possible that some contacts will fit into two of your networks – typically the personal and organizational ones, or the organizational and professional ones. In certain exceptional cases, a contact will fit into all three networks.

Developing your professional network

YOU CAN DEVELOP *your network of professional contacts through career-related associations, special-interest groups, clubs, institutes, and guilds. To identify professional organizations that may be appropriate for your profession, trade or craft, consult the* Encyclopedia of Associations, *a standard reference directory that's available in print and electronic versions. The associations are listed by keywords (Advertising, Healthcare, Publishing, Communications, etc.), not all of which are industry-specific. Some keywords refer to associations that are formed to serve specific member groups (women, blacks, MBAs, for example).*

■ **A professional association** *can provide you with much-needed support.*

Which groups are for you?

Identify the associations you'd like more information about. You can select them according to several criteria, including membership size, geographic location, frequency of meetings, and others. Then contact the associations (the Encyclopedia provides contact information) and find out when upcoming meetings will take place, where they'll be held, and whether or not meetings are open to non-members. Typically, associations will charge annual dues for membership and offer members a lower per-meeting attendance fee than non-members. You may wish to pay as you go, until you're sure you want to spring for a year's membership dues.

Finally, spread the word about the associations, clubs and institutes you like. Encourage some of your coworkers and colleagues to attend meetings with you. Pass along the information to contacts you already have. Keep current on the activities of the associations you follow. Read any publications or newsletters they distribute and (in true networking fashion) pass them along to others who may be interested in them. Continue to attend the meetings, develop relationships, and follow up on them – don't just attend meetings for the sake of being there. Meet people, and get people to meet you.

■ **Why not invite** *colleagues to clubs or institutes that you would like to attend.*

Network online

You can also take advantage of a wealth of online networking resources. These include professional organizations like the American Society of Association Executives (www.asaenet.org) and the U.S. Chamber of Commerce (www.uschamber.org), both invaluable sources of information and direction. You can also uncover networking resources by accessing a host of different mailing lists that you can search by keyword or browse by category. You can also tap into a variety of newsgroups and, if you're selective, chat rooms.

How you can benefit professionally

Your professional network can offer you the benefits of career-related information, development, influence, and personal support. It's in your best interest to give your professional network the lion's share of your networking time and effort. Your contacts there can provide you with invaluable perspectives on your professional role, including feedback, resources for development, problem-solving techniques and, occasionally, firsthand knowledge about people in your organization.

INTERNET

www.egroups.com

eGroups also provides lists to browse and search. Each category group offers access to additional networking services and resources.

INTERNET

www.liszt.com

If you're looking for contacts, this is the right site. It's a directory that offers access to more than 90,000 mailing lists that you can browse by keyword or by subject category.

You can also look to professional contacts for guidance and perspectives on your career progress. They may be able to assist you in gaining exposure and visibility within your profession, both by informing you about what forums and arenas to investigate and by promoting you through word of mouth. Your professional contacts will likely be in a position to give you big-picture feedback about your company, as well as your industry and your profession. Some may be able to provide you with signals and information about coming events and trends that may have an impact on your career – in effect, an informal but reliable warning system.

How you can benefit personally

Finally, your network of professional contacts can enrich your personal life. Remember that the three networks are not completely independent, but are linked. As you build and develop relationships, you will heighten the interaction among the three networks. It is not unusual for professional contacts to offer recommendations and referrals that will expand and enrich your network of personal contacts. For example, you may be in need of a referral to a financial planner or advisor. Your professional network will be a valuable source of leads and recommendations, since some of its members may share lifestyles similar to your own, and may understand and relate to your needs. In addition, some members of your professional network may be able to make personal introductions that might enrich your life.

Often, simply demonstrating your openness to and belief in the process of exchange with others will yield tremendous benefit. In other words, personal and professional enrichment are likelier to come your way when you're in a receptive frame of mind.

How you can give back

Many people who could benefit tremendously from the networking process hesitate to participate in it or develop relationships with contacts because they fear they have nothing to give or contribute. Nothing could be further from the truth. If you're a thinking person, you have ideas to offer – and, very likely, opinions. People are interested in them.

■ **Networking relies on** *the exchange of information and ideas, so don't hold back!*

If you are an information gatherer, you have information to offer. You can share your findings with other people in your network. They may be interested in them. You can also share information about developmental resources – courses, professional seminars, conferences, and workshops. Your network of contacts may be interested in them. You can exchange viewpoints and insights about organizations and industries, as well as professions. People are interested in your thoughts.

As you build your networks, you can make referrals to each of them, and facilitate other people's career and personal pursuits. There are many ways to reciprocate the contributions of your contacts – don't underestimate the value of any of those ways. Even if people are not highly interested in the information you are directing to them, they will appreciate your thoughtfulness. Often, those represent more than enough reciprocation for information received.

■ **What goes around** *comes around. If you have some interesting information don't keep it to yourself.*

The exchange is enough

Keep in mind, too, that engaging in the reciprocal process of networking gives people the opportunity to know and experience you. That alone is reason enough to participate. Donna Fisher and Sandy Vilas note that "power networking" is an opportunity to tap into your inner resources while working wisely with your outer resources: your contacts. It provides a framework for living up to your potential. Many people engage in networking and aspire to the process of exchange simply for its intrinsic value.

■ **Unless you make the effort** *to get to know others, how will they get to know you?*

Networking more effectively

IF YOU'VE BEEN READING this chapter and waiting to learn what you should talk about in networking conversations and read the words you should say, you're going to be disappointed. You won't find that kind of advice here, because this chapter is mostly about how networking can promote career vitality and the frame of mind you need to engage in it effectively. Remember, networking for career vitality is about developing and maintaining reciprocal relationships. Consistent with that theme is an appeal – far easier said than done in professional networking activities – to be yourself and allow others to see who you are.

However, networking is both a skill and an art, and there are techniques that you can practice and master in order to maximize your effectiveness – especially in the specialized area of job-search networking. If you feel you might benefit from guidance about phrases to use, topics to talk about and questions to ask during networking exchanges, help is available.

NETWORKING TO READ ABOUT

The resources listed here include books that have been mentioned in this chapter, along with others that deserve special note:

Information Interviewing: What It Is and How to Use It in Your Career,
    by Martha Stoodley (Ferguson, 1997)
Job Notes: Networking (The Princeton Review series),
    by Meg Heenehan (Random House, 1997)
Networking for Everyone!
    by L. Michelle Tullier, Ph.D. (JIST Works, 1998)
Power Networking: 55 Secrets for Personal & Professional Success, by Donna Fisher
    and Sandy Vilas (MountainHarbour, 1992)
Successful Networking,
    by Dena Michelli and Alison Straw (Barron's, 1997)
Why Should Extroverts Make All the Money?
    by Frederica J. Balzano, Ph.D. & Marsha Boone Kelly
    (Contemporary Books, 1999)

The networking code of conduct

While there's no single, surefire method for doing career-vitality networking, there commandments you can follow to ensure you're preserving the spirit of reciprocity and mutual benefit. Chief among those is one that relates to expectations: Never feel entitled to anything from your participation in the networking process. You will undoubtedly receive many benefits, but think of all of them as gifts.

There's a small but toxic breed of self-centered careerists who hoard information and assistance. They may promote the networking process and say they value it, but typically they don't engage in it. And if they do, they're usually the worst abusers of the process because they don't give out at the same level they want to take in. It's important to be wary of one-sided networking. Obviously, you'll want to engage in networking activities only if you're willing to honor the relationships you build and the process of reciprocity.

INTERNET

www.ncna.com

The National Career Networking Association's website offers guidance on a range of career management topics, including finding a career counselor.

You'll also want to steer clear of the users and abusers who engage in networking only for personal gain. Consider that kind of one-way street a no-way street.

The 10 commandments

Here are the 10 Commandments of career-vitality networking – the unspoken rules that are shared, understood and practiced by sincere, co-active networkers.

a) Hope to receive support and assistance, but expect to receive nothing in return for the support and assistance you give.

b) Do not keep track of the assistance you give, the favors you provide, or the ways you say yes to people. Networking is not a game that involves scorekeeping.

c) Maintain an open-mindedness and receptivity to the process of exchange. Be willing to learn from others and help them to learn from you.

d) Invest in the idea that it's easier to reach your goals when you have help and assistance. No person is an island.

■ **Networking is a process** *of exchange – not a one-way street.*

(e) In all of your networking efforts and activities, apply the golden rule: Do unto others as you would have them do unto you.

(f) Honor your contacts and yourself by doing the things you say you're going to do, by keeping your commitments, by following through, and by following up.

(g) If you need support or assistance, ask for it – if you don't, you won't get it. Asking is not a sign of weakness, but of self-confidence and self-worth. Are you worth the help you need?

(h) Give back, in any way you can. Don't just take out of the process – put in as well. Be thoughtful and inventive about how you can.

(i) Engage in networking for its intrinsic value. Find meaningfulness and satisfaction in the ongoing reciprocity involved in the process.

(j) Be thankful for the fellowship and support of your contacts, and express your thanks often.

■ **A positive attitude** *to networking will help you make useful and interesting contacts.*

An investment, and a commitment

KEEPING YOUR CAREER *vital through networking is a commitment that requires time and energy. Most of all, it requires your to buy in to the idea. If you don't truly believe it will work for you, you'll never make the kind of investment that will allow it to.*

■ **If you believe** *in what you are saying while networking, others will believe in you.*

Remember that networking is about cultivating and maintaining spirited relationships with other career-minded people. It's about inclusion, not exclusion – of you and of others.

Anyone who thinks that networking seems calculated and impersonal is not focusing on people, but strictly on agendas.

Networking for career vitality is about people helping other people advance worthy career goals. Very possibly, the only people who can't benefit from thoughtful, intentional networking are those who don't need to reach career goals. If you've gotten to this point in the book, you're not among them.

■ **Be to others** *in your network as you'd have them be to you.*

A simple summary

✓ Networking is an activity that involves interactions and exchanges among people, typically for recommendations and referrals.

✓ Career networking has a specific focus: Researching a career choice or change; advancing a job search campaign; or actively managing your career while you're working.

✓ Networking for career vitality involves an ongoing process of relationship building with other professionals. It is a process of exchange and reciprocity – sharing resources.

✓ Career networking is about giving, as well as getting, valuable information and ideas.

✓ Your network of professional contacts will be the most valuable in helping you manage your career. You can develop and pursue your professional network through career-related associations, special interest groups, clubs, institutes, and guilds.

✓ Career networking is both a skill and an art. To engage in it effectively and respectfully, follow a set of ten simple guidelines that are honored by sincere, co-active networkers.

More resources

Good books

Kristina M. Ackley. *100 Top Internet Job Sites: Get Wired, Get Hired in Today's New Job Market.* Impact, Manassas Park, Va., 2000.

Jeffrey G. Allen. *The Complete Q & A Job Interview Book.* 2nd ed. John Wiley & Sons, New York, 1997.

Joseph Anthony. *Kiplinger's Working for Yourself: Full Time, Part Time, Anytime.* Kiplinger Books/Times Business, Washington, D.C., 1995.

Frederica J. Balzano and Marsha Boone Kelly. *Why Should Extroverts Make All the Money?: Networking Made Easy for the Introvert.* NTC Publishing Group, Lincolnwood, Ill., 1999.

Richard Nelson Bolles. *What Color Is Your Parachute?: A Practical Manual for Job Hunters and Career Changers.* Ten Speed Press, Berkeley, Ca., 2000.

Nick A. Corcodilos. *Ask the Headhunter: Reinventing the Interview to Win the Job.* NAL/ Dutton, New York, 1997.

Karmen N.T. Crowther. *Researching Your Way to a Good Job: How to Find and Use Information on Industries, Companies, Jobs, Careers.* John Wiley & Sons, New York, 1993.

Debra A. Dinnocenzo. *101 Tips for Telecommuters: Successfully Manage Your Work, Team, Technology and Family.* Berrett-Koehler Publishers, San Francisco, 1999.

Caela Farren. *Who's Running Your Career?: Creating Stable Work in Unstable Times.* Bard Press, Austin, Tex., 1997.

Marian Faux. *Successful Freelancing: The Complete Guide to Establishing and Running Any Kind of Freelance Business.* St. Martin's Press, New York, 1997.

Richard Fein. *101 Quick Tips for a Dynamite Résumé.* Impact, Manassas Park, Va., 1999.

Howard Figler. *The Complete Job-search Handbook: Everything You Need to Know to Get the Job You Really Want.* 3rd ed. Henry Holt, New York, 1999.

Donna Fisher and Sandy Vilas. *Power Networking: 55 Secrets for Personal & Professional Success.* Bard Press, Austin, Tex., 1992.

Melvyn N. Freed and Virgil P. Diodato. *The Business Information Desk Reference: Where to Find Answers to Business Questions.* Macmillan, New York, 1991.

Kim Johnson Gross, Jeff Stone, and Rachel Urquhart. *Chic Simple Women's Wardrobe.* Knopf, New York, 1998.

Kim Johnson Gross, Jeff Stone, and Woody Hochswender. *Chic Simple Men's Wardrobe.* Knopf, New York, 1998.

Carol A. Hacker. *Job Hunting in the 21st Century: Exploding the Myths, Exploring the Reality.* CRC Press/St. Lucie Press, Boca Raton, Fla., 1999.

Christy Heady and Janet Bernstel. *The Complete Idiot's Guide to Making Money in Freelancing.* Macmillan, New York, 1998.

Heenehan, Meg. *Job Notes: Networking.* Princeton Review, New York, 1997.

David P. Helfand. *Career Change: Everything You Need to Know to Meet New Challenges and Take Control of Your Career.* 2nd ed. VGM Career Horizons, Lincolnwood, Ill., 1999.

Sandra Krebs Hirsh and Jean Kummerow. *LifeTypes.* Warner Books, New York, 1997.

Christopher W. Hunt and Scott A. Scanlon. *Job Seeker's Guide to Executive Recruiters.* John Wiley & Sons, New York, 1997.

Fred E. Jandt and Mary B. Nemnich. *Using the Internet and the World Wide Web in Your Job Search.* JIST Works, Indianapolis, 1997.

James H. Kennedy. *Kennedy's Pocket Guide to Working with Executive Recruiters.* 2nd ed. Kennedy Publications, Fitzwilliam, N.H., 1996.

Caryl Rae Krannich and Ronald L. Krannich. *Interview for Success: A Practical Guide to Increasing Job Interviews, Offers, and Salaries.* 7th ed. Impact, Manassas Park, Va., 1998.

Ronald L. Krannich. *Change Your Job, Change Your Life: High Impact Strategies for Finding Great Jobs in the Decade Ahead.* 7th ed. Impact, Manassas Park, Va., 1999.

Otto Kroeger and Janet M. Thuesen. *Type Talk: The 16 Personality Types that Determine How We Live, Love, and Work.* Delta, New York, 1988.

————. *Type Talk at Work: How the 16 Personality Types Determine Your Success on the Job.* Dell, New York, 1993.

Jean Kummerow, Nancy J. Barger, and Linda K. Kirby *WorkTypes.* Warner Books, New York, 1997.

David Lord. *National Business Employment Weekly Guide to Self-Employment: A Round-up of Career Alternatives Ranging from Consulting and Professional Temping to Starting or Buying a Business.* John Wiley & Sons, New York, 1996.

LaVerne Ludden. *Franchise Opportunities Handbook: A Complete Guide for People Who Want to Start Their Own Franchise.* JIST Works, Indianapolis, 1999.

LaVerne Ludden, and Bonnie Maitlen. *Mind Your Own Business!: Getting Started as an Entrepreneur.* JIST Works, Indianapolis, 1994.

Dena Michelli and Alison Straw. *Successful Networking.* Barron's, Hauppauge: N.Y., 1997.

Susan Morem. *How to Gain the Professional Edge: Achieve the Personal and Professional Image You Want.* Better Books, Fairfield, Ia., 1997.

Barbara Moses. *Career Intelligence: The 12 New Rules for Work and Life Success.* Berrett-Koehler, San Francisco, 1998.

Mary B. Nemnich and Fred E. Jandt. *Cyberspace Résumé Kit: How to Make and Launch a Snazzy Online Résumé.* JIST Works, Indianapolis, 1999.

Daniel Porot. *The 101 Toughest Interview Questions ... and Answers That Win the Job.* Ten Speed Press, Berkeley, Ca., 1999.

Résumés! Résumés! Résumés!: Top Career Experts Show You the Job-landing Résumés that Sold Them. 3rd ed. Editors of Career Press, Franklin Lakes, N.J., 1997.

Laurie Rozakis and Bob Rozakis. *The Complete Idiot's Guide to Office Politics.* Macmillan, New York, 1998.

Mark Satterfield. *VGM's Complete Guide to Career Etiquette: From Job Search Through Career Advancement.* VGM Career Horizons, Lincolnwood, Ill., 1995.

Edgar H. Schein. *Career Anchors: Discovering Your Real Values.* Jossey-Bass/Pfeiffer, San Francisco, 1990.

Martha Stoodley. *Information Interviewing: What It Is and How to Use It in Your Career.* Ferguson, Chicago, 1997.

Tieger, Paul D., and Barbara Barron-Tieger. *Do What You Are: Discover the Perfect Career for You Through the Secrets of Personality Type.* Little, Brown, New York, 1995.

L. Michelle Tullier. *Networking for Everyone!: Connecting with People for Career and Job Success.* JIST Works, Indianapolis, 1998.

L. Michelle Tullier, Tim Haft, Meg Heenehan, and Marci Taub. *Job Smart: What You Need to Know to Get the Job You Want.* Princeton Review, New York, 1997.

Tom Washington. *Interview Power: Selling Yourself Face to Face.* Mount Vernon Press, Bellevue, Wash., 2000.

Kate Wendleton. *Building a Great Résumé.* Five O'Clock Books, New York, 1997.

————. *Job-Search Secrets: That Have Helped Thousands of Members.* Five O'Clock Books, New York, 1997.

————. *Targeting the Job You Want: Featuring Special Sections throughout on Using the Internet to Identify and Reach Your Job Targets.* Five O'Clock Books, New York, 1997.

Yaeger, Neil and Lee Hough. *Power Interviews: Job-Winning Tactics from Fortune 500 Recruiters.* John Wiley & Sons, New York, 1998.

Yate, Martin. *Knock 'em Dead: The Ultimate Job Seeker's Handbook.* Adams Media Corp., Holbrook, Mass., 1998.

Web sites

At the time of writing, all the web sites listed in this book were completely state-of-the-art. But web sites come and go very quickly. Therefore, while every effort has been made to ensure the accuracy of the Internet information contained here – and within the book – please accept our apologies if a site you are interested in no longer exists. Furthermore, the publisher can accept no responsibility for the information contained within these sites, or any links from them. Happy surfing!

www.aarp.org
People over 50, individuals seeking a late-career change, and anyone approaching or enjoying retirement can find a wide range of useful information and services at the web site of the American Association of Retired Persons (AARP).

www.altavista.com/careers
This site is among the most useful career links of the major search engines and will serve you as an Internet pathfinder for career management information and resources.

www.americasemployers.com
Sponsored by the Career Relocation Corporation of America (CRC), this site features information on job search essentials, recruiters, electronic networking and more, along with a resume bank, job listings and a company database.

www.asaenet.org
This site is run by the American Society of Association Executives. It's an invaluable resource for online networking in the business world.

www.asktheemployer.com
This site provides perspectives on many career-management topics, including managing your reputation and succeeding at work. It also provides e-mentoring insights for career enhancement.

www.asktheheadhunter.com
This "insider's edge on job search and hiring" is presented by Nick Corcodilos, real-life recruiter and author of *Ask the Headhunter* (Plume, 1997).

www.assessment.com
As you move through the process of self-assessment, you can visit the web site of the International Assessment Network. It's all about finding personal fit and fulfillment at work. The site offers specialized material for corporations, students, educators, and others. Membership enables you to take an assessment tool called MAPP (Motivational Appraisal of Personal Potential).

www.bls.gov
To look at current and projected demographic trends in the workforce, check out the extensive web site maintained by the U.S. Bureau of Labor Statistics. This site also provides online access to an indispensable career guide, the *Occupational Outlook Handbook* (see Chapter 11).

www.bls.gov/ocohome
The U.S. Department of Labor's Bureau of Labor Statistics makes its valuable *Occupational Outlook Handbook* (OOH) available online here.

www.careerbuilder.com
Career Builder links with more than two dozen other career sites, and provides information and advice on many areas of job search, including interviewing.

www.careerconnex.com
This site presents general career guidance on such topics as choosing a path and forging a new beginning. There's also a career forum.

www.career-index.com
www.CareerPerfect.com
Several web sites bring together a variety of career- and job-related resources that are useful to individuals considering a major change or planning a search campaign. You'll find advice and direction on issues relating to work here.

www.careermag.com
Career Magazine's web site features valuable articles (by Caela Farren and other specialists) on managing and advancing your career, and on a host of topics that relate to employment and working life.

www.careermosaic.com
Career Mosaic features access to a cross-section of job "communities" (actually industries) like accounting and finance, human resources, and technology. Click to check out jobs, company profiles, and online job fairs, or post your résumé or a job.

www.careerpath.com
CareerPath provides a compilation of job listings from major newspapers and employers across the country. You can search companies by industry, geographic location, or keyword.

www.careerpathsonline.com
This site can help you navigate your self-assessment. It features a ten-step career-planning guide, links to articles about careers, and other useful components. It even has a theme: "Life is a journey . . . enjoy the ride."

www.careerresource.com
Whether you're new in your job or a veteran, you'll find valuable career-management information and insights here. Designed to help you enhance your career and improve your performance, this site presents learning strategies, tips for managers and executives, solutions to workplace problems, and a host of other resources.

www.careers.wsj.com
Whether you're new in your job or a veteran, you'll find valuable career-management information and insights here. Designed to help you enhance your career and improve your performance, this site presents learning strategies, tips for managers and executives, solutions to workplace problems, and a host of other resources.

www.careershop.com/careerdr
This site enables you to "Ask the Career Doctor" for advice on managing your career.

www.careervoyager.com
This easy-to-use portal offers hundreds of links to career management sites.

www.companiesonline.com
www.companysleuth.com
www.corporateinformation.com
Go to these sites to do online research about companies you may be interested in working for.

www.dbm.com
This site is sponsored by Drake Beam Morin, a large firm that specializes in business-to-business career consulting and transition services. You can access information categories on online learning resources; news, tips, and trends, and managing your career.

www.defenselink.mil
Small business research programs tap into the resources of government agencies such as the Department of Defense. Check out this site for details.

www.doe.gov
Small business research programs tap into the resources of government agencies such as the Department of Energy. Check out this site for details.

www.dol.gov/dol/asp/public/futurework
For a wealth of information and insight about current and future workplace trends, visit Futurework, maintained by the U.S. Department of Labor.

www.doleta.gov/programs/onet
At this site, sponsored by the U.S. Department of Labor's Education and Training Administration, you'll find the online version of Occupational Information Network and its new O*NET Dictionary of Occupational Titles, an extensive database with comprehensive information on job requirements and worker competencies.

www.egroups.com
eGroups also provides lists to browse and search. Each category group offers access to additional networking services and resources.

www.employmentspot.com
The Employment Spot features a compendium of must-see career and employment sites, an archive of feature articles on search, and capabilities for finding a job or posting a job.

www.entrepreneur.com
Packed with guidance for aspiring and existing small business owners, this site features e-zine articles, a compendium of small business tools, and several entrepreneur's databases.

www.entreworld.com
Sponsored by the Kauffman Center for Entrepreneurial Leadership, this site offers a wide range of resources for entrepreneurs. You can click on "Starting Your Business," "Growing Your Business,"or "Supporting Entrepreneurship." There's also a Business Information Center with links to sites in five key categories.

www.excite.com/careers
This site is among the most useful career links of the major search engines and will serve you as an Internet pathfinder for career management information and resources.

www.fiveoclockclub.com
The Five O'Clock Club is a national membership organization that focuses on implementing effective job-search strategies. The club is run by Kate Wendleton, who contributes to the content provided on the site.

www.4resumes.com
At this specialized site from the 4Anything Network, click to access résumé writing tips, guidelines, postings, coaches, and more.

www.franchise1.com
This site promotes itself as "the #1 franchise destination on the Internet." You'll find a directory of franchise opportunities, profiles of featured franchises, and a list of worldwide franchise associations.

www.franinfo.com
"A world of information about franchising," this site provides links that pertain to buying a business and franchising your business.

www.freeagent.com
Click on this information hub for freelancers, consultants, and independent contractors to locate work and connect with other "free agents."

www.hhs.gov
Small business research programs tap into the resources of government agencies, such as the Health and Human Services. Check out this site for details.

www.hoovers.com
This site will provide you with up-to-date information on companies you may be interested in working for.

www.hotbot.com/careers
This site is among the most useful career links of the major search engines and will serve you as an Internet pathfinder for career-management information and resources.

www.hotjobs.com
This site enables you to do a job search by keyword, by location, and by company. Also references jobs by industry sector. You can also access a 411 feature for sharp, advice-filled articles by expert career counselors.

www.jobhuntersbible.com
This site is sponsored by Dick Bolles, author of What Color Is Your Parachute?, and is designed as a supplement to that seminal book on career change and job search.

www.jobprofiles.com
This site focuses on interests and the personal side of work. It describes jobs in a variety of occupational categories and provides links to many career exploration and planning resources.

www.jobs.com
Jobs.com promotes itself as "the Internet's fastest-growing website." It offers a job search resource center, an employer list, a résumé bank and other useful tools. It's especially helpful for students making the transition into the workforce.

www.jobtrak.com
This helpful employment site features information and resources for students, alumni, and college staffs. It also provides access to a variety of valuable services.

www.jobweb.org
This site of the National Association of Colleges and Employers (NACE) features employment information and an e-zine on job choices. Students transitioning into the workforce may find this site especially useful.

www.keirsey.com
This site focuses the character and temperament types personal-style theory. Related to (but distinct from) the MBTI, temperament theory also seeks to trace and celebrate differences among individuals. You'll find more detailed explanation, along with links to many other related resources.

www.knockemdead.com
Here you'll find advice and strategies on managing the interview process and other aspects of job search, modeled on the format of Martin Yate's popular book Knock 'em Dead.

www.liszt.com
If you're looking for contacts, this is the right site. It's a directory that offers access to more than 90,000 mailing lists that you can browse by keyword or by subject category.

www.monster.com
Not called Monster.com for nothing, this comprehensive job search site includes some 175,000 jobs and more than 30,000 employers. It also offers job-hunting advice by expert columnists.

www.careers.msn.com
This site is among the most useful career links of the major search engines and will serve you as an Internet pathfinder for career management information and resources.

www.nase.org
Sponsored by the National Association for the Self-Employed in Washington, D.C., this site offers articles and news on self-employment. You can also pose queries and search for links to a host of related resources and information.

www.ncna.com
Sponsored by the National Career Networking Association's, this site offers guidance on a range of career-management topics, including finding a career counselor.

www.iccweb.com
This is a noteworthy site for career-minded individuals. It features a wealth of career-related categories, which link to clusters of related sites such as business for sale, career articles, job sharing, networking, older workers, self-employment, and others.

www.planetclick.com
This easy-to-use portal offers hundreds of links to career management sites.

www.provenresumes.com
This site very possibly has more information about résumé writing than you could ever use. It includes listings of workshops and resources, and booklets that you can download immediately.

www.quintessentialcareers.com
Several career and job-search web sites offer special resources and information for new graduates who are looking to begin their careers in earnest.

www.rileyguide.com
This popular job-hunting web site with sharp advice and guidelines from search strategist Margaret F. Dikel offers a host of resources on many facets of a job search.

www.sba.gov
The Small Business Association provides a panorama of information and guidance on starting and maintaining a small business. If you're serious about launching yours, this site is indispensable.

www.sbdc.org
For valuable information and counseling on planning and launching a small business, check out the Small Business Development Center, a cooperative venture between the SBA and community businesses.

www.score.org
The Service Core of Retired Executives (SCORE) hosts this site to provide expert advice to individuals pursuing self-employed business options.

www.self-directed-search.com
Access this site for a detailed explanation of the Holland career system and the Self-Directed Search. Click on "What is the SDS?"; "Find a Career Counselor"; and, if you like, "Take the Test."

www.shrm.org
Sponsored by the Society for Human Resource Management, this site provides access to a wealth of work-related news, information, and

resources. It also keeps you in touch with the hot workplace issues and trends that the HR community is thinking about.

www.smartbiz.com
Although the Smart Business Supersite positions itself as a "how-to resource for small business," serious career-minded people in many different workplace situations will find useful resources "to help you run your business or department smarter."

www.snap.com/careers
This site is among the most useful career links of the major search engines and will serve you as an Internet pathfinder for career-management information and resources.

www.temp24-7.com
This is an informative e-zine for workers pursuing or holding temporary jobs.

www.temperament.com
This site focuses the character and temperament types personal-style theory. Related to (but distinct from) the MBTI, temperament theory also seeks to trace and celebrate differences among individuals. You'll find more detailed explanation, along with links to many other related resources.

www.typelogic.com
Here's a site devoted to MBTI resources. You can access links to articles and information about the MBTI and its origins, history, interpretation, and uses.

www.uschamber.org
This site is run by the U.S. Chamber of Commerce. It's an invaluable resource for online networking in the business world.

www.workingsolo.com
Visit this site for a trove of information and resources "for the self-employed, home-based business owners, e-lancers, telecommuters, consultants and other independent professionals."

www.workingtoday.org
This informative site is sponsored by Working Today, a national nonprofit membership organization that promotes the interests of people who work independently.

www.yahoo.com/careers
This site is among the most useful career links of the major search engines and will serve you as an Internet pathfinder for career-management information and resources.

A simple glossary

Accomplishments In career management terms, goals you've attained or achievements you've realized.

Age-stage career theory A view that links career advancement to early, middle, and later phases of adult growth and development.

Ageism Discrimination in the workplace based on an individual's chronological age.

Aligning with work Thinking about your career in relation to your personal identity and your life needs.

Assessment instruments Inventories or information tools that measure personality traits, aptitudes, skills, or interests.

Baby Boomers Individuals who were born between 1946 and 1964, the period of the largest boom in infant births in American history.

Career The progression through a variety of work situations throughout your lifetime. Not just your current job or profession, but the sum of all your work experiences.

Career change A radical remaking of working life – not merely a switch of jobs or organizations but, more typically, the undertaking of a different profession.

Career commercial A concise overview of your career background, skills, and personal style attributes.

Career configuration The shape of your career within the greater context of your life activities and experience.

Chronological résumé A résumé that organizes career and educational history in reverse chronological order, beginning with the most recent and working back in time. See also Combination résumé and Functional résumé

Combination résumé A résumé that organizes career and educational history by emphasizing functional experience within a reverse chronological time line. See also Chronological résumé and Functional résumé

Congruence The favorable match of an individual's personality traits and characteristics with the facets of a particular work situation.

Consultants Professionals who are hired to bring knowledge and expertise to a business situation, often with recommendations for improving or realizing it.

Contingency workers Professionals who are hired on a time-defined or per-project basis.

Core values The ideals most prized and cherished by an individual. In career management terms, the things or conditions that are likeliest to promote job-person match.

Craft A discipline of work activities that exists to serve basic human needs, endures and evolves over time, and usually requires specialized education or a long apprenticeship.

Electronic résumé A résumé that synthesizes career and educational information in a format especially designed for online use.

Entrepreneur A career-minded individual who organizes and assumes the risk of some kind of business or enterprise. Also, an individual who works in a self-employed way.

Farming out See Outsourcing

Freelancing Generating income by working in a nonemployment, work-for-hire capacity for one or more clients or organizations. See also Independent contracting

Franchising Operating a branch of an established enterprise within a framework of guidelines established by the owner or owners.

Frequently used skills Abilities an individual brings to a variety of personal and career situations.

Functional résumé A résumé that organizes career and educational history by functional areas, drawn from the entire span of one's work experiences. See also Chronological résumé and Combination résumé

Gatekeepers Professionals, such as human resources managers and recruiters, or headhunters, whose positions enable them to control access to other individuals within organizations.

Hierarchy A classification of individuals according to their standing within an organization.

Honeymoon A time of adjustment during an employee's earliest days and weeks with an organization, typically colored by mutual admiration and idealism.

Job An ever-evolving bundle of tasks and activities that helps an organization reach its goals.

Headhunter A professional contracted to identify ideal candidates for open positions within organizations. Also called a recruiter

Hidden job market The sector of the job market that is out of public view and that is tapped through informal channels and by word of mouth.

Holland theory The view that individuals who work in occupations and environments compatible with their interests are more likely to experience career satisfaction and fulfillment.

Independent contracting Generating income by working in a non-employment, contract capacity for one or more clients or organizations. See also Freelancing

Industry A field of work, with definite boundaries and borders, that exists to provide essential products or services.

Interests Subjects areas or topics that arouse innate attraction or natural curiosity.

Job-person match The degree of alignment of the factors of a work situation with those of an individual's personality.

Marketable skills Workplace activities that have measurable value to organizations.

Mentor A person who can provide valuable career guidance, advice, and assistance, typically by drawing from a wealth of experience.

Motivated skills The activities an individual does well and enjoys doing.

Multitasking Working at a number of activities simultaneously.

Networking Building relationships with people through an exchange of information and resources.

Occupation A career activity, such as a job or a profession, in which one engages as a livelihood.

Organization A business, foundation, association, or institute that unites people from various professions to pursue a well-defined set of goals and objectives.

Organizational culture The formal and informal customs, policies, and procedures that define the work environment for an organization.

Outplacement A program of career management services that may include office space, career assessment, job-search counseling, and research resources, typically available only on a business-to-business basis.

Outsourcing The organizational practice of contracting a third party to complete projects.

Passive job search The activity of posting electronic résumés online, without selectivity or diligent follow-up effort.

Personal style The sum of the qualities, traits, values, interests, attributes, and other factors that make you unique.

Primary profession A discipline of work that is central to an industry or organization, and indispensable.

Profession A discipline of work activities that exists to serve basic human needs, endures and evolves over time, and usually requires specialized education or a long apprenticeship.

Recruiter See Headhunter

Reputation How you are known and regarded by the people in your organization, industry, and profession. Also, how people talk about you and what they say about you.

Search engine An Internet program that seeks and locates online information about a specific topic requested by the user.

Search firm An organization of professionals who may be contracted to identify ideal candidates for open positions within other organizations. See also Headhunter

Secondary profession A discipline of work that is subordinate in importance to others within an industry or organization, and not necessarily indispensable.

Self-assessment The deliberate process of investigating and inventorying your career interests, skills, values, and style qualities.

Self-reporting instrument An assessment instrument that measures only information known to the individual completing it.

Situational view of careers Thinking about your career only in terms of your current or most recent job.

Skills Activities that reflect a high level of proficiency. Also, an ability that is learned through practice and application, rather than innate.

Talents Abilities that are innate and that can be cultivated and advanced through practice and application.

Telecommuting Working out of a home office and interacting with coworkers, customers, or clients via phone, fax, and e-mail rather than in person.

Temping Working in a situation that is officially recognized as interim or "temporary" by employer and employee.

Trade A discipline of work activities that exists to serve basic human needs, endures and evolves over time, and usually requires specialized education or a long apprenticeship.

Upward mobility Achieving career success by advancing through traditional, ascending organizational channels and earning progressively more income.

Values Those things, which may change and evolve over time, that are most desirable and prized within the context of your life and career.

Workplace politics The strategic positioning and tactical maneuvers workers undertake to gain favor and advantage.

Index

Acknowledgements

AUTHOR'S ACKNOWLEDGEMENTS
This project is the culmination of an intricate career story. A number of people deserve special recognition and thanks for their role in this effort, and I'd like to single them out here.

Letitia A. Chamberlain, Ph.D., Director of the Center for Career, Education, and Life Planning at New York University's School of Continuing and Professional Studies, inspired and encouraged me to pursue the career counselor's work with individuals and groups, and offered me abundant opportunities to do just that. I am grateful for her genuine and unwavering support, and – like so many of my colleagues – I value her insight and dedication to the counseling profession.

Amy Friedman and Jaye Smith have provided me with a wealth of opportunities to do rewarding career management work as a counselor, coach, consultant, and trainer, and have supported my efforts on this project without qualification. They and my colleagues at their firm, Partners in Human Resources International, have enabled me to enjoy the most satisfying career situation I've known.

Editorial consultant and Fordham good guy Tom Ranieri brought this project to my attention after trading career transition stories with me for six months. The entire team at DK Publishing deserves hearty applause for pulling this book together and giving it a special character and style. Beth Adelman, the series editor, offered valuable perspective throughout the writing process, and kept me on the right track. Matt Kiernan graced the text with sharp thinking and deft editing skills. And Kristi Hart added extra precision to the pages with her contributions as copy editor.

I'd also like to thank the hundreds of individuals I've worked with since becoming a career management professional. It's their career experiences and biographies that have drawn the lines and shapes of the perspectives in this book, and provided me with the momentum for a unique and gratifying career episode of my own.

K.A.L.

Picture credits